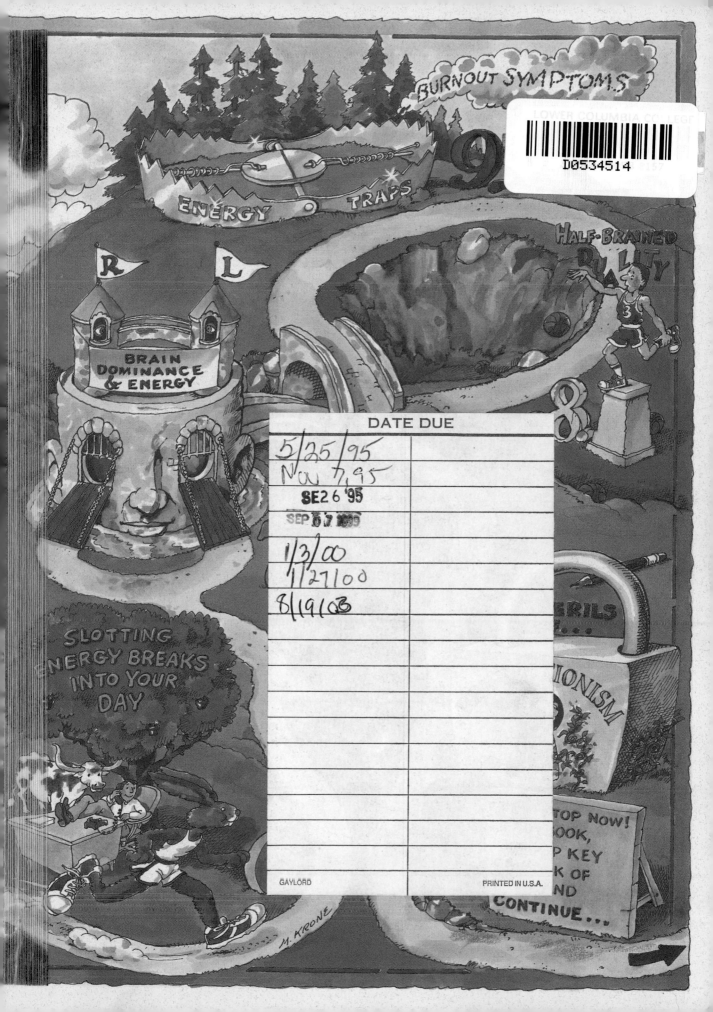

Top Business People Praise
"You Don't Have to Go Home from Work Exhausted!"

" *Working with someone as talented, multidimensional, open, honest, and, yes, as vulnerable as Ann McGee-Cooper has unlocked many energy doors for me. The initial understanding of the importance of balance in work and play is critical. Appreciating that these are not mutually exclusive ideas is so exciting and yet so fundamental to continued growth. The things I used to feel somewhat guilty over – a cluttered office, a quick daydream, a catnap, shifting from one task to another before completion – are now sources of sustained energy, a daily revitalization. Ann explodes the myths that so many of us have lived with. Her ideas on Energy Engineering offer the opportunity of exponential payout.* **"**

—Leslie G. McCraw, Vice-Chairman and CEO, Fluor Corporation

" *Desire for accomplishment is often overruled by one's limited energy. Ann McGee-Cooper has taught us there is a greater energy resource available to each of us. These insights are like a gentle, quenching rain in the middle of a major management development drought in this country.* **"**

—Robert J. Gary, Executive Vice President, TU Electric

" *A great book – absolutely on the mark! Ann McGee-Cooper has produced an excellent handbook on how to be more productive, have more energy, and lead a more balanced life while HAVING MORE FUN. This is a MUST READ book!* **"**

—Jim Young, Assistant to the Chairman, Electronic Data Systems

" *This is a charming, delightful book that will entertain as well as give invaluable advice on managing your life.* **"**

**—Tony Buzan, founder of Brain Clubs International and
author of *Use Both Sides of Your Brain***

" *A great book for being up-to-date on living life rather than merely existing. It is delightful, fun, and easy to read. The lessons are simple, yet profound.* **"**

**—Ted L. Edwards, Jr. MD
Specialist in Preventive and Sports Medicine
and co-author, *Weight Loss to Super Wellness***

You Don't Have to Go Home from Work Exhausted!

THE
ENERGY ENGINEERING
APPROACH

BY

Ann McGee-Cooper

WITH

Duane Trammell & Barbara Lau

BOWEN & ROGERS
DALLAS

For information write
Bowen & Rogers
P.O. Box 64784,
Dallas, Texas 75206,
or call 214 / 357-8550.

ISBN 0-9625617-1-1

Library of Congress Data
90-080410

A BARD PRODUCTIONS BOOK

Illustrations:	Mike Krone
Text /Cover Design:	Suzanne Pustejovsky
Copy Editing:	Alison Tartt
Typography:	Schweers Typesetting, Austin, Texas

DEDICATION

We dedicate this book to two masters of Energy Engineering. The first is Georgia Ulrich, who at age eighty-two enjoys a full-time career as a business partner with us, reads six to eight books per week both for fun and for our research, manages a household for three, enjoys daily exercise, and claims to have more fun than most people with a variety of hobbies and friends of all ages. To celebrate her eightieth birthday she went up in a hot-air balloon. She exemplifies through her actions the rich rewards of living life fully. When asked her secrets for staying so fully invested in living, Georgia shared these tips:

- hang on to your humor,
- don't ask for permission, just do it! and
- make everything fun.

The second great inspiring Energy Engineering role model is Bob Gary. For the past four years we have watched him turn problems into opportunities as he has coached us and several hundred others in applying the secrets of brain integration to our daily lives. We would gather and synthesize the research and he would show us how powerful it can be by putting it to work in real situations. Bob has literally saved lives with his intuitive genius, and with his whole-brained team, turned impossible situations into innovative business wins. On weekends you can usually find him having a grand time on his farm with his wife, Joyce, and his grandchildren. A master of play and mischief, Bob personifies the genius of abundant energy, innovation, and servant leadership.

CONTENTS

PART FIVE

Energy Engineering Strategies

PREFACE

The Story of Two Companies, Three Researchers, and the Quest for Unlimited Energy

fter writing *Time Management for Unmanageable People*, which discusses brain dominance and its effect on a person's preferred work style, office environment, organizational habits, and ultimate productivity, Duane Trammell and I realized that finding enough time in the day just wasn't enough. Another major challenge was finding enough energy to keep working— *and* relaxing *and* playing—at 3:00 p.m., 6:00 p.m., 9:00 p.m., and so on. We found, for instance, that we could teach our clients how to budget their time for a big project at 2:00 p.m. But if they didn't have a good reserve of energy stored up, the project either dragged on forever or was done in a mediocre fashion.

Our clients complained of needing more energy for these activities:

- to put in a truly productive and creative eight to ten hours on the job day after day;

- to do more than flop on the couch and watch mindless TV sitcoms at night;

- to develop new interests and activities in their spare time;

- to take up a physical activity or sport; and

- to spend quality time with family and friends on the weekend.

Yes, without abundant energy, these things rarely seem to get accomplished. Or we do them half-heartedly, merely going through the motions, so that the satisfaction we could derive from them is greatly diminished.

Our team at Ann McGee-Cooper and Associates, Inc., in Dallas decided to study *how to maintain and maximize one's energy, productivity, and overall zest for life each day of the year.* As we began our research, we discovered that very little had been written on the subject. A profusion of material on stress management, however, had flooded the market over the past ten years. Although stress can definitely be a factor in low energy, getting stress under control does not necessarily result in sustained high-energy levels and increased motivation. In fact, managing stress and maximizing energy are two different functions, each with separate solutions and problem areas.

In addition to collecting whatever data we could find on factors contributing to low and high energy, the team interviewed many of our clients on the topic. Then we tested our ideas on ourselves, our friends, and interested clients. During the course of our research we also looked at three key populations:

1. highly successful executives who manage to get a tremendous amount of work done plus enjoy a full range of outside activities;

2. people recognized as geniuses—inventors, scientists, artists, and others who were very productive and creative throughout their lives, even into their seventies and eighties; and

3. preschool children, perhaps the most energetic population of all, who seem to have an inexhaustible supply of energy.

We searched out patterns these several groups held in common and were both surprised and delighted to discover several significant new insights regarding strategies adults can learn to recreate the abundant energy of small children. At first we set about seeing whether our discovery would generate more energy for ourselves, our team, and our families. The success rate was unusually high, so in 1984 we designed these strategies into a two-day seminar that we took "on the road." We crisscrossed the country teaching these concepts to hundreds of very diverse groups: educators, Junior League members, government agencies such as the Environmental Protection Agency and Naval Weapons Center, health-care professionals, and dozens of corporations like International Business Machines, American Banking Institute, Electronic Data Systems, Steak and Ale Corporation, Federated Department Stores, and Atlantic Richfield Company. Other groups included the American Heart Association, American Association of Operating Room Nurses, American Society of Civil Engineers, World Future Society, and American Library Association. The response was overwhelmingly enthusiastic, so we decided to take our work a step further. We looked for a way to study the long-term outcomes of these strategies in greater depth.

As a result, we shifted our research efforts accordingly. For the past four years we have worked almost exclusively with two large corporate groups, Texas Utilities and Fluor Daniel, Inc.

Fluor Daniel, Fluor Corporation's principal operating business unit, provides a broad range of services to clients in five business sectors: Industrial, Process, Power, Hydrocarbon, and Government. Recognized as the number one contractor for the second year in a row by the major engineering publication, *Engineering News-Record*, which yearly ranks all engineering firms for performance, Fluor Daniel's services include feasibility studies, conceptual design, project management, engineering, construction, procurement, technical services, project financing, maintenance, and plant operations. Fluor Daniel provides global capability from more than fifty offices located around the world through the teamwork of over 40,000 people.

Texas Utilities Company is an investor-owned holding company for an electric utility system with six wholly owned subsidiaries. The principal subsidiary is TU Electric, which provides electricity to more than five million people—about one-third of the population of the state of Texas, including the Dallas-Fort Worth Metroplex. TU Electric ranks in the top ten nationally in kilowatt-hour sales revenues and utility plants in service. Other subsidiaries include fuel, mining, and service companies and two nonutility companies involved in energy-related activities. There are more than 15,000 employees in the Texas Utilities system.

To date, close to 200 corporate leaders as well as their direct reports and spouses have participated in Energy Engineering programs. In addition, over 2,500 employees in Texas Utilities and approximately 625 employees in Fluor Daniel have become involved in testing and applying our energy strategies. As a significant part of our research process we have collected hundreds of their personal stories. From these we are finding both strong validation for our basic assumptions (based on what is working for them) and a rich diversity of possibilities because each person must "engineer" his or her own process. Therefore the majority of personal stories throughout the book come primarily from these two companies.

And what is their assessment of our ideas? Top executives, who already were operating at a commendable energy level, subjectively rated their energy increase at an average of 40% on our follow-up evaluations. Several executives reported a 100% energy boost! And women struggling to balance their careers and family responsibilities have been extremely enthusiastic as well. Thus we know these energy strategies work for lots of different people in lots of different ways.

Ann McGee-Cooper
January 1, 1990

ABOUT THE AUTHORS

Y ou might find it helpful as you approach this book to know a little more about the authors in terms of our own energy management, past and present. We were united because we each experienced serious problems with energy. As we explored solutions, we were delighted to discover common patterns which worked for us and many of our clients. One guiding thread is that people have to choose for themselves what fits their style. But overall, the principles have been so universally successful that we have been repeatedly asked to produce this book.

Ann's Energy Case History

"I grew up with two distinct role models for Energy Engineering. My dad used the typical business model: work hard, go to the office early, stay late, come home exhausted, always meet deadlines, etc. We took annual vacations and did fun things together, but I remember that he spent most of his evenings just being tired, listening to the radio, and going to sleep in his big easy chair. My mom, on the other hand, had a different energy style. To this day, she gets more work done than anyone I have ever been around. Yet she has more fun in the process! She has always been a master at finding ways to get two goals met with one effort. She knows how to recruit others to assist her. She has lots of interests, gets plenty of exercise, has a great sense of humor, and at the age of eighty-two works at a full-time career while running a household for three people! She also enjoys a wide range of friends of all ages, reads several books a week, and keeps us all entertained with her ideas and new things she is learning.

So you can see why it came naturally for me to grow up expecting to work hard and accomplish many things at once. When I was young, I picked up my father's work patterns by keeping busy in all my after-school hours with small jobs, extracurricular activities, and summer jobs to help pay for college. In addition, while in high school I earned a scholarship to museum classes and completed the equivalent of a university program in art by the time I graduated from high school. To compound my work load, I was dyslexic (which I did not discover until I was much older). This forced me to do more school work in order to keep up and make good grades. Thus, working hard was an everyday phenomenon to me.

Then in college I filled up every waking hour with a heavy course load, volunteer work, and college organizations. When I graduated with a B.S. in design and a minor in architecture from the University of Texas at Austin, I immediately married and put my husband through Drew Seminary while teaching grade school plus museum art classes on Saturdays. It was not unusual for me to have four jobs going at once while I supported the family and raised my son.

Next came graduate school with an M.F.A. at Southern Methodist University, then an Ed.D. from Columbia by commuting from Dallas to New York and finishing with highest honors earned in record time. This was a very fertile time for me as I continued my thirty-five years of research in the areas of creativity and began to explore brain hemisphericity. My doctoral project was to develop a Teacher Survival Program.

It was based on my observation that often the most creative young teachers become targets of the system and drop out, frustrated and drained of their creative energy. I decided to study this pattern and see whether I could develop a support system to help these creative change agents stay effective and happy within the demands of their job.

I designed a dual program of studying creative problem solving along with the more specific challenges facing the teachers. During this time I read everything I could find by the gifted psychologist and author Rollo May. I went to hear him speak and interviewed him by phone to get his insights on my project. Another motivating element built into my doctoral work was my meetings with Margaret Mead. We met several times to review my research and to gain valuable insights from her own findings.

I poured all of my energy into my academic work and my very demanding job, taking it for granted that I would have to forgo fun times during this period of my life. But once the pattern was set, I seemed unable to break out of it. Playing "Superwoman" as a single mother, full-time college instructor at SMU, part-time business consultant, and an active volunteer, I went seven years without taking more than an occasional weekend off. I established the Experimental Arts Program at SMU and supervised its growth into an internationally recognized project involving 5,500 teachers, students, and parents. Then in 1978 I was invited to a world conference in Hawaii to present the work I was doing on gifted adults.

For the next several years I taught graduate courses at four different universities to help prepare teachers to work with gifted students. I also served as a consultant for scores of schools, developing programs, educating parents, and training teachers. In addition, I served on the board of the Texas Association of Gifted and Talented Students and as an advisor, consultant, and panel member to both the National Endowment for the Arts and the National Endowment for the Humanities.

My involvement in all of these areas provides the groundwork for many of the ideas presented in this book. But at that time I had not yet learned how to balance and sustain my energy reserves. Finally I reached my breaking point, both physically and mentally. I developed a serious case of burnout and had a major physical problem that required surgery. It was then that I realized that life was controlling me more than I was controlling life. I learned the hard way about trying to do too much at once, about the perils of playing Superwoman and not balancing my life.

So I took a one-year sabbatical to rethink my life, my priorities, and my use of time. After taking stock of my goals and the advice of some special mentors, I began from scratch to restructure my work and leisure time. I said good-bye and good riddance to some exhausting work habits and behavior traits. Around five years ago I also tried a new weekly work schedule that my husband, a dentist, uses with great success. He sees patients three and one-half days a week. Then he goes into "retirement" the rest of the week, using that time to pursue his outside interests and to renew his energy. During the years I experimented with that schedule, I found that I was producing more than I had previously because on the days I worked, I felt utterly refreshed, creative, and motivated. Although my current work and travel schedule have expanded so that I once again have a five-day work week, I still integrate work with periods of play and recreation so that my energy is constantly being replenished. I also try to keep my weekends free for family, fun, and personal growth.

Experiencing the benefits of these new work and life-styles made me want to show others how to achieve a better balance between work and play. The writing of this book represents a synthesis of many aspects of my life and work: doctoral studies, ongoing research on brain dominance and learning methods, training programs with corporate leaders, seminars with a wide range of professionals, fieldwork with Texas Utilities and Fluor Daniel and, finally, my own experiences in balancing career goals with personal needs."

uane Trammell, my managing partner, is a constant source of inspiration for me. Before joining me in 1981, Duane served as a classroom teacher for seven years. In 1984, Duane was awarded one of the top recognitions in his field—Dallas Teacher of the Year. And in the previous year he received the Ross Perot Award for Excellence in Teaching. Duane has a master's degree in gifted education in addition to postgraduate studies in creative problem solving.

During his years in the classroom, doing one of the most demanding of all jobs, Duane observed many energy patterns among his colleagues. Some had limitless vitality and enthusiasm even in the most frustrating conditions, while others merely hoped to make it until the 3:30 dismissal bell rang. By working together and discovering the sources of his energy drains and gains, Duane learned to engineer a high-energy life-style for himself.

Duane's Energy Case History

"I was a new teacher in an impossible teaching situation. I had thirty-eight students performing three grade levels below their age in an urban area with all the related problems that go with that. My answer was to work harder, stay later at school, and become stricter on discipline. By the end of my second year, I was ready to quit and find another line of work. Then I met Ann.

Ann conducted a three-hour seminar for the Dallas school district, and it literally changed my life. She presented information on hemisphericity and explained the right brain's need for joy, playfulness, and relaxation. She suggested I approach the school day from this perspective—interspersing play and fun into my serious, disciplined subject matter throughout the course of the day. She also suggested I take time out for myself and leave school at school and use weekends and weeknights to renew my own energy.

I knew that the advice and concepts fit for me, so I began to implement them. I relaxed. I stopped yelling at the kids. I approached every subject from the viewpoint of asking, how can I incorporate fun into these lessons while still teaching the basics? My students and I underwent an incredible transformation. My discipline problems vanished. My attitude changed from feeling "overwhelmed" to feeling challenged and excited. Everyone was

smiling and laughing more. Students came early and stayed late. Parents wanted to be a part of the excitement and learning going on in the room. The energy level was incredible! We worked together off an energy high all day long— because I had learned to skillfully balance and interject play and fun into "serious" work. One other thing: hugs became an important energy booster for us. I needed to be hugged as much as the students did. When we would become tired or frustrated working together on a concept that just wouldn't stick, we would stop and hug each other for mutual encouragement—encouragement to the student to keep trying and encouragement to me to keep explaining. This application of Ann's insights yielded these results:

1. I went home with abundant energy, looking forward to an energizing evening.

2. I got fresh energy from working on a new teaching lesson sometimes in the evenings. Before, I barely made it home to fall into bed, let alone even think about doing more lesson planning.

3. My physical health improved; this new-found freedom to play and enjoy life gave me the energy to want to take care of my body. With a healthy diet and exercise program, energy was compounding more energy because of a desire to change habits.

4. Others began to recognize the excellence that my new teaching program begot, and I won several wonderful awards.

All during this time, I worked with Ann, reporting results of energy-building techniques and what was working for me, my students, and their families. We collaborated on *Time Management for Unmanageable People* and toyed with a beginning understanding of energy-building concepts. Then in August of 1984 we retreated to the upper Hudson River in Tarrytown, New York, and wrote the first summary of our research on personal energy. As we walked along the foothills among the tall pines, Ann and I processed insights both of us had collected over the past year. We organized our notes and presented these findings in a two-day seminar in Dallas in October 1984."

This book would never have been written without Duane's significant participation in the design, implementation, evaluation, and ongoing revisions of our applied research. He has become my highly valued, left-brain-gifted counterpart. So even though my role is to present our ideas and serve as the primary writer of this book, it would be inappropriate to not have his name credited for this work equally with mine.

In 1984, Barbara Lau, a nationally published free-lance writer and co-author of *Weight Loss to Super Wellness*, called me after reading an article on our unorthodox approach to time management and its tie-in to brain hemisphericity. She was already familiar with some of our concepts, having already published articles on mind mapping, creativity, and journal writing. After attending two of our seminars and having some extensive talks with us, Barbara began a successful series of articles in magazines such as *Savvy, Family Circle, Management Quarterly, The Executive*, and many other publications. Here are some of Barbara's Energy Engineering secrets.

Barbara's Energy Case History

"I first encountered Ann's unique and unorthodox ideas in an article published in a slick Dallas magazine. At the time I was publishing articles mainly in the fields of health and business. The article was about a popular time management consultant who brazenly contended that some people actually thrive on working amid clutter, that some things worth doing aren't worth doing well or even worth finishing, and that brain dominance is the real key to discovering an individual's best work methods. Many of her explanations fit me to a tee. They also validated some work habits of mine that I had previously regarded as faults. Intrigued by her ideas, I asked to interview her.

After visiting Ann's amazing office—which looks part playroom, part artist's studio—and attending two of her seminars, I knew I could develop many articles around her and her methods. In addition, I could see the value of her suggestions for my own time management and energy problems. As a free-lance writer working on my own, I was responsible for developing all my own projects, opportunities, and work schedules. And since I always had an unlimited number of potential projects to market, I usually felt guilty whenever I granted myself free time away from work.

But Ann taught me the many benefits of taking energy-restoring breaks. She also taught me the importance of granting myself time for fun and of working in an attractive office. After returning from her first seminar, I immediately spent two days reorganizing and redecorating my office. Since I had never taken time to fix it up much, it was a less than inspiring place to work. I turned it into a setting that reflected the quality of writing and creativity that I was striving for. I also learned how to tell when my concentration and energy were waning and when I was pushing myself to write beyond the point where I was still productive."

Unlike many other writers who simply help an author express ideas in more readable ways, Barbara has also chosen to add her own personal research to our data bank. In addition to applying our concepts to her own life, she has used them in many writers' workshops and university courses she has taught. So even though the book reads from the perspective of my life and insight, without the talent and unselfish teaming of both Duane and Barbara, the project would never have happened.

As you can see, it has taken all three of us much change and experimentation to find our best energy solutions. But now we and our entire team are committed to enriching our lives by increasing the amount of energy we can apply to each activity we do. For it's not simply a matter of managing your time wisely; it's having enough energy to make the most of your time and to enjoy each moment fully.

INTRODUCTION

s Duane, Barbara, and I began the task of researching and writing this book, we had seven goals in mind. Since knowing where you are going with your work (having a clear purpose) and visualizing the rewards you stand to reap are two ways to build energy, we want to share those initial goals with you:

1. We planned to learn as much as possible about how people could continually replenish their reserves of personal energy and could live life with the verve and enthusiasm of a child.

2. We wanted to use ourselves and our workshops for examples and role models.

3. We wanted to learn how to arrive home from work at 6:00 or 7:00 p.m. with enough energy left to enjoy our families and to revitalize our energy supplies for the following day. (Of course, this meant breaking

some bad habits, such as falling into an uninspired heap on the couch.)

4. We wanted to write a very practical and usable text rather than a theoretical discourse. We were committed to evaluating a broad range of strategies and options in order to give readers a wealth of practical ideas to use both at work and in their leisure time.

5. We wanted to focus primarily on the business community. Even though these ideas can work and have worked for people of all ages in all walks of life, the majority of our work in the past four years has been with the business community.

6. We wanted to include many real case studies and testimonies from a wide range of clients to make the book more relevant to our readers.

7. Finally, we wished to make the book fun and intriguing, because fun and curiosity are primary sources of energy not only for children but for adults as well.

So why not begin learning the great energy value of fun in the process of becoming acquainted with these ideas? Of course you,

the reader, must be the ultimate judge of our success in meeting these goals. *You Don't Have to Go Home from Work Exhausted* will give you many new insights into the causes of energy drains and energy gains—both for you as an individual and for your associates—because there is an energy and productivity link to individual brain dominance, work habits, personal expectations, and personality types. We designed the text, therefore, in a highly usable and visual, whole-brained style that allows each reader to evaluate his or her distinct energy problems and solutions. In true workbook format, *You Don't Have to Go Home from Work Exhausted* features a multitude of exercises titled "Action Items" as well as an array of practical suggestions—from both our team and from many top corporate leaders around the country—for maximizing your energy levels at the office and at home.

Reading Intuitively

There is one word of caution to add before you dive into this book. Since each person is uniquely different, we are convinced that it is essential for you to read and process this book based on your own sense of what is right for you. Much of what we share will probably ring so true you may wonder why you didn't think of it on your own. This reaction is a pretty reliable signal that the information is something you need to listen to, think about, try out, and evaluate. And chances are, the information will be appropriate for you.

For that matter, all our concepts are backed up with practical exercises and activities. If an idea works for you—if it adds new energy and creativity to your life—then explore a variety of ways to put it into your daily habits and life-style. But if it doesn't ring true, feel right, or seem to fit, then read on, knowing that it may help someone else but not work for you at this time. Only you can know what is right for you at each moment. Indeed, this in itself seems to be one of the key secrets to living in balance at high energy.

Here's another point about individuality. Since the Industrial Revolution, our culture has tried to standardize everything from dress codes to production methods to cures for illnesses. In addition, when we were kids in school we were systematically taught not to trust our intuitive inner voice. We were rewarded for conforming and for being obedient. In fact, we were typically rewarded as being good girls and boys almost directly in proportion to how well we turned off the inner voice and stayed tuned in to the voice of the authority . . . our parents, teachers, coaches, and so forth. Yet when contact is lost with this inner sense of what is right for us, something very vital dies within us.

We are just now coming to realize that people are not only very different from each other but are changing from day to day. What is right on one day for someone may be out of balance on another. So how do we know which rules to follow? The answer is only partly out there. The other half of the answer is within yourself. The more you learn to trust it and listen to it, the stronger and more responsive this inner sense of knowing will become. And the more you live in balance with your inner feelings, the less emotional stress you will experience and the more energy you will invite into your life.

In fact, you can begin to get back in touch with your intuitive and unique self as you read this book. No doubt some of our ideas and techniques will seem rather off-the-wall or unbusinesslike at first. Many of our concepts will challenge some age-old work rules that your parents and society have taught you. But if you will suspend the rational, judgmental side of your consciousness long enough to try our ideas, then let your intuition cast the deciding vote, you will be better able to know which ideas feel right for you. Furthermore, if you give yourself permission to have fun with this book and to change some of your current ways of doing things, you will be much more receptive to the new ideas you are about to encounter.

Calling Your Own Shots

Stop for a moment and think of one or two people you have known who have lived with unusually high energy and spirit. Now ask yourself, were they staunch conformers, reluctant to think and act apart from the norm? Or did they "march to their own drummer?" More often than not, we think you will find the latter to be true. As we listed people who lived with this abundant, unlimited vitality and reservoir of personal energy, there seemed to be a pattern: they called their own shots and knew which path was right for them.

Thomas Edison, for example, was thrown out of school as unteachable in the third grade. Yet he went on to patent more inventions than any other person before him or in his time. He was known to go to work and spend six days on a project before he came home. He had a sleeping pad under a back stairway in his lab, and when he felt tired he would go take a nap. Then when he awakened, he would get back to the search for solutions. And often there was fun and good humor mixed in with all the work. There are reports of his having all types of musical instruments at his lab. Sometimes at three o'clock in the morning his team would break from work and strike up the band. The neighbors complained and didn't understand this nonconventional sense of time. Yet it produced some highly creative people with some highly creative solutions inspired by some uniquely high levels of energy.

As you read this book, you are encouraged to contemplate solutions of your own—to find your own energy "leaks" and "wellsprings." Energy comes from doing things your own way at your own pace. In addition, you will get many more personal insights from this book if you read it actively rather than passively. Active reading involves doing the exercises, testing out our ideas, and discussing the concepts with friends and family. It also involves making notes and doodles in the margin and highlighting favorite sections. This will boost your learning curve and give you "more juice for the squeeze."

Developing Your Own Energy Networks

Sharing this experience with someone else can also boost your understanding and use of the material. Often participants in our workshops have developed small networks to try our ideas, to compare results, and to motivate each other toward a common goal of high-energy maintenance. But if you try working with a group, remember that no two people and their working styles are exactly alike; what works well for one person may not work well for a business partner, best friend, or spouse. So discard those ideas which don't seem to be right for you. That's one reason the book presents such a diverse number of exercises and techniques to try.

You will soon learn for yourself what a difference high energy can make in your life. You will discover how extra energy will enable you to get more done of higher quality in less time—with more time left each day to enjoy the things and people that renew your energy. And get ready to feel young again! As author Wayne Dyer reminds us, "It is never too late to enjoy a happy childhood."

"It is never too late to enjoy a happy childhood."

PART
ONE

Tired of Being Tired?

ENERGY MYTHS:

Fables That Foil Our Energy

> 66 *Unbearable mental fatigue. Work alone could rest me; gratuitous work, [and] play . . . I am far from that. Each thought becomes an anxiety in my brain. I am becoming the ugliest of all things: a busy man.* 99
>
> — **Andre Gide, quoted in *When I Relax I Feel Guilty***

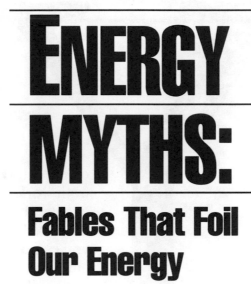

Y ou don't have to go home from work every day feeling tired and exhausted. Through creative Energy Engineering, you can bring vitality and enthusiasm to your evenings and weekends as well. But you must begin by *unlearning* some comfortable habits that are unproductive and that drain you of precious energy.

At our seminars, we often tell a story that is popular among those who teach creativity. It describes a professor who visits a Japanese Zen master. The wise teacher immediately sees that the professor is rather set in his ways and needs to be taught a vital lesson. The master picks up a pot of tea and begins filling the man's outheld cup. He fills the cup to overflowing, tranquilly watching the tea spill out of the saucer onto the table and floor. "Master!" shouts the student in dismay. "Can't you see? My cup is already full. There is no room for more tea in it."

"Just like your head," replies the master. "If you wish to make room for new ideas, first you must empty your head of the old ideas that are blocking your mind."

This lesson serves as excellent advice for reading this book and reevaluating your own filled-to-the-brim cup of notions. For it is difficult to abandon "the way it's always been done before" in order to risk thinking and trying something new. But you must be open to this if you wish to change things for the better in your life.

Myth 1: Energy Can Only Be Restored by Sleep

Wrong!

To begin with, there are many ways to restore energy during the day and night, and sleeping is just one of them. Time spent exercising, playing, laughing, having fun, being creative, relaxing, meditating, and switching to other activities can also renew your momentum and increase alertness. And you can do these energy-building activities throughout the day rather than wait for bedtime to restore your energy. For instance, Albert Schweitzer and Thomas Edison—both notorious for having unusual sleep patterns—would play the organ and piano as a form of relaxation and stimulation. In *Genius in the Jungle*, a biography of Schweitzer, author Joseph Gollomb writes: "By that time a little sleep was even worse than none at all, as so often happens when one has overdrawn on one's reserves. He [Schweitzer] had to have something that would rest him more than sleep. At such times . . . he would climb to the organ loft and play." Biographer Robert Payne (*The Three Worlds of Albert Schweitzer*) also emphasizes this key source of energy renewal in Schweitzer's life. He writes that while Schweitzer was studying medicine, in addition to completing two long pieces of writing, "he slept little and sometimes forgot to eat. When the strain became altogether intolerable, he would slip into St. Wilhelm's church, to play Bach for an hour with Ernst Munch. Then the weariness vanished, and he was calm again."

Sometimes sleep can actually drain your energy more than restore it. If you fall asleep while you are experiencing anxiety, muscular tension, and exhaustion, stress toxins can remain in your body rather than being expelled through exercise and relaxing activities. Often this is the case when people complain that they feel like they "hardly slept a wink" or "fought a battle in their sleep." Moreover, it is a fallacy to assume that all people are at their maximum energy upon waking up. Some people feel most energetic and alert at other times in the day, such as late at night or by mid-morning.

The main point you should remember regarding this myth is that you are not like a car that starts off with a full tank in the morning but is destined to run out of gas after eight hours of driving. Rather, there are many techniques available to you for refueling your energy reserves a little bit at a time throughout the day.

Myth 2: We All Need Seven to Eight Hours of Sleep Per Night

Wrong again!

Although the majority of people seem to feel best with from six to eight hours of sleep each night, by no means is this a requirement for all people. Many of our most celebrated geniuses and other very active folks do well on much less sleep or on unusual sleep patterns. For example, R. Buckminster Fuller's spontaneous sleep habits allowed him to work vigorously nearly around the clock. He would be actively engaged in some activity (designing, reading, conversing, playing, etc.) for about six hours. At that point he would usually feel drowsy, and wherever he was, he would lie down on the floor and sleep for about thirty minutes. Refreshed, he would wake up and start another six hours of intense activity, continuing this pattern throughout the day and night. That amounts to only two hours of sleep per day. Explained Fuller (as quoted in *Bucky* by Hugh Kenner): "I was trying to find out how much I could get done, and noticed that a dog, when he gets tired, simply lies down and sleeps. So it could be that if the minute you're tired you just lie down, you'd need far less sleep. So I just tried it out." He kept up this pattern for many years until he reached his seventies and needed five or six hours of sleep each day. Bucky called this "dymaxion sleep," *dymaxion* meaning doing more with less.

Edison took a similar "catnap" approach to sleep, often working throughout the day and night, lying down for a short snooze whenever fatigue overtook him. Assistants who worked with him reported that he could go to sleep almost instantly, and "upon waking twenty to thirty minutes later, would return to his work just as if he had not stopped," write authors Roselyn and Ray Eldon Heibert in *Thomas Edison, American Inventor*. A surprising number of our creative geniuses went full speed ahead using shortened sleeping patterns like this one.

For a more contemporary example, Don Frick, a self-employed writer and producer in Indianapolis, often breaks his sleep time into two to three intervals during a twenty-four-hour period. He explains: "I've found that I don't need eight hours of sleep at one stretch. If I just listen to the signals my body gives me, then there are naturally occurring times when my productivity is high and when it crashes. I'm no good after lunch, for example, so I've gotten into the habit of sleeping one and one-half hours after eating. Then I often work at nights, but around 3:30 a.m. there's absolutely no productive work left inside me. So I'll sleep until 6:00 or 7:30 a.m. I feel fine going on this way for about five days. Then my body gives me a cue, and I'll let myself sleep for a nine-hour shift, which totally revives me."

These examples are not meant to encourage you to attempt such shortened sleep patterns unless you have a two-week vacation period to experiment with them. In addition, factors such as illness, heavy work loads, sadness, and stress can increase the amount of sleep your body needs. However, our main point is that these highly creative people listened to their internal voice when it told them they needed rest. And like children usually do, after restoring their energy with a nap or recreation, they were able to jump back into high gear.

Many executives follow a modified version of these sleep patterns as well. Once or twice a day they have their secretaries block all calls and interruptions while they stretch out on their office couch (or floor!) and take a fifteen- to thirty-minute nap. Others have a short deep-breathing or meditation session. Armand Hammer, for example, writes in his autobiography that he got into the habit of taking a half-hour nap each day after lunch. At age ninety, he is working circles around his younger business associates.

DO NOT DISTURB, PLEASE.

Doing daily aerobic exercise can also decrease the amount of sleep people require. Exercise provides some of the benefits of sleep in that it helps to release tension and stress toxins, thereby producing a feeling of relaxation and well-being. It also tends to produce deeper and less fitful sleep. Finally, many people find that they need less sleep when they reach sixty years and older.

In fact, learning to listen to and trust what your own body is telling you is another of the key insights we gained in our research in this area. Each person's body seems to have its own unique way of working best. And if we just trust that this is so and begin to intuitively follow what our body is requesting, an amazing new level of energy usually follows.

Myth 3:
Loss of Energy Is Part of the Aging Process

Wrong once again!

Energy does not have to slowly burn out as we age, like a flame on a candlestick. Instead, our individual energy plateaus appear to be linked much more closely to our health and to our enthusiasm for our work and our life. Other fundamental factors include being in sync with our brain dominance; having energizing eating and exercising patterns; being interested and involved in different projects; having a purpose in life; being curious about learning new things; having a passionate involvement in life; spending time in playful, fun activities; and daring to dream dreams that really matter to us. Once again, many noteworthy people—Georgia O'Keeffe, Pablo Picasso, Thomas Edison, Albert Schweitzer, R. Buckminster Fuller, to name a few—continued to be highly productive and energetic beyond their ninetieth year. In addition, many business leaders we have worked with have maintained the vitality and spontaneity they had in their youth.

George Waldon in the November 1988 issue of *SPIRIT Magazine* reported that Sam Walton, the seventy-one-year-old entrepreneur who, according to *Forbes,* is the richest man in America, "vowed to do the hula on Wall Street if [his company] could tally up a net pretax profit of more than 8%." When the company did it, Sam "donned a grass skirt over his business suit . . . and shimmied along with some traditional Hawaiian dancers and musicians on the sidewalk in front of a downtown Manhattan office building."

Myth 4: The Main Source of Energy Is Physical Health

Wrong again!

Although feeling healthy certainly contributes to your well-being and energy levels, you also need to be interested and engaged in life in order to want to be active in the first place! And two of the key elements that cause people to vigorously embrace life are having a strong purpose for living and having a commitment to reaching a certain goal.

Larry Dossey, former chief of staff at Medical City Dallas Hospital and a leading reformer of medicine, both traditional and holistic, takes this idea even further. He believes that energy in his own work comes from these two important sources:

1. **A sense of purpose that goes beyond the details of "the job," whatever the day-to-day details of "job" might mean.** There must be a sense that what I do is somehow congruent with the overall purpose, design, and flow of the universe as I experience it. I've got to feel that my work fits with the Big Picture. For example, I don't think I could energize myself for work every day if I were a corporate executive of a breakfast foods company that made only sugar snacks for kids, or pesticides that cause cancer, or chemicals that deplete the ozone layer. I can't overemphasize the importance of this factor. I believe it is some sort of "megatrend"—the need to feel that one's work is somehow aligned with what's best for the earth itself. The increasing concern for the environment is today a global issue and is expressing itself through the actions of many corporations; and I would suggest to you that the energy drain many workers feel is because they

sense they're not aligned with what's best for the earth. This frequently leads to a feeling of malaise and emotional/spiritual poverty. In short, personal energy can't be discovered if it conflicts with the way of nature.

2. **A sense of the "top line."** This is opposed to the "bottom line," which we usually say is the ultimate criterion of the worth of our work. Great achievers have an abiding sense of what the top line is (a concern for people and quality of life), and it is one of the most energizing aspects of their lives. The work of psychologist Abraham Maslow is leg-

endary here. He did a lot of work interviewing these sorts of people, the great accomplishers, trying to uncover what made them tick. These are high-energy people who have learned something many people never learn. Although the top-line factor is related to the ideas above, they go further and begin to border on something spiritual, something transcendent, something that is difficult to put into words. People do all sorts of things to hide from their greatest possibilities and deny any sort of top line, a behavior that Maslow called the "Jonah Complex."

Jerry Farrington, chairman and chief executive of Texas Utilities, Dallas, reflects on a part of his work philosophy: "It is important to genuinely like what you do—to enjoy your work, your home life, your life-style. I have always been fortunate to work within a company that has a lot of integrity. I have always felt good about working in this industry . . . because it provides a vital service to the public. I also feel very enthusiastic about the people I work with. It is important to feel that you are a part of a team at work, to enjoy accomplishing something together."

Another fundamental source of vitality is feeling passionately about something. It may be a cause, a person, a creative hobby, or your life's work. Many people get an entirely new lease on life by becoming enthralled with something new. Yes, passion will rejuvenate you in a deeper, more long-lasting way than simply getting enough sleep and feeling healthy. In fact, feeling passion for something in your life is so vital to high energy that we are devoting the next chapter to it.

Along with passion, the most important and undergirding element of high-energy living seems to be balance. Learning to live in balance, allowing time for both work and a rewarding personal life, will bring synergy, joy, enthusiasm, and creativity to your life.

> "It is important to genuinely like what you do—to enjoy your work, your home life, your life-style. I have always been fortunate to work within a company that has a lot of integrity. I also feel very enthusiastic about the people I work with. It is important to feel that you are a part of a team at work, to enjoy accomplishing something together."

Summary

1. You have an abundant amount of energy available to you throughout each day. The key is to learn ways to constantly be refueling and adding energy as other behaviors use up energy.

2. Sleep is not the only way to restore your energy, nor does everyone require seven to eight hours of continuous sleep. Time spent exercising, having fun, doing something artistic, relaxing, and meditating can also revive your momentum.

3. As you age, your energy need not burn out like a flame on a candlestick. Having a strong purpose in life and feeling passionately about something will fill you with youthful vigor and will maintain your enthusiasm for life.

4. A healthy balance of both work and play is needed in life.

5. The need to feel that one's work is contributing significantly to making the world a better place is a key to high energy.

6. Balancing the "top line" (concerns with people and quality of life) with the "bottom line" (concerns with things, productivity, and profit) is essential for long-term quality energy and vitality.

2

HOW PASSION AND DREAMS BEGET ENERGY:

Nothing Much Happens Without a Dream

66 *Hold fast to dreams*
For if dreams die
Life is a broken-winged bird
That cannot fly.
Hold fast to dreams
For when dreams go
Life is a barren field
Frozen with snow. 99

—Langston Hughes

66 *Whether you believe you can or can't, you're right.* 99

—Henry Ford

s you search out people who can serve as role models of high and inspirational levels of energy, look for passion in their lives. We're not referring to sexual passion, though often there is a high level of sexuality that seems to be part of the pattern. For some people, it's a person—a new friend, mate, grandchild, or acquaintance they are committed to helping—that instills their lives with fresh vitality and meaning. For others, it's the blossoming of a new talent or interest, such as taking singing lessons at the age of fifty, learning to ice skate at thirty-five, finally finding the "perfect job" at forty-five, restoring an old house into their dream home at sixty, or going back to college to get that degree they never earned.

Live Outside the Bounds of What's Safe and Familiar

When we speak of passion, we are also referring to a general enthusiasm for life—for learning, for music, for government reform, and for whatever else might capture one's interest and imagination. People of uniquely high energy seem to live outside the bounds of quiet interest. You may find them up at all hours, as when Edison stayed up for forty hours watching his first light bulb to be certain it didn't flicker.

Applying this description to yourself, stop and think, "When did I last feel passion? And what or who inspires my passion?" Did you ever notice that passion seems to be contagious within your life? When you were courting and madly in love, didn't the sky seem bluer and the flowers smell sweeter? If you fell in love all over again at the age of fifty, didn't you find yourself enjoying "foolish things" such as flying kites, buying fresh flowers, or taking a walk barefoot in the rain and discovering a new, abundant energy source within yourself?

The point is, when you allow the governor of self-control to be withdrawn so that you *begin to experience life again as you did as a child*, without the tight restrictions of how others might judge you, you live with greater energy. And the energy drawn from one part of your life will leak into other parts of your life. Now you begin to challenge worn-out rules and restrictions in other areas of your life that no longer seem as necessary and significant. You might also begin to wonder whether there isn't a more meaningful way for you, as a unique individual, to live.

Fresh Circumstances Can Add Energy and Passion to Life

For example, last week you may have given a typical cocktail party and been somewhat bored with the same polite conversations with the same people. But this week you become inspired to think of new possibilities for the next of such parties. These

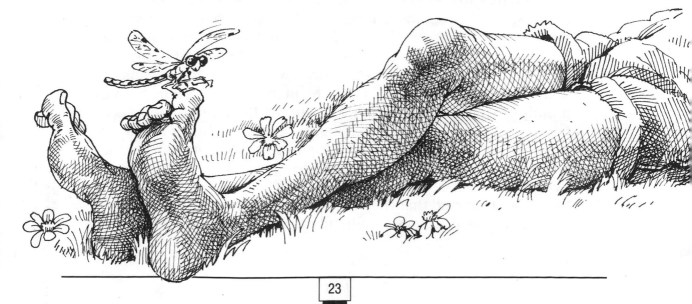

people aren't boring, but the unchallenged guidelines of the usual cocktail party may be. Instead, what if you threw a fantasy party and everyone came dressed as their fantasy career? Or what if the party centered on childhood, with guests bringing a childhood game and pictures of themselves in their youth? Instead of only having people of the same general age and background, what if you invited people of a wide range of ages? What can you learn from the elderly? from young children? from teenagers? And before you toss this book away as completely loony, think again of what new energy might be unleashed with such a mixture of people and fun ideas.

So how can you bring passion to everyday life? We're not suggesting that you leave your mate at middle age for a fresh young lover. But we are encouraging you to find something you care so much about that you would willingly give your life for it (since *something* is devouring your time and energy, wouldn't you rather it be something you feel passionately committed to?).

Here's another example of how fresh circumstances can add energy and passion to life. We had a gathering at a church one evening and invited all ages. Each family brought homemade ice cream for the close of the celebration. The group of about forty people was divided into teams of six persons each. There were young children, teenagers, young parents, middle-aged people, and elderly grandparents.

Each team was given a problem to solve, such as world hunger or air and water pollution. Then they were given all kinds of art materials and ideas for ways to solve these problems through fantasy inventions, such as stuffing pantyhose with crushed newspaper and dressing them in odds and ends of clothes. Each group was challenged to create a working model to present to the group within forty-five minutes. On one team a distinguished surgeon worked feverishly with a ten-year-old to stitch up an agricultural engineer who would farm the oceans and develop hydrogardens. Other team members, a teenager and grandparent, worked together to write out the story of how their fantasy invention worked. Still another group, a banker in his sixties and a young mother in her early twenties, designed a sound-effects tape to accompany their space-age solution to overpopulation.

Many reported that they had misgivings about attending such an evening. They were already tired by the time 6:00 p.m.

ACTION
ITEM

Stop and ask yourself: What are you passionate about? Where, or when, do you allow yourself to experience passion? If there is little passion in your life now, why? When and how did you lose it? What could rekindle your passion? If skepticism or cynicism has crept in, you might want to take a look at what price you are paying for these two qualities. Age and experience are not necessarily strangers to passion. Ben Franklin, Thomas Jefferson, Eleanor Roosevelt, Madam Curie, Lee Iacocca, and Georgia O'Keeffe all knew defeat and dis-couragement. Yet in spite of their difficulties, all were able to hang on to a sense of passion about those things that really mattered to them. Perhaps passion is linked to a degree of caring about something. And perhaps we learn to protect ourselves from disappointment and defeat by not caring too much, by suppressing our emotions, and by not risking things that seem far out of reach. But if we sacrifice high energy, deep involvement, and making a difference in life, is the price of our apathy and indifference too great?

rolled around. And they weren't sure this was their "cup of tea" anyway. Yet by the time each invention was shared, complete with original poetry, lots of laughter, and the risking of creative ideas, plus ice cream and a worship service about the gift of cre-ativity and the great resource of individual differences, each per-son left with a new sense of hope, renewal, dedication, and quality energy. There is something here to be learned for us all.

How Do We Lose Our Passion?

If we choose the safer route, to lower our goals and only hope for realistic, sure possibilities, we limit our lives to the mediocre and

"**Far better it is to dare mighty things, to win glorious triumphs, even though checkered by failure, than to take rank with those poor spirits who neither enjoy much nor suffer much, because they live in the gray twilight that knows not victory nor defeat.**"

—Theodore Roosevelt

rob ourselves of the chance for a really big win and all the excitement that goes with it.

When weighing the options of living fully versus living safely to avoid potential pain and disappointment, we vote for the high road. This means choosing to risk experiencing big disappointments and great losses by investing heavily in dreams and goals. To live with great passion means to "bet the farm" on each day of life. Yet we find we have to reconfront this choice again and again. For often, without realizing it, we slip back into the comfort of not caring quite so much, not risking, dreaming realistic rather than innovative dreams, not adventuring forth. Life becomes safer (and this may be needed and appropriate for a time). But it lacks the depth, the challenge, the richness, and the vitality that we have grown to love and enjoy. If our passion has been lost, we need to discover ways to rekindle it.

Dreams for a High-Energy Future

The writer Robert Greenleaf has said, "Nothing much happens without a dream. For something really great to happen, it takes a really great dream." Greenleaf and others who have spent their lives studying leaders and leadership qualities have discovered that one characteristic these leaders hold in common is dreaming great dreams and sharing their visions with others.

What is your dream or vision for your life? Is it a practical, fairly easy dream to obtain, or is it a very challenging vision, one that falls under the "in your wildest imagination" category?

Without an inspiring dream, life loses its zest, its purpose, its energy. As children leave the nest to start their own lives, many women—especially those who have chosen to remain home and raise their children—suffer from the "empty nest" syndrome.

Their main purpose has been successfully fulfilled and now they must ask themselves what life is all about. Another common problem people face is becoming so busy helping others around them (children, spouses, friends) achieve their dreams that they forget to generate any dreams of their own. In addition, many men and women experience a mid-life crisis as they reach or fail to reach certain goals, then suddenly realize that old age is fast approaching. They may foolishly try to recreate their youth. Or they may spend time soul-searching and reestablishing new and meaningful dreams for the second half of their lives.

I learned ten years ago when my life got too easy that without big dreams, I lost my energy and drive. I require challenges and wonderful, "impossible" dreams to energize my whole life process. Yet we are all different, and some people thrive on much more "do-able" dreams. The breadth and extent of dreams is not so much the issue. But giving yourself permission to dream and invest in your dreams *is essential to high-energy living*.

Viktor Frankl, during his four-year imprisonment in a Nazi concentration camp, discovered that of the prisoners who escaped the gas chambers, those who had a life purpose (or dream) were far more likely to survive. Those who didn't, died. Bernie Siegel, a surgeon and teacher at Yale Medical School, and oncologist Carl Simonton also report that having a meaningful purpose is a primary factor for patients who successfully recover from cancer. In a new field of study called psychoneuroimmunology, we are learning that just thinking vividly about an exciting dream or goal, and imaging it as complete with all its benefits, can cause our body to create chemicals and hormones (such as endorphins) which activate our immune system, counter stress, and seem to create new energy.

"Nothing much happens without a dream. For something really great to happen, it takes a really great dream."

Test this idea by recalling which people, in your experience, have the most dynamic energy. Do they have a dream and does it seem to energize them? Is their dream contagious to others around them? Martin Luther King's "I have a dream" speech is a wonderful example of this quality.

In addition, dreaming is a safe way to test options for the future. It is also the first step toward finding ways to make the impossible possible. "If you can dream it, you can do it," said Walt Disney. I have a personal anecdote to share along this line. Several years ago in a workshop, I was encouraged to make a list of ten outrageous, inviting, challenging dreams for my life. If there were no limits, what would I wish? I made my list, but was careful to keep my ideas covered, for to me they were so impossible that I was embarrassed to have anyone else see them. Then a few years later I moved and was unpacking boxes. Out fell my list. At first I didn't recognize it. But as I read through the ten dreams, to my amazement, eight of the ten had been realized. I had earned my doctorate from a prestigious university, published not one but two books, started my own successful business, found and married a marvelous mate, designed and built a greenhouse off my bedroom, enjoyed a year's sabbatical exploring and pursuing a new direction in life, enjoyed an exciting cruise in the Caribbean and sailed in the West Indies, and designed the ideal job for myself and found a client to pay me to do what I most enjoy doing.

We encourage you to entertain yourself each day with vivid images of your dreams as though they have come true in the best possible ways.

Summary

1. Feeling enthusiasm and emotional involvement for people, activities, and causes is a key ingredient to high energy. Controlling your emotions and "playing it safe" will diminish your vitality for life.

2. Without an inspiring dream, life loses its zest, its purpose, its energy.

3. Expanding your life by entertaining courageous, enticing dreams is the first step toward programming your brain to produce original solutions.

PART TWO

Reclaiming KidSpirit: Joy Breaks and Other Energy Secrets

3

ROLE MODELS FOR HIGH ENERGY:

Recapturing the Vitality of Childhood

66 *In every real man a child is hidden that wants to play.* **99**
— **Friedrich Nietzsche**

66 *My father always reminded me that I should enjoy life, and he practiced what he preached. No matter how hard he worked, he always made sure to leave enough room to have a good time. He loved bowling and poker as well as good food, drink, and especially good friends.* **99**
— **Lee Iacocca**

66 *One of the high-energy items in my office is a baseball cap that says, 'I refuse to grow up.'* **99**
— **Peter Van Nort, President, Power Sector, Fluor Daniel, Inc.**

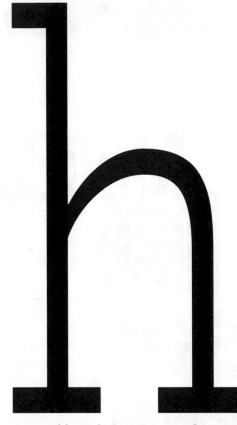

ow many times have you watched your own children or the neighborhood kids and remarked enviously, "Where do they get all that energy?" or "They never seem to slow down!" or "Ah, to have that kind of energy again." Yes, childhood seems to be a time of limitless energy, the one period in our lives when we rarely felt tired, worn out, and pressed for time. Children seem to be in motion constantly—exploring, searching, trying, mimicking. But they also get a significant amount of rest during the day. And when their bodies tell them it's time to rest, they usually will switch gears to a more passive activity or will fall asleep wherever they are, then bounce into action again.

The Secret of Childhood Energy

What is their secret? Is this tremendously high energy level only granted to us during the earliest years of our lives? Or is there a way for us to maintain, or regain, much of the vitality we had in our youth?

We believe there is. A supple body, hormonal growth spurts, and a high metabolism are not the only sources of their vitality.

Childhood behavior patterns and attitudes also contribute greatly to their energy levels. Consider the way healthy children go about their day, then compare this with the way you spend your average day. Study the list of fifteen childhood characteristics that we have observed among children.

Characteristics of Childhood

Little kids characteristically

1. seek out things that are fun to do, or else they find a way to have fun at what they are doing;
2. spontaneously jump from one interest to another, giving themselves permission to leave one activity whenever they feel bored or more interested in something else;
3. are curious, usually eager to try anything once;
4. smile and laugh a lot;
5. experience and express emotions freely;
6. are creative and innovative;
7. are physically active;
8. are constantly growing mentally and physically;
9. will risk often—i.e., aren't afraid to keep trying something that they aren't initially good at and aren't afraid to fail;
10. rest when their body tells them to (and if they resist nap time, they become cranky and have shorter attention spans);
11. learn enthusiastically;
12. dream and imagine;
13. believe in the impossible;
14. generally don't worry or feel guilty; and
15. are passionate.

Unfortunately, most of us learned to "act our age" as we grew up. Yet this meant abandoning some of the most natural and powerful high-energy stimulants available to us. For example, remember how you felt the last time you were really angry at someone. Did you experience a surge of emotion and aggression flowing through your body, so that it was difficult to sit passively in your chair or the driver's seat? Did you feel like yelling at the offensive person, shaking your fists, or even striking the person? The incident might have left you so agitated that you had difficulty sleeping that night.

On a more positive note, what about the last time you achieved something wonderful? Perhaps you were chosen to receive a community award, or your ad campaign was selected over ten other companies vying for the commission, or you won your first game of tennis against a challenging partner. Can you remember the burst of emotion and momentum that surged through you? You probably wanted to shout for joy, jump up and down, and hug someone. And you probably felt pretty enthusiastic and "revved up" for several days following the news.

What you experienced was a big dose of adrenaline or endorphins along with emotional energy coursing through your brain and body, making you alert and passionate and ready to respond. Of course, in most emotional situations, especially at the office, frequent unabashed displays of your feelings would be considered inappropriate and immature. So you probably had to do some deep breathing or aerobics to calm down those pent-up feelings, especially in the case of anger.

Or perhaps you have such "grown-up" control over your emotions that you can quickly talk yourself out of reacting to them. You can regain your com-

ACTION
ITEM

Examine your overall life-style and work day, and honestly ask yourself how many of the fifteen characteristics of childhood describe you now. Next think of some of the most active and successful adults you know and decide whether any of these childhood traits fit their mode of behavior.

If you discover a large disparity between your current work/personality style and these characteristics of children, perhaps you have left behind some of the most valuable high-energy behavior traits of your youth. Each of these normal childhood experiences and behavior patterns are releasers of energy.

posure and keep the lid on. Often adults purposely never allow themselves to get too high or too low so that they can "retain their objectivity."

As adults and professionals we can't allow ourselves to be on an emotional roller coaster every hour of the day. Yet can you recognize how this tempering of our feelings and actions has stifled many of our most natural sources of energy? By eliminating most of our opportunities for fun, laughter, joy, physical activity, curiosity, adventure, and unrepressed emotional expression, we adults are in fact denying ourselves many positive energy boosts throughout the day. Furthermore, we must expend a great deal of *mental* energy to repress *emotional* energy, as in the case of controlling feelings of anger. And instead of leading the invigorating yet sufficiently restful life of a child, many of us have tied ourselves down to routine (guaranteed successes) or to so many responsibilities that life becomes more exhausting than joyful.

Other adults lead such programmed, single-focused life-styles that there is little room for unstructured fun, spontaneity, and relaxation. Is it no wonder we end up using artificial stimulants such as caffeine to perk us up and alcohol to loosen us up?

In addition to emotional expression, there is a strong link between play and energy. Normal children spend the vast majority of their day playing and having fun. Even when they are doing a chore for Mother and Dad, they often make a game out of it. And the fact that they are experiencing so much fun and intrigue and so many adventures and emotional "highs" throughout the day is a major source of their high energy levels.

When adults "play with an idea" at work, they are also incorporating some of the elements of play. In addition, they let down mental barriers and relax the limits—or inhibitions—on their thinking. This allows for a greater flow of blood to the brain and for a release of energizing endorphins.

Being grown up doesn't have to mean leaving all our positive childhood traits behind. On the contrary, we have experimented with a variety of ways to incorporate the fifteen energy-producing behavior patterns into the office and home environment. And by relearning these strategies you can recapture much of the energy you had in your youth.

Yes, physical activity, the free expression of emotions, a sense of adventure and challenge, and feelings of joy, anger, curiosity, fascination, surprise, apprehension, and satisfaction— all a daily part of a healthy child's life— affect either brain chemistry or metabolic and mental processes in a way that produces energy.

One reason we have concluded that high energy is *not* the sole property of youth is that we know of many adults who have had the energy of children throughout their lives. Our sources are through our field research with top business leaders and their teams and families, plus the biographies and autobiographies of scores of highly active and productive people. R. Buckminster Fuller, Leonardo da Vinci, Ben Franklin, Thomas Jefferson, Eleanor Roosevelt, Winston Churchill, Armand Hammer, and Louise Nevelson are just a handful of the genius personalities we have studied. In fact, most of

Study the following components of play and consider how they help to release energy. When preschool children are playing, they are usually

- looking at and touching toys and equipment that have stimulating colors, shapes, and textures (notice how few black-and-white and single-colored toys there are);

- being challenged to solve something, such as putting together a puzzle and making the jack-in-the-box pop up;

- fantasizing about being something other than themselves, such as being a lion or a firefighter or their mommy;

- getting exercise, and therefore increasing their metabolism, by climbing on a jungle gym, playing tag, jumping rope, etc.;

- testing the limits, as in how far out on a tree limb they can climb or how much they can get away with before being punished;

- exploring and discovering relationships, such as cause and effect (what happens when I step on a bug, drop an egg, etc.?);

- discovering their personal power, such as swinging high in the air or winning a game; and

- creating new possibilities, such as blending two colors together to make a new color.

These activities renew energy—for both children and adults—by

- relieving stress buildup;

- creating an interplay and balance between the right and left brain hemispheres;

- releasing energizing hormones and endorphins;

- producing challenging situations and the satisfaction of solving them; and

- building bridges between people.

them sustained their vitality well into their seventies, eighties, and nineties.

Our key discovery about them was that their work and play styles were remarkably similar to those of children. And when we integrated these behavior traits into our own work habits and life-styles, our energy and productivity levels increased significantly as well.

Business Leaders Apply Traits of Childhood as Energy Builders

When we asked several corporate leaders which of the fifteen traits of childhood still fit them today, it was not unusual for their answer to be, *"Most of them!"* Here are some of their comments to show how they have retained these childhood strategies:

1. **Seek out fun things to do, or else find a way to have fun at what they are doing:** "I definitely seek out fun, and I find it difficult to push myself to do things that I don't view as fun. Of course, my definition of fun is different from a child's. I find most of my activities at work as being fun; watering the plants in my office is fun to me, too, as is cleaning off my white board at the end of the day. So I guess I'm pretty good at turning work into fun."

2. **Spontaneously jump from one interest to another:** "I demand that I get to do that. I believe in responding to every mind stimulus unless it is truly hazardous. I feel free to pick up on my ideas as they come, to stop in mid-sentence if another thought hits me, and to jump from topic to topic."

3. **Are curious and usually eager to try anything once:** "People who to me are truly alive and curious are not passive when

they have the chance to learn something new. I am always appalled when I sit through a meeting in which complex ideas and material are being discussed, and many of the people aren't even taking notes. Yet they are supposed to understand this new data and bring it back to their staff. But I know there is no way they have really involved themselves in the learning process. Instead, I try to participate in every new situation that presents itself to me and to learn from it."

4. **Smile and laugh a lot:** "That's me. In fact, I refuse to have a picture taken of me when I'm not smiling. Sometimes a photographer at work will ask me for a serious, businesslike pose, but I never comply . . . because that's not me."

5. **Experience and express emotions freely:** "I definitely experience them freely. I only limit my expression of emotion to those times when the protocol of the situation will not allow it. Still, I'd say that I express my feelings 80% of the time."

6. **Are creative and innovative:** "This is simply the fine art of thinking of every problem as an opportunity and a challenge. The more I do this, the easier it gets. I truly believe this is what put me and others at the top!"

7. **Are physically active:** "I can feel the difference in my energy when I am physically active. This is a daily gift I give myself to boost my performance."

8. **Are constantly growing mentally and physically:** "I'm a strong believer in the idea that there are only two directions your mind can go—forward and backward. And there is no such thing as resting on your laurels in terms of your mind. Physically, I don't feel very susceptible to the standard notions of age slowing you down. Also, I like to frequently learn new physical skills, such as juggling or skiing."

The Lord must have realized that folks need a shot in the arm when they get to my age because he gave us grandchildren.
—Bob Gary

9. **Are willing to risk often—i.e., aren't afraid to try something they aren't initially good at and aren't afraid to fail:** "In my line of work there is always a certain risk factor. I'd say that I'm not afraid to go against the system or to at least go back and challenge it. There is a tremendous opportunity that is often missed by people in business who never question the way things are . . . and what change might bring. Another factor that allows me to risk often is that I have absolute confidence that I will survive no matter what happens. I think I have always felt this way."

10. **Rest when their body tells them to:** "I try to respond to my body's apparent demands in many areas. And if I feel tired and I'm in a situation where I can catch a nap during the day, I'll do it."

11. **Learn enthusiastically:** "Definitely. For example, one thing I make a point to do when I fly is to sit next to someone interesting-looking and to learn as much as I can about him or her."

12. **Dream and imagine:** "Absolutely. I can't imagine my life without my dreams."

13. **Believe in the impossible:** "I'll even go so far as to say that there is no such thing as the impossible. It's a belief I've had ever since I can remember. Now, I'm not saying that I want to try jumping out of a twenty-story window. But I basically believe that if you put your mind to something, you can find a way to do it. Plus we often prove we can accomplish the impossible at work. For example, recently my company was asked to overhaul and manufacture a particular piece of equipment. Some experts told us it would take at least sixty days, but we did it in thirty-seven. And with experience, now we have the time down to five and one-half days."

14. **Don't worry or feel guilty:** "I don't worry much and rarely dwell on guilt. In fact, I have never kept myself awake at night worrying over some problem. Now, I do spend time analyzing how I might have done something better. But once that's done, I feel I have resolved the matter. I basically feel satisfied if I know I have put my best effort into something, no

matter how it turns out. Otherwise, I think most worrying is a waste of energy."

15. **Are passionate:** "That really leads back to feeling free to express my emotions and to being an avid learner, both of which are true about me. And another thing I'll say about having these traits is that one of the fun things I have in my office is a baseball cap that says, 'I refuse to grow up.'"

Energy Profiles

As you read the following excerpts from biographies and articles on Thomas Edison, Margaret Mead, Georgia O'Keeffe, Albert Schweitzer, Winston Churchill, and Liz Claiborne, notice how many of their behavior and work habits match the fifteen characteristics of children listed earlier.

Thomas Edison

Thomas Edison, the American father of invention, perfected the incandescent electric bulb, started the electrification of the United States, improved on the telephone and storage battery, made the first phonograph, and pioneered motion pictures—to name just a few of his accomplishments. In *Thomas Edison, American Inventor* Roselyn and Ray Eldon Heibert write, "From the time he was 12 years old until he reached his middle eighties he worked, often day and night. By trial and error he patiently attacked problems until he found their solutions."

Edison frequently napped to enable himself to work long hours. "He continued this practice throughout his adult life, and it is known that he had the peculiar ability to sleep anyplace—on the floor, on a table, on a pile of coal, or even in a rolltop desk!" report the Heiberts. At times, visiting dignitaries found him sleeping in one of his unorthodox spots. Finally his wife moved a cot into one of his alcoves and demanded that he use this instead.

Although Edison punched a time clock that recorded sixteen-hour days throughout his seventies, he also gave himself extended periods of leisure time away from work. He was fond of traveling and

> **Edison's strict habits and demanding routine were balanced by a prankish sense of humor and zest for life.**

camping in the country with fellow inventors Harvey Firestone and Henry Ford and the naturalist John Burroughs. In what the Hieberts describe as "many carefree expeditions across the country," the men often toured the back roads of New England. "Edison had a wonderful time on these trips. He loved to sit by the campfire at night and tell funny stories. He slept happily in his clothes, washed in the icy waters of mountain streams, and stopped to admire the views and vistas of the countryside," they write. In addition, his "strict habits and demanding routine were balanced by a prankish sense of humor and zest for life."

This zest for life could be seen in his work nook as well. The Hieberts describe Edison's desk as being strewn with paperweights, bottles of chemical solutions, parts of phonographs, assorted incoming letters, a bottle of jelly, throat antiseptic, photographs, some soda-mint tablets, and cubbyholes jammed with notes, reports, memoranda, and stale cigars.

Margaret Mead

Margaret Mead, America's foremost anthropologist, wrote thirty-four books and scores of articles, made ten films, lectured constantly across the United States and the world, frequently lobbied the government for more funding for scientific research, authored a monthly column for *Redbook* for some fifteen years, kept up with an extensive network of friends, and taught for many years at Columbia University. Writes Jane Howard in *Margaret Mead: A Life*, "With her daring journeys, provocative ideas and unbounded energy, she built on that celebrity [image] until she achieved the status of myth throughout the English-speaking world." In fact, Howard likens Mead's extensive lecture travels to "those of Air Force One."

So remarkable were Mead's stamina and enthusiasm that one of her young colleagues mused on the need for a project "to study the source of her energy, her creativity, and her appetite for and ability to encompass the complexity of very many lives within her own life and intellect." Surely one source of her energy was her fervor to communicate her findings and to continuously gain new insights on a culture's effect on its people. Her work routine began at 5:00 a.m., when she wrote 1,000 words before sitting down to breakfast. "She had a great talent," Howard quotes another colleague as saying, "for producing ideas and never mind how many secretaries it kept up all night . . . she never wasted a minute or a meal. All her meals were business meals, and why not? She'd take trains back and forth to New York and her time was so calibrated that she probably wrote a book each way." In addition, rather than ride alone in a cab to the airport, Mead was often driven by her students while she viewed videotapes of their work.

Mead's passionate spirit was another wellspring of her energy. She could be as temperamental as she was generous and supportive, and her "jabbing, aggressive manner," quotes Howard from a close friend of Mead's, helped generate "incredible amounts of work. She invoked and evoked the best there was in other people. She'd get them off their butts and tell them, 'Of course you can write this dissertation.'"

Yet Mead enjoyed many hobbies and interests as well as her work, among them cooking, sewing, knitting, socializing, and raising her daughter Cathy. Although Mead could have afforded a cook, she once commented, "If I had a cook I would be tempted to go to dinner conferences, but this way I have to come home to make dinner for Cathy." She also believed in incorporating her child into her daily routine, as her parents had done with her. In every room of her house, reports Howard, were things for her daughter to play with. Beneath the coffee table was a shelf filled with sand so that Cathy could play while the grown-ups had cocktails. And next to Mead's dressing table was an easel so that Cathy could paint while her mother got dressed to go out.

"I expect to die, but I don't plan to retire," Mead said in her late sixties. Indeed until she began to suffer from various illnesses in her last years, she seemed to attack her work with increasing vigor, calling it "post-menopausal zest." Leo Rosten commented that her insatiable curiosity kept her learning "all the time, through her pores. She had a brilliant flair for seizing ideas from children, colleagues, historians and every other source that came her way. She was the greatest picker of brains I've ever known, the greatest girl reporter in the world."

Of course, Mead needed to stop to "refuel" just like the rest of us. Like Edison, one way she restored her energy was to take catnaps whenever the opportunity presented itself. Once she passed up a formal prespeech luncheon in order to revive herself before giving her address. Other times she would instruct her staff to wake her up just minutes before she was to begin her speech.

Georgia O'Keeffe

Georgia O'Keeffe was a highly creative and productive contemporary of Mead's. O'Keeffe composed nearly 900 completed canvasses depicting her unique vision of Southwest landscapes, clouds, flowers, stones, and evocative abstractions. She was always setting new goals and challenges for herself, using new hues of colors, trying difficult techniques, or painting a picture so it could be hung with any of the sides serving as the top. In her later years she experimented with large sculptures and ceramics. In her seventies, in fact, she created her largest canvas—a spectacular twenty-four-foot by eight-foot cloudscape.

O'Keeffe's usual work style was to paint intensely, from several hours up to an entire day if she was pleased with her results. But her work was often broken up by short, reviving breaks and "mini-vacations" away from her work. In *Portrait of an Artist: A Biography of Georgia O'Keeffe*, author Laurie Lisle reports that O'Keeffe as a young student "sometimes worked intensely, and other times, refused to work for days and instead pestered the other girls in the studio . . . indulging in antics." During her many years of living in New York, she would start on a painting by midday, absorbed in her work until the fading light of dusk forced her to stop. Then she would take to the sidewalk for a long walk.

Throughout her life, O'Keeffe balanced the stillness of her painting sessions with daily exercise. During her many years of living in Texas, New Mexico, and other Southwest sites, O'Keeffe would typically be out before sunrise for a two-hour hike across the desert. She was also fond of swimming, camping, and climbing, and enjoyed exploring the countryside of every place she visited. O'Keeffe was also an avid gardener, and she loved to start off her day by tending to her herbs and flowers as well.

Perhaps because most photos of O'Keeffe show her wearing a serious expression, some people regarded her as being rather austere. But there was definitely an emotional and joyful side to her. For instance, during a walk O'Keeffe took with a faculty couple in Texas, she "let out a loud whoop," reports Lisle. When the couple checked to make sure she was all right, O'Keeffe shouted back, "I can't help it—it's all so beautiful!" In addition, the newly released letters of O'Keeffe are riddled with exuberant feelings of love, astonishment, joy, uncertainty, and courage, all of which were manifested in her emotionally-charged paintings.

Although she maintained many strong liaisons throughout her life, O'Keeffe also needed times of daily solitude. Even as a

> **"O'Keeffe sometimes worked intensely, and other times, refused to work for days and instead pestered the other girls in the studio . . . indulging in antics."**

small child, she often played alone, creating imaginary households and lives out of ordinary objects from nature. She took most of her walks alone; she used the time to focus on the landscape and muse on the latest technique she was experimenting with. This habit may have contributed to O'Keeffe's individualized and daring visions, such as one painting of fuchsia-colored snow. And although most of the male artists of her era made it plain to her that as a woman she couldn't hope to succeed, O'Keeffe stubbornly persevered until in her thirties her work began to earn enthusiastic reviews. O'Keeffe continued producing her art until her death at age ninety-eight.

Albert Schweitzer

Nobel Prize–winner Albert Schweitzer was a physician, respected philosopher, renowned biblical scholar, prolific author, accomplished organist and organ builder, manager, and crusader for world peace. As committed as he was to his mission in Africa, he could not "surrender his gifts" of music, theology, writing, and lecturing, writes Robert Payne in *The Three Worlds of Albert Schweitzer*. Furthermore, Schweitzer shifted from project to project, interest to interest, throughout the day. In the winter of 1906, for example, Payne shows Schweitzer continuing to pursue a full agenda of writing assignments while attending medical school. That winter he wrote a long essay on organ-building and completed the last chapter of his book, *The Quest for the Historical Jesus*. In order to find enough hours in the day and night to accomplish his many endeavors, Schweitzer "learned to take short naps in the middle of the day and to sleep easily on trains. He was pushing himself to the utmost, and vastly enjoying, in his rare moments of tranquility, his capacity to squander himself in so many directions," reports Payne.

Despite Schweitzer's demanding schedule at the mission, he still needed recreation and a creative outlet. "Above all, his fruit orchard gave him intense pleasure," writes Payne, as did "the stimulus of music." Payne also notes that the doctor "worked better after playing seriously."

During his years in medical school, for example, "he had turned with relief to the organ, and with Ernst Munch at his side he had played strenuously for an hour or two before returning to his studies." Schweitzer once explained to someone who asked him the secret of his serenity, "Appreciate fantasy. When I play my piano in the evening in Lambarene I shut my eyes and can make-believe I am playing a great organ and this gives me true repose."

Winston Churchill

Winston Churchill is best remembered as a brilliant statesman and military leader who had unflinching courage, fortitude, and energy. In fact, the British admiral J. H. Godfrey described Churchill as having "demonic energy and extraordinary imagination." A closer look at the man, through biographies and his own writing, reveals that much of his vitality and vision came from his ability to retain the sense of inventiveness, spontaneity, spunk, and belief in the impossible that children possess.

For example, in William Manchester's biography of Churchill, entitled *The Last Lion*, Churchill is depicted as having a passionate "love of gadgetry and wildly improbable schemes." During the war, he was forever coming up with ideas for innovative types of weaponry, such as a trench-cutting tank. Although many of his inventive ideas seemed outlandish to his more conservative military leaders, he was not afraid to risk failure by trying what had never been conceived of before. This characteristic led Franklin Roosevelt to comment later, "Winston has fifty ideas a day, and three or four are good." Explains the author, "Most of his schemes were politely discussed and then dropped. The difficulty was that his Admiralty staff was dealing with genius, with a man who thought in cosmic terms, and that the price for some of these excursions was beyond the grasp of career naval officers." By the end of the war, however, many of Churchill's ideas were integrated into successful military strategy and weapons.

Churchill also had a fluid mind which "had many tracks, and if one was blocked, he left it and turned to another," writes Manchester. Similarly, his moods and personality were equally diversified, like a "kaleidoscope." Furthermore, the prime minister had a strong artistic bent. He authored numerous biographies and history books, and in 1953 won the Nobel Prize for literature. In addition, he enjoyed painting and gardening in his retirement years.

You don't, however, have to be a scientist, artist, or world leader to possess these high-energy characteristics of children. Many, many business leaders, young *and* older, have personalities and life-styles that produce continually high reserves of human energy.

Liz Claiborne

At the vibrant age of sixty, Liz Claiborne has built a thirteen-year-old fashion enterprise (with a $255,000 initial investment) into one of the youngest companies ever to land on the Fortune 500 list. She has accomplished this feat as much through her ability to innovate, dream big, and risk often as through her sharp business sense. She captured a market that other designers had overlooked—the thirty-years-and-older professional career woman who does not have the fat-free figure of a fashion model and who prefers classic, softer styles and casual wear over short-lived trends.

> **Claiborne is a physically active person and often walks many blocks to work from her apartment. She doesn't put herself above her staff, but enjoys getting into the thick of things right along with them.**

Claiborne is often described as a "pathfinder" and a "reluctant revolutionary." Working for years as the chief designer for other clothes manufacturers, she tried unsuccessfully to convince her former bosses to create clothes for the older, professional woman. Then in 1976, she and her husband/partner risked their entire savings to market their own line of womenswear. Not one to rest on past laurels, Claiborne has continued to dream big, take risks, and break into new merchandizing areas such as menswear, fragrance, accessories, and retailing.

Claiborne typically puts in a ten-hour work day, but she knows the tricks for replenishing her energy supply. A physically active person, she often walks many blocks to work from her apartment. She also runs for aerobic exercise. In addition, she and her husband spend most weekends far removed from their work, walking, reading, and watching birds at either their beach house on Fire Island or at their ranch in Montana. And Claiborne does not seem to allow unrelieved stress, worries, or pent-up emotions to diminish her energy. People describe her as being intense but candid, witty, and fun-loving with her staff and peers. Wednesday mornings, for example, she jumps into a company van with her design staff for a trip to a fitting session in New Jersey. She doesn't put herself above her staff, but enjoys getting into the thick of things right along with them.

Retaining High-Energy Traits throughout Adulthood

In addition to noticing how energetic and productive life can be for people in their sixties up to their nineties, we hope you saw many parallels between the behavior patterns of children and these men and women. We think these traits, plus a fervent dedication to their fields and a clear vision of what they wish to accomplish, are the primary reasons they were able to remain so highly energized. Outstanding leaders always seem to have a strong vision of where they are headed and what they are capable of doing, even when others consider that vision impossible. We remember as children being inspired to "dig a hole to China" for hours, digging many days in a row. We made blisters on our palms but still we continued. Other times we would set out to build a fort or a tree house. We would work tirelessly, dragging junk down the alley, hammering and building until after supper time. Then we would beg to go back out after dark. There is enormous energy to be had from a goal if it is your personal dream. Yet only small children, fools, geniuses, and highly energetic people give themselves permission to dream so boldly.

The success of the energetic geniuses and business leaders profiled above also depended on several other traits that are not on our list for children. You probably can name them yourself. They are *perseverance, purpose,* and *discipline*. Unless someone is incredibly lucky, these usually make the difference between someone being highly successful or just managing to get by. Schweitzer, for instance, used to plunge his feet into cold water in order to study throughout the night during medical school. Edison worked many years with frustrating failures and skeptical critics until he perfected some of his key inventions.

Actually, children know how to persevere or else none of them would accomplish the arduous task of learning to walk or talk. But since children appear to be having fun all the time, this quality isn't as obvious to us as we watch them. Discipline is a mature quality that is acquired through practice and self-control.

> There is enormous energy to be had from a goal if it is your personal dream. Yet only small children, fools, geniuses, and highly energetic people give themselves permission to dream so boldly.

Turning back to the high-energy behavior traits of children, how many similarities did you find between those and the six adult profiles? Jot down some of your reactions in the margins, if you wish.

FIRST, did you notice that all of them were avid learners and were constantly experimenting with something new? Edison was unwilling to rest on his past laurels but continued to improve on everything he invented. And O'Keeffe went from specializing in black and white sketches to colored paintings to making sculptures in her later years.

SECOND, all of these highly successful men and women were passionately involved in a diverse number of interests and activities. Witness, for example, Schweitzer's continual dedication to his musical talents, his writing, his orchards and gardens, and his contributions to world peace. He could easily have become totally consumed by his medical practice and mission, but he chose not to deny himself the enjoyment and constant stimulation he received from the many other engaging areas of his life.

THIRD, most of the people profiled worked on a variety of projects during the day and would jump from one to the other according to their moods and interests. Remember that this is the normal play pattern of children, one that is often tagged as a "short attention span." But this label would hardly be used for geniuses who have the habit of doing three things at once.

FOURTH, all adults profiled were willing to try new endeavors, to experiment and learn new skills, to become an imperfect beginner at something. Witness how Churchill, Edison, and O'Keeffe were so curious about some new aspect of their work or plans that they were willing to start from scratch, risking disappointment or even failure, to pursue their new endeavor. Their highly developed senses of curiosity and adventure frequently led them into new territories to challenge their creative and intellectual skills.

FIFTH, most of these people believed in the value of play. They broke away from their work to enjoy stimulating and light-hearted activities by playing frequently with their children, taking extended vacations, socializing with their co-workers and friends, decorating their offices with their favorite trinkets (can't we call them toys as well?), and so on. Edison's work styles are particularly good examples of putting fun breaks into the work day (and night).

SIXTH, creativity and innovation were central to these people's works and activities, even among the nonartists in the group.

FINALLY, even though this book has not yet discussed the phenomenon of brain hemisphericity, we will interject our seventh similarity—that each of these men and women appear to have well-balanced and well-integrated brain hemispheres. Having a balanced, or "whole-brained," orientation enables a person to have a smooth and flexible flow between doing step-by-step work based on logic and reason supported by doing more creative, conceptional work based on intuition, the emotions, and artistic appeal.

If you are as convinced as we are that generating abundant and unlimited energy is linked to reclaiming many characteristics of childhood, you will want to test this hypothesis for yourself.

Learn to Let the Child within You Live

Now let's look at some ways to help you tap into the abundant energy of kids. Four strategies that can be great fun will get you started. First just remember what it was that you loved doing as a kid. Find ways to go back and indulge in these fond memories. What did you miss out on as a kid that you longed to experience? Find ways to claim those adventures now. Become aware of what inner fears and messages block or spoil your fun. Creatively find ways to challenge or turn them off. And, finally, you'll really get into the fun if you recruit an expert or two to coach you. Little kids are just such specialists, so be sure you let them take the lead.

We have collected a few high-energy stories from the research experiences of several of our participants to convince you to find your own ways to reclaim KidSpirit.

Tom Baker, senior vice president at TU Electric, shares his story:

> "*My daughter Kim graduated from Lake Highlands High School this spring (thank you, Lord!). At the end of each school year the senior class puts on a senior show in which they sing, dance, and put on skits. Three or four weeks before the show was to take place, I received a telephone call from another father. In a hushed voice he asked me to meet him along with several others at a local dance studio within the hour and not to say a word to Kim about it. He was drafting volunteer fathers of graduating seniors to appear in a surprise skit in the school's senior show. I had no idea what to expect although I feared the worst. When I showed up at the appointed hour at Kitty Carter's Dance Studio, I discovered that about thirty fathers were going to learn a dance routine, taught by one of the senior girls. We attended several secret practice sessions each week. We learned a complete routine to Michael Jackson's song titled 'Bad.' We dressed up in old jeans, Harley Davidson tee shirts, and chains. I used about half of a tube of Dep to slick my hair into a duck tail on the sides and combed the front forward into a point. Apply a couple of stick-on tattoos and there you have it. The act was appropriately called 'The Bad Dads' and needless to say was the hit of the show.*
>
> *With regard to recapturing childhood vitality, don't ever let anyone tell you that 'you can never go back.' I went back during the month of rehearsals and was in high school again (except I didn't have to take finals!!!).*

ACTION
I T E M
▼

What was most fun for you when you were a child? Make a list of things you enjoyed as a child. Better yet, invite a friend to join you as together you recall and each make a list. To help get you started, we will share some of our first ideas:

- building tree houses
- playing with paper dolls
- having tea parties
- making mud pies
- giving plays and shows
- making and flying kites
- playing in the sand pile
- building models
- digging a hole to China
- playing dress-up
- building rubber guns and having wars
- having water fights
- building soap box racers
- thinking up scary stories to frighten other kids

Let this list continue. Now begin to think of creative ways you can begin to enjoy some of your childhood pleasures. A stockbroker realized he would love to own one of those fancy, remote-controlled model sailboats his family could not afford when he was young. He found one in a hobby store and was amazed at the breakthrough of new energy he experienced as a result of this purchase. Claiming the joys of childhood can awaken that abundant energy resource in your life.

It was interesting to watch a group of pinstriped captains of industry as we practiced and put on our skit. There was total role reversal. During the rehearsals, the 'boys' cut up and clowned around while our eighteen-year-old teacher, whose father was one of the group, chided us to pay attention and quit talking. As we were getting dressed for one of the shows, one of the Bad Dads commented that it was rather scary how comfortable some of us looked in our costumes! I actually had an increase in energy level after each rehearsal and experienced a bit of a 'high' after the performance. Recapturing the vitality of childhood works. I can't wait for my next trip back!! That trip will be in a few weeks when I put the pinstripe back in the closet and get out the Harley tee shirt when the family vacations in Disney World. Although there are a lot of very interesting things to see there, I can't wait to ride the rides!!"

For each of us there most likely were dreams we missed out on while growing up. These can be even more delicious to realize as an adult, having waited decades to claim them. For me such a dream was to learn to tap dance.

As a girl we couldn't afford the shoes or the lessons. So at the age of forty-nine I bought a pair of shiny black tap shoes and a videotape called "Let's Tap" by Bonnie Franklin and learned three dances to perform for my fiftieth birthday! This generated lots of new energy for me, and it's a great way to enjoy aerobic exercise. To my amazement, many of my friends who had learned to tap dance as kids were also excited when I invited them to tap again as adults in a playful, spoof birthday-party recital.

I must have built ten or twelve tree houses in my early days. But never so grand as I could build now. This past year I gave myself permission to build a marvelous tree house as a second-floor addition to our home, which surrounds a favorite sweet gum tree in our backyard. It has a dumb waiter that lifts loads of things up into the tree house. A group of engineers built a wonderful tire swing that hangs invitingly from a nearby live oak. A shiny red spiral stairway allows adults easy access to the tree house. And I am amazed at how much energy we get by giving ourselves permission to live this fantasy.

Barbara's lost dream was ice skating. She relates this story:

"It wasn't until I was in my mid-thirties that I lived in a place where I had the chance to learn to ice skate, something I had always wanted to do. I admit I was scared of falling and break-

What did you miss out on when you were a kid that might be fun and energizing now? Make your own list of things you always wanted to do but missed out on. Maybe it's learning to play a musical instrument; to paint, sculpt, build with clay, or take and develop your own photographs; to write poetry or a murder mystery; to act in a play, learn French, or take singing lessons; to own your own ice cream stand or become a D.J.; or to build a sailboat or sail the Caribbean.

Realize that for some people, it takes some poking around before you can dig up those old fantasies and start dreaming again. You might go to your local library and see what interesting books you can find on fun things to do. Or try becoming a scout leader or girl's club leader, and in the process of helping youngsters discover new talents and fun, you might discover some of your own.

Then don't deny yourself the chance to revive these old dreams and interests. All you need is the awareness that you still would enjoy these activities (or slight variations on these fun ideas) and the permission to pursue them.

When we validate our playful self by taking time to listen to and fulfill wishes and dreams, we bring back to life our optimistic, outrageous, enthusiastic, little-kid energy. Find ways to make some of these unrealized dreams come true.

ing something—and I certainly took many a hard thump during that first month on the ice. But after going to the rink about three times a week, I felt stable enough to acquire adequate speed and confidence for it to become exhilarating. Going round and round the rink faster and faster in time to rock music made me feel as if I were flying. And my energy felt boundless, as if I could keep skating for hours without any fatigue. At my age, I rarely challenged myself to learn a new physical skill, so this experience gave me an extra sense of vibrancy, excitement, and physical freedom."

We have encouraged the executives in our Perspective III program (executive development seminars which teach the benefits of whole-brain thinking) to spend time with a very young child to learn how they play and how they process or think as they play. The idea was to see what we can learn from them and how we might use these insights to develop our right-brain thinking.

Bob Gary, a Dallas executive, tells this story which illustrates the fresh perspective children bring to our lives.

"The Lord must have realized that folks need a shot in the arm when they get to my age because he gave us grandchildren. They are great examples of high energy, always ready for hugs, always giving out great, long belly laughs. Once my wife leaned over to tie my three-year-old grandson's shoe. He looked her in the eye and said, 'Mimi, did you know you can't ever run out of hugs and kisses? All you do is just hug 'em tight again and kiss 'em like this as many times as you want to.' Yet as adults, we do run out of them because society has taught us not to behave this way even though physical affection gives us a great emotional boost.

Kids instinctively know how to have high energy. Just watch them breath deeply all the time. And everything they do, they give their all through their laughter, play, and emotions.

Another lesson we can learn from kids is how they seem to know how to avoid things that will steal their energy. Back when my grandson was three years old, he had the irritating habit of saying 'I don't like you.' It was driving everyone up the wall. One day I had him on the tractor with me and he said it again. So I asked him what he would do if I told him that I didn't like him. 'I wouldn't listen to you,' he answered. Basically what he meant was that he wouldn't give someone else permission to hurt him. If you let someone hurt you—and no one can really hurt you unless you allow them to—then you're also letting pent-up hurt drain your energy from you. Of course the flip side to that is that nobody will love you without your permission, either. So if you want to build up your energy, let someone express kindness and love to you."

Bob Payne, a Dallas engineer, shares his story:

"One weekend a close friend had asked my wife, Wanda, if she would look after her four-year-old son one Saturday morning. Seeing the opportunity to do some interesting research, I volunteered for the job. It was a cold, wet winter day so John Mark suggested we go play in the garage. There he found a ladder, an

old broom, a bent bucket, and a partially deflated basketball. All four items were things I had stacked to throw away because they were no longer useful (left brain). Yet he was immediately drawn to them and discovered dozens of new ways to play with them (right brain). For four hours the youngster played happily with these four objects. I was amazed that none of the uses of John Mark's were the practical, work-oriented uses I would have explored. I might have been inclined to try to hammer the dent out of the bucket, find a way to inflate the basketball, sweep up some dirt with the broom, or sweep cobwebs off the ceiling. He did things like climbing up the ladder to drop the ball in the bucket, laying the ladder on its side to build a kind of fort, wearing the bucket on his head as a helmet, and marching with the broom over his shoulder. John Mark created action games, in no way the typical things I would do with these objects."

What stops you from awakening childhood energy? Make a list of "funstoppers" (admonishments from others or yourself that discourage participation in childhood activities). Some examples are:

"What will the neighbors think?"

"Don't start anything you're not going to finish!"

"Grow up!"

"Be perfect!"

"Act your age!"

"Anything worth doing is worth doing well!"

"You look ridiculous. Don't make a fool of yourself."

"What will my friends think?"

Be sure you don't contaminate your energy-building fun with adult expectations. If you hear these kinds of warnings creeping into your consciousness, it might help to stop and acknowledge their potential effect on you by writing them in the margin. Then realize they come from an entity we call "the Merciless Taskmaster." It's the part of you that expects you to adhere to the all-work-and-no-play Puritan ethic, that won't accept any tasks done less than perfectly and completely, that cares more about other people's expectations of you than your own needs. But turn off that nagging taskmaster voice long enough to discover how much fun and energy you can get by unleashing your natural instincts for free, creative play and hobbies.

Where can you find an energy coach to relearn the secrets of getting energy from your fun? Find a child to play with! If you find it difficult to turn off adult "should" messages, a child can be a good role model. Being with children often gives us permission to open and explore our playful right brain without contaminating the wonder and fun with left-brained restrictions. Collect a list of possible playmates who could become your energy coach—perhaps a kid down the block or a grandchild.

Rather than seeming like a chore, Bob's baby-sitting session flew by in a magical way, as time does when you get immersed in childhood fantasies. This is a big part of the energy secrets of children. When you lose yourself in timelessness, your left hemisphere has time to refresh and renew itself.

Summary

1. Most of the high-energy behavior characteristics of kids can be used by adults to increase their energy as well. In fact, research indicates that most geniuses and top performers have retained these characteristics through adulthood.

2. There is a strong link between play and energy. That's one reason why children have so much energy—they spend most of their day playing!

3. Learn to let the child within you live. Abundant energy is linked to this joyful playfulness.

4. Get busy reclaiming childhood fun and even wishes that never came true and see what happens to your energy reservoir.

5. Become aware of fun-stopping messages from the adult world and learn to ignore all but those essential for health and safety. (Most come from fear of change.)

6. Seek out kids as role models of high energy, high creativity, and the open, curious, joyful thought processes that use both.

4

BALANCING WORK AND PLAY:

Are You Joy-Starved?

66 . . . I'm constantly amazed by the number of people who can't seem to control their own schedules. Over the years, I've had many executives come to me and say with pride: 'Boy, last year I worked so hard that I didn't take any vacation.' It's actually nothing to be proud of. I always feel like responding, 'You dummy. You mean to tell me that you can take responsibility for an $80 million project and you can't plan two weeks out of the year to go off with your family and have some fun?' 99

—**Lee Iacocca,** *Iacocca: An Autobiography*

66 We do not stop playing because we are old, we grow old because we stop playing. 99

—**Source unknown**

We've talked about the importance of reawakening childlike qualities to generate and reclaim unlimited energy. Let's also stop to consider why play is specifically so important in generating energy and how society discounts and discredits childlike play.

The All-Work, No-Play Mentality

It is easy to fall into an all-work, no-play mentality in our culture. As author and social critic Jeremy Rifkin writes in his book *Time Wars*, "The modern age has been characterized by a Promethean spirit, a restless energy that preys on speed records and short-cuts . . . existing only for the quick fix . . . Despite our alleged efficiency . . . we seem to have less time for ourselves and far less time for each other . . . We have become more organized but less spontaneous, less joyful."

Many businesses, including private law practices, public relations and advertising firms, large corporations, and owner-operated companies, consider a work week of sixty to ninety hours as routine. In addition, the United States has one of the shortest average vacation leaves in the industrialized world. In most Western European nations, a five-week vacation leave is standard for new employees as well as longtime employees. Maternity and paternity leaves are also much more generous for our European counterparts.

The U.S. business world's mentality tends to be, the more hours worked, the more work produced. This idea applies not only to the stretch of hours worked on a given day and week but also to the minimal amount of personal break time allotted to each day. Yet for many reasons, this myth of a productivity curve continually rising throughout the day is being refuted. Numerous studies show that people usually hit a productivity peak at a certain point each day (or over a span of a certain number of hours worked), then their efficiency, carefulness, motivation, and creativity steadily wane. Working much beyond that effective productivity point, when fatigue is setting in, will often result in errors, poor judgment, accidents and injuries, and overall uninspired thinking. And in the area of learning, other studies indicate that sixty-minute periods may be the maximum time a person can comprehend and process information at his or her peak learning level. Steadily decreasing mental and physical energy levels are the primary causes of decline in each of these areas.

There is a way, however, to stay alert and productive throughout an average work day. Our method involves restoring your energy reserves *before* they have dropped so low that, like Albert Schweitzer, you have to dunk your feet, or perhaps your head, into a bucket of freezing water to revive! Our studies clearly support the value of *integrating a variety of short, brain-balancing breaks into each work day.*

A growing number of businesses are incorporating these energy-renewing breaks into their work structure and envi-

> **Numerous studies show that people usually hit a productivity peak at a certain point each day (or over a span of a certain number of hours worked), then their efficiency, carefulness, motivation, and creativity steadily wane.**

ronment. For instance, at E. I. DuPont de Nemours & Company, employees have scheduled frequent breaks to juggle, walk, do puzzles, and draw maps in the company's recreation room. At a huge shipping firm in Sweden, the staff often relax and test their new ideas in "the Brain Room," a converted storage area that features employee artwork, classical music, comfortable chairs, and brainstorming tools like flip charts and colored pens.

Within our own company in Dallas, we encourage our team to balance intensive, demanding work periods with frequent energy breaks. Most of us are on flex time, which means we are accountable to get our part of the job done but can plan around our personal and family needs. Rayo, our production director, takes an extended lunch break every other day to play basketball at a nearby YMCA and chooses to work later in the evenings. Our office is closed from noon to 1:00 p.m. to ensure time for an energy-restoring lunch break. Often two or three of us will take a brisk twenty-minute walk when we need an energy lift. There are also musical instruments for music breaks. A stationary bike invites anyone to take an exercise break. Some days there are morning breaks for peppermint tea and muffins and afternoon fruit and cheese breaks outside on the deck. Errands might include a joy break to stop by a toy store or card shop and browse for new ideas for our seminars. There are frequent five-minute breaks to celebrate news of a client's creative breakthrough or personal growth.

In addition, we each have a learning partner within the team. We become role models for each other as we review our creative plans for work *and* play. We share stress management strategies and make a serious personal commitment to live what we teach and then teach each other from our experience. Each of us also invites our family and friends to participate and teach us from their experiences. This process brings abundant energy into our team.

The Link between Play and Energy

Play and leisure time is critical and essential to maintaining abundant energy because it

1. allows the left hemisphere to rest while the right hemisphere creates new options and possible solutions to problems;

2. helps release built-up tension;

3. can open blocked thinking and trigger creative ideas;

4. stimulates an energy boost and thus restores your energy resources;

5. builds bridges between people;

6. creates hormones, endorphins, and other substances which activate your immune system;

7. allows you to safely explore new perspectives and new interests; and

8. creates new links between ideas.

Often, as we become adults, we lose our capacity to play. We may participate in games or sports, but we do so with our serious, ego-centered, competitive, "do your best" left brain hemisphere. In order to accomplish the goal of energy renewal and refreshment, we simply need to learn to shift gears and participate from the right hemisphere of our brain, which is open, spontaneous, flexible, joyful, loving, and eager to play for no purpose other than to enjoy experiencing and possibly sharing the moment.

If you find yourself on the golf course or tennis court working hard to do it right, irritated because you are playing badly or feeling tense about doing your best, then try to relax, be gentle with yourself, and remind yourself that you need to shift gears. To get the full benefit from play, first you need to learn to love yourself unconditionally just because you are you rather than because you are good at something. Next, extend that love to others and to life itself. Then just enjoy being and sharing and laughing and being open to all that is. Can you remember this wonderful open quality of childhood, demanding nothing from self or life other than to simply participate in life? Some call it "being time." To rediscover your ability to enjoy "being time" is the beginning of the discovery of not only new energy but of a new quality of energy. Learning to play is a critical step in discovering abundant energy.

The Link between Play and Well-Being

As Norman Cousins reported in *Anatomy of an Illness*, joyful laughter causes the brain to create endorphins which relieve stress and activate the immune system. These neuropeptides also seem to be linked to energy renewal. Notice the next time you leave a high-pressured meeting to have a few minutes of joyful laughter and relaxed, playful talk with a trusted friend. You are very likely to feel a sense of renewal, new balance to your judgment, and a fresh commitment to appropriate priorities. The same is true of any play that stimulates the senses, such as listening to music, seeing colorful photos and drawings, and drinking a delicious glass of juice.

The Link Between Play and Innovation

Stop for a moment and recall the times of your best ideas, your breakthrough solutions. Maybe you came up with a way to resolve a staff dispute, to phrase a perfect slogan for your new ad campaign, or to end a short story you were writing. Try to recall where you were and what you were doing when the creative "Aha!" popped into your head.

If your experiences have been similar to the many inventors and artists we have studied, you probably got that wonderful idea not when you were struggling to find an answer, but precisely when you weren't trying to think about it. Perhaps you were on the running path, in the shower, at a symphony concert, reading the funnies, or driving home from work. For many people, their great "aha" moments of insight come upon waking in the middle of the night with the answer. Albert Einstein, for example, claimed he got his best ideas while he shaved in the morning. O'Keeffe solved some of her painting technique problems during her walks.

Psychologist Rollo May has written an excellent book on this phenomenon entitled *The Courage to Create*. He discusses "the necessity of alternating work and relaxation, with the insight often coming at the moment of the break between the two, or at least within the break." Likewise, he details a personal breakthrough that came to him after he had spent an exhausting day struggling with a conflicting set of data. "I was tired. I tried to put the whole troublesome business out of my mind. About 50 feet away from the entrance to the Eighth Street station, [the answer] suddenly struck me 'out of the blue' . . . ," he writes.

> **When forced to concentrate too long on the same problem, the brain can end up going in circles, rehashing the same factors, coming to the same end point again and again.**

Quoting from the autobiography of the brilliant mathematician Jules Henri Poincare, May cites a fascinating pattern to these moments of insight. Poincare wrote that for fifteen days he strove to prove a theory but "reached no results." Then, he reports: "One evening, contrary to my custom, I drank black coffee and could not sleep. Ideas rose in crowds; I felt them collide until pairs interlocked, so to speak, making a stable combination. By the next morning I had established the existence of a class of Fuchsian functions, those which come from the hypergeometric series; I had only to write out the results, which took but a few hours."

After a frustrating struggle, suddenly everything became crystal clear to him. Poincare documented many such breakthrough ideas coming while he was relaxing, physically removed from his work. Another insight broke through while he was on a cross-town bus trip. Still another came during a vacation. Poincare explained: "Then I turned my attention to the study of some arithmetical questions apparently without much success and without a suspicion of any connection with my preceding researches. Disgusted with my failure, I went to spend a few days at the seaside, and thought of something else. One morning, walking on the bluff, the idea came to me, with just the same characteristics of brevity, suddenness and immediate certainty . . . ."

One reason that the brain needs to be distracted from the problem it is being asked to solve is that it can get deadlocked. When forced to concentrate too long on the same problem, the brain can end up

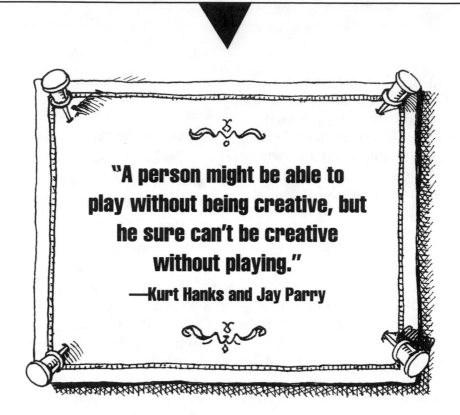

"A person might be able to play without being creative, but he sure can't be creative without playing."

—Kurt Hanks and Jay Parry

going in circles, rehashing the same factors, coming to the same end point again and again. In the future when you think that you've come to a stalemate, put the problem aside, take a relaxing break, and turn to some other work for a while (or until the next day if possible). And if you've been working with no progress for an entire week, try to totally block the problem and related pressures from your mind for several days. Then as your conscious mind is allowed to switch hemispheres and to focus on other topics, the subconscious mind can take over the details of the problem you need to solve. Many theorists think the subconscious mind has greater access to the huge storehouse of data in your brain. Furthermore, they say the subconscious can operate much more freely when you are sleeping or are engaged in an entertaining, or "mindless," activity. The subconscious can also break through to the surface of your conscious mind more easily while you are in a relaxed, nonworking state.

A word of caution is due, however, before we go on. If you begin to *expect* your play to produce creative thoughts, this will destroy the relaxed, free-thinking nature of your play. So learn to play strictly to enjoy yourself and to revive your energy.

Summary

1. Adults often lose their capacity for unstructured, non-competitive fun. Their lives become out of balance, weighted down by all work and little or no play.

2. Even when adults participate in activities for the purpose of playing, they often continue to process from the left hemisphere of their brain, pushing for success and a certain performance much as they do during work. As a result, they don't experience the balance and refreshment that comes from free, open-ended play.

3. Play builds energy by releasing tension, producing positive endorphins, and stimulating fresh thinking.

4. Play, laughter, and fun trigger hormones in our bodies which activate our immune system and contribute to our health.

5. Play is an essential quality for increasing innovation. This is literally how we get ourselves out of the mental ruts of the status quo. To quote Kurt Hanks and Jay Parry in *Wake Up Your Creative Genius,* "A person might be able to play without being creative, but he sure can't be creative without playing."

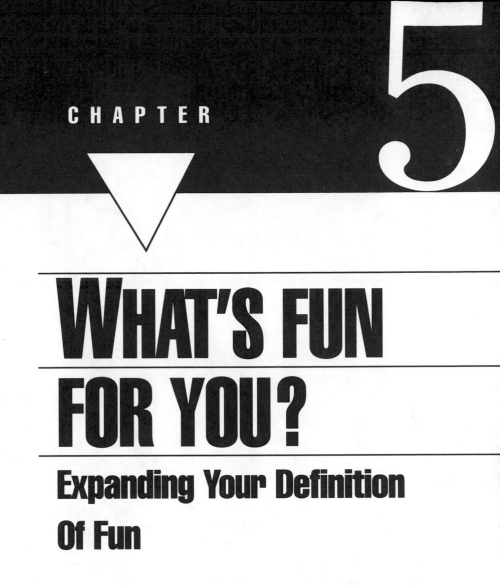

CHAPTER 5

WHAT'S FUN FOR YOU?

Expanding Your Definition Of Fun

66 *Playfulness is my basic nature. And we work so many hours here that the job has to be playful.* 99

— **Betty Hudson, Vice President, Government Relations, Fluor Corporation**

66 *I think the most important thing for people to do [in order to unwind on weekends] is some activity that is totally different from their work. For instance, doing some form of physical activity, like gardening, is good if your office work keeps you sitting still most of the day. I used to get my therapy from taking care of horses on the weekend. I enjoyed fussing around with the hay, tending to my horse, and so forth. It feels like getting back to the basics, just as running your fingers through soil gives you the same feeling. I also need to do a noncompetitive type of activity; golf, for example, would not relax me.* 99

—**Vince Kontny, President and CEO, Fluor Daniel, Inc.; President, Fluor Corporation**

ne of the basic prob-
lems for most adults is
twofold: not only do they
have trouble finding time
to play, but when it comes
right down to it, they have
lost touch with what's fun for
them. The Action Item in this
chapter will help you test your Fun
Quotient. Before reading on, it is important to complete the
inventory in the Action Item so that you will get an unbiased
insight into your current awareness level (see pp. 78–79).

When I first tried the inventory in the Action Item, I had most
of my ideas on the second half of the sheet. And most of my
ideas were such lengthy undertakings that I was not likely to ever
get around to them. They were activities such as making a wall
hanging of stitchery to cover one wall of the bedroom. To do this,
I envisioned converting a bedroom into a sewing room and working for about a year on the project. Well, I'd have to wait for one
of the kids to start college, so that would be a while! Another
idea was to buy a potter's wheel and make hand-built pottery.
This would require converting a room into a studio, building a
damp room for drying the clay, putting in a special commercial
drain, and buying about $2,000 of special equipment.

Then I began to realize that perhaps I didn't have inner permission to have this fun. If I really wanted to make hand-built
pottery, all I had to do was to enroll in an art course at the com-

munity college, which was about ten minutes from my home. In less than a week and with about $40 in tuition, I would be enjoying this process.

As I analyzed my fun inventory I discovered that I knew of very few ways to have fun that required less than thirty minutes. *Yet most of my free time open for fun was only small bits of time.* I also realized that because I didn't have permission to have fun, I kept it safely out of reach by dreaming up projects so lengthy or so expensive that I would never be able to find the time or money to get into them.

The third reason I was missing out on fun was not planning ahead so that I had what supplies I needed when I had a few free minutes between projects or phone calls. If you come to work armed with ideas for short breaks and any accessories you'll need (such as fishing, golf, or special-interest magazines, a portable tape player with earplugs and your favorite relaxing music, colored pens and drawing paper, a puzzle or a book of your favorite cartoons), then you can easily find time to schedule some moments of fun and relaxation into each work day. And you can achieve a healthy balance of work and refreshing play or relaxation time during the week instead of postponing fun for the weekend.

With these three insights, I began to reorganize my work/play quotient. I made the longest list I could of ways to have fun in two to five minutes, and I would urge you to do the same. We have included some of our ideas to get you started. Don't stop till you get at least twenty or thirty good ideas.

Two- to Five-Minute Breaks

1. Read the comics or your favorite columnist in the paper.
2. Read a poem.
3. Hear a favorite song with a tape recorder and headphones.
4. Relax with a cup of herb tea.

ACTION
I T E M
▼

Jot down things that are fun for you. Put them into columns according to the amount of time they take.

As you begin recalling what's fun for you, write down as many possibilities as you can. For example, you might think, "It's fun to read a novel." How long do you typically need to enjoy this fun? "Well, I'd like to have at least an hour to get into it," you might answer. So you would enter this idea for fun in the third column, "30 Minutes to 1/2 Day." An idea for fun might fit in all four columns, such as spending time with a special friend. If so, just put an arrow across to indicate all the columns it will fit in. You might want to time how long it takes before you begin to run out of ideas. Draw a line when you find the ideas are no longer coming quickly and you have to stop and think awhile between ideas.

Take time for this list-making activity. If you like, invite a friend or mate to be making a similar fun list while you make yours.

How many activities did you come up with? You might be interested to know that most busy adults run out of ideas between ten and fifteen. (Ten-year-olds have easily generated fifty-five ideas in the same amount of time.) And how many could you think of quickly before having to really search for ideas?

Now, just for fun, count up how many ideas you have in the first two columns (ways to have fun in thirty minutes or less) and how many ideas you have in the last two columns. Which has the larger number? And what does this tell you about the problems you are having finding time for fun?

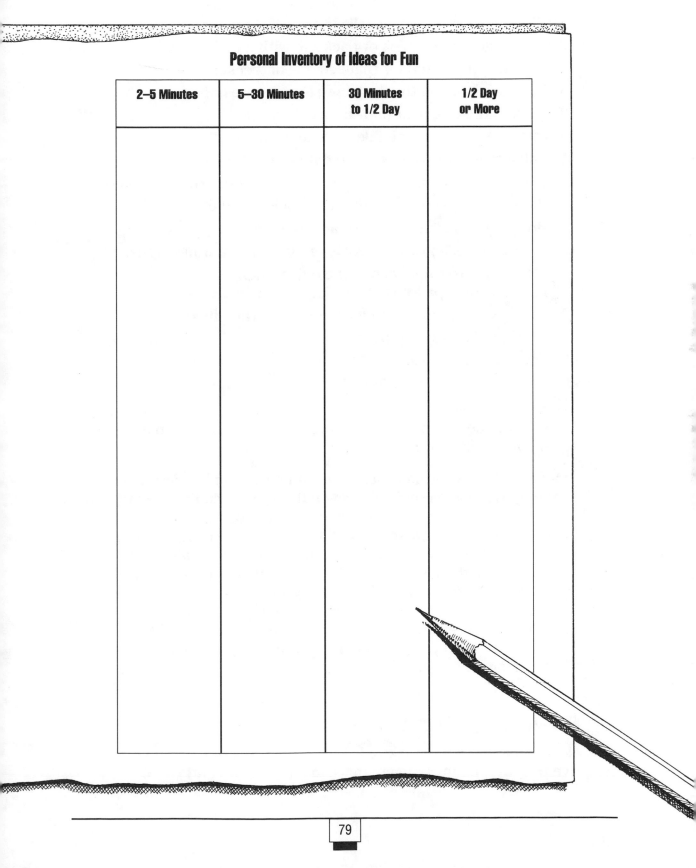

Personal Inventory of Ideas for Fun

2–5 Minutes	5–30 Minutes	30 Minutes to 1/2 Day	1/2 Day or More

5. Close your eyes and visualize yourself skiing down a slope.

6. Exchange a quick neck or back rub with a colleague.

7. Plan something fun for that evening or weekend.

8. Lay your head on the desk for a five-minute nap.

9. Walk to the cafe next door for a cold drink.

10. Check the movie schedule in the daily paper.

11. Call a friend and plan a lunch date.

12. Make a list of what you want for Christmas or your birthday.

13. Praise a secretary or co-worker for a job well done.

14. Browse through a catalog or art book.

15. Look at travel books and brochures and plan your next vacation.

16. Play with a toy you keep at the office, such as a yo-yo, kaleidoscope, paddle ball, or dart board.

17. Take a walk around the block or around the office.

18. Work on a crossword puzzle.

19. Tell someone a joke.

20. Breathe deeply or meditate for five minutes.

21. Wash your face.

22. Play the perfect hole of golf in your imagination. Choose your favorite golf course.

Then, go to your daily schedule and begin to plan your play as thoughtfully and creatively as you do your work. For the first week, you might just practice taking several two- to five-minute joy breaks each day. Observe both the quality of your energy and the quality of your work and mental processing right after your joy breaks. We think you will find a noticeable improvement in all three areas. On the way home each day, mentally reward yourself for risking and exploring with this new process. Remind yourself of the potential rewards of becoming more whole-brained (being in touch with both your left and right brain hemispheres) and more balanced.

Five- to Thirty-Minute Breaks

Now you are ready to make a longer list of ways to have fun in five to thirty minutes. Again, this can be more fun and you can

get a much better list if you do this with a friend or two. We have included some of our favorite ideas to prime the pump for you. You might edit or rewrite any on our list that don't quite fit you but that give you an idea that you like.

These are just to get you started thinking of many of your own favorite ways to make life more fun. Note which ideas you could use to give you more energy and a better balance of work and play during your day plus your lunch breaks, evenings, and weekends.

1. Listen to some inspiring or career development ideas from a seminar casette tape.

2. Learn French or another language on cassette.

3. Plan extra walking into your day—park so as to give yourself a brisk walk to and from your office, the grocery store, etc.

4. Spend ten minutes reviewing all the positives from your day.

5. Recall or read an inspirational poem, psalm, or prayer.

6. Read an article in a favorite magazine.

7. Select and order a present for a friend or yourself from a favorite mail order catalog.

8. Take a sack lunch and a good book to a nearby park.

9. Stop by a bookstore during your lunch hour or on the way home from work.

10. Have a collection of activities, hobbies, and crafts that you can easily pick up and put down in twenty- and thirty-minute increments, such as whittling, needlework, weaving, puzzles, single-hand card games, juggling, and crossword puzzles.

11. Remember in detail a time when you were an outstanding success. Recall each detail as vividly as possible. (This activity helps you expect good things to happen and helps you get comfortable with success.)

12. Carpool with someone you enjoy. Try to focus your conversation primarily on positive, energy-building topics rather than problems.

13. On the way to work in the morning, see your day in vivid, positive detail. See applause, success, appreciation.

14. Plan something special to look forward to this evening, making whatever arrangements are necessary.

15. Plan a surprise for someone you love or appreciate. It might be a phone call or note to be found later in a coat pocket.

16. Get up in time to welcome the sunrise with a brisk walk.

17. On your way to work, have breakfast with someone you enjoy.

18. Take a different route home from work, stopping to walk in a beautiful neighborhood, to sit by a pond, to shop at a rural produce stand, or simply to drive through the countryside with your windows down.

19. Enjoy a tape of James Galway's golden flute or other relaxing music you love.

20. Take your children out for a surprise treat or visit to a park before dinner.

Weekday evenings require special planning because typically there are several routine chores to fit into that time and not a lot of open time just for fun. Also, if you wait until evening to decide upon and arrange your break, you may be too tired to even consider what would be fun for you that evening. Thus, we recommend making a habit out of choosing at least one fun thing to look forward to each evening, even if it's only twenty minutes for a neck massage or fast gin game. In addition, planning ahead so that you anticipate your evening fun will give you another, earlier energy boost.

Weekday Evenings: Fun Ideas in Thirty Minutes to Two Hours

To whet your appetite for fun, consider the following list of thirty-minute to two-hour activities to do after work.

1. Get out old photo albums and share memories.

2. Enjoy making music on the piano, guitar, kazoo, or whatever you play. Learn to have fun playing badly. Most of us learned

to play some instrument as kids but gave it up because we didn't enjoy lessons. Pick it up and play just for the fun of it this time. Have fun with friends putting together trios and quartets of strange combinations as you renew early interests in the piano, clarinet, trombone, horn, or drums. Or look in the newspaper ads and buy a second-hand instrument you've always wanted to play.

3. Take a long walk and watch the sunset.

4. Trade rubs for sore feet, backs, or necks with your family.

5. Have a cookie-baking evening and make several kinds to freeze for later. Mail them to kids in college or take them to work to share with the office team. Why not make "gingerbread people" and decorate them with raisins and frosting?

6. Teach a pet an unusual trick.

7. Design an artistic creation or a new arrangement of your house or yard—whether you intend to execute it or not.

8. Get out old games—checkers, dominoes, Parcheezi, Monopoly, or puzzles—and have an ongoing tournament for the week. The winner takes the loser to dinner and a movie of his or her choice, or prepares dinner for the loser. Short games make good homework breaks for students.

9. Enjoy a good book with a cup of hot tea, soft music, and perhaps a crackling fire in winter months.

10. Call or write someone special you've been out of touch with; tracking down lost friends can be half the fun. Satisfy your curiosity—most people will be flattered by your interest.

11. Break out of your routine. For example, enjoy a chilled cup of fresh juice or gazpacho before preparing dinner while sharing pleasant thoughts from your day.

12. Plan your next vacation—collect maps, books, articles, or vacation lore from friends. Even total strangers may enjoy discussing their travel experiences with you and offering tips, especially if you share a common interest (opera, Indian ruins, botany). Planning a trip well in advance not only saves you money and headaches but also allows for more options and spontaneous fun once you're on your way. And planning, like reminiscing afterward, stretches your enjoyment of your vacation over time.

13. Join the family in a game of backyard badminton, croquet, Ping-Pong, or perhaps a good game of hide-and-go-seek before dinner.

14. Review old pictures with your parents and tape their memories to accompany them. What treasures for later years and generations!

15. While the weather is good and sunsets are late, enjoy gardening. Trade cuttings from favorite plants with a neighbor; create raked or hand-fashioned designs on sand or pebble surfaces that you can change with your moods or the seasons (an idea taken from Japanese gardening).

16. Get out old musical albums and enjoy memories of years gone by. Dance in your own living room.

17. Spend an evening making a long list of things that would be fun to do, people whom it would be fun to see, places that you've always wanted to visit, and so forth.

18. Keep a journal—pick a format you really enjoy so that it's not a chore. You can even keep a journal of delightful developments and quotes from a growing child. Looking back at old journal entries can provide perspective, surprises, insights, direction, and energy.

19. Have a bad day? Role play with your friends and/or family about outrageous, silly things you might have done differently or said to people who tried your patience. (Laughter is a great cure for relieving pent-up stress and frustration.)

20. Before dinner, gather your family to survey recipes and choose one that is totally new to you. (Have ingredients on hand for your family's favorite zero-effort meal, and agree that whoever doesn't like the experiment will fix his or her own alternative meal.)

Half-Day or Longer Breaks: Fifty-Two Mini-Vacations

Just as weekdays are focused on achieving work goals, to maintain a balance between work and play, weekends need to be focused on renewal. So even if you are a single parent or both you and your spouse work outside the home, be sure to make some part of each weekend fun to look forward to, even if it's only for an hour or two.

We credit Tim Hansel with his wonderful idea of planning for fifty-two mini-vacations a year. In his book *When I Relax I Feel Guilty,* he helps readers rediscover the vital role of re-creation in their lives. Doesn't the idea of having a vacation waiting for you at the end of every week sound great?

You can have lots of fun just generating your list (unless you feel trapped by your schedule or circumstances and are unable to claim even the most meager play time). We have found the secret to be in brainstorming options. At first many of the ideas do seem unlikely. But as the list grows, so does our awareness of ways we can fit more and more refreshing fun into our lives.

See if our list doesn't help to get your own ideas flowing. Each part of the country has its own special sites, festivals, and opportunities, so let our list of mini-vacations remind you of opportunities in your neck of the woods.

1. Schedule a ride in a hot-air balloon or go to a balloon festival.
2. Visit a zoo.
3. Organize a Christmas caroling group and take it on tour. Or brush up on a collection of patriotic songs for a Fourth of July celebration.
4. Locate an environmental center in your area and take a class such as natural basketry. Bring home wildflower seeds for your own yard.

5. Cool off on a summer weekend at a water theme park or create your own park with sprinklers, kids, and wading pools. (Discount stores can provide lots of ideas.)

6. Have a stay-home-and-sleep-in vacation, complete with breakfast in bed.

7. Enjoy bird-watching. Local Audubon societies can recommend good birding spots and the best times to see birds.

8. Get off the beaten path and take a ride through the country or interesting but out-of-the way parts of the city.

9. Visit historic houses in your area. Often these homes offer tours at Christmas, early spring, and other special times.

10. Check out the farmers' markets in your area. They provide fresh fruits, vegetables, nuts, and local flavor and can be a great place to talk with interesting people.

11. Visit a museum.

12. Take in a game of polo.

13. Attend a music festival. Plan your own. Provide nonmusicians with spoons, tamborines, or perhaps a string bass made of a washtub, broomstick, and tight string.

14. Make Halloween special—invite all the family to dress up and answer the door in full costume.

15. Throw a quilting party.

16. Plan a bicycle trip.

17. Go horseback riding.

18. Enjoy a long walk.

19. Enjoy a massage from a professional masseuse.

20. Dig into your memories and come up with some of the fun things you did as a kid. Teach them to others or to your own kids.

21. Go square dancing or folk dancing, or sign up to learn push dancing or other styles you may not know.

22. Make holiday preparations a joyful part of the year. What if you invited someone who lives alone, perhaps an elderly person or a foreign student, to come join your fun? Ideas for holiday activities include trimming a Christmas tree, decorating the front door, and preparing family recipes for Passover.

23. Locate the local Sierra Club for ideas for weekend trips.

24. Go on a wildflower-picking hike or photograph samples of all you find.

25. Pack a lunch and enjoy a picnic. There are lots of unusual kites to build and fly. Or if the weather turns bad, spread out your blanket at home and be glad there are no ants!

26. Take some fun and love to the elderly and celebrate life and living together.

27. Go rock climbing. Learn new skills from an expert.

28. Fish from an inner tube and enjoy looking into the water.

29. Watch a model airplane tournament. Check with craft stores for place and times or make your own plane and fly it.

30. Go antiquing for the fun of it.

31. Enjoy fall leaves. Pile up a huge stack and jump in them.

32. Organize your neighborhood for a block party—have games, music, and maybe a parade for the tricycle set.

33. Get involved in your child's school carnival.

34. Go roller skating or ice skating. Take lessons if this is new for you.

35. Change roles for a fresh outlook on life. Whoever usually cooks, drives, selects the entertainment, calls for reservations, or cleans the kitchen swaps roles with a partner. There can be a bonus of renewed appreciation for each other.

36. Volunteer at an archaeological dig.

37. Visit a state fair.

38. Take a let's-learn-something-new vacation. Visit the library or bookstore for ideas to get you started.

39. Try some star gazing or take an astronomy class.

40. Have a spiritual growth weekend. Retreat to the woods with reading material to challenge or expand your spiritual awareness. Plan time to be alone and listen.

41. Play tourist for a day. Drop by your local chamber of commerce and get a visitor's guide.

42. Go to a garage sale or estate sale.

43. Visit an out-of-the-way cemetery. See what you can learn by reading grave markers. Or you might make rubbings of unusual tombstones with thin paper and oil pastels.

44. Visit a state park in a scenic setting.

45. Find a hotel with special mini-vacation rates. You don't even have to leave town for a get-away treat.

46. Pick a concert, sporting event, or theater to attend.

47. Go bowling.

48. Throw a "hero's party." Invite your friends to come dressed as their favorite hero.

49. Spend a night at a bed and breakfast.

50. Rent a Winnebago or camper for a weekend getaway.

51. Check with local veterinarians for pet shows.

52. Enjoy a game of miniature golf.

Summary

1. Become as dedicated to planning and experiencing creative, refreshing play as you are disciplined about getting your work done and notice the tremendous boost you will experience in both energy and productivity.

2. If you think you need an hour or more to have fun, then you probably will be joy-starved much of the time, rationalizing and procrastinating over work projects simply because the little kid within you needs a few minutes to stretch and play.

3. Discover some relaxing and enjoyable breaks that take less than five minutes, then schedule several short joy breaks during your work hours each day and notice the difference in your productivity, energy, and innovative thinking.

4. Taking one fun break, thirty minutes or longer each evening, will help to revive your energy for the following day.

5. To maintain a healthy balance between work and play, find creative ways to claim some part of every weekend as a mini-vacation. When your brain gets the message that there is a play break around every corner, you will experience a new vigor and enthusiasm for your work.

66 *When my work pile is getting deeper than I can handle or want to handle, I'll let myself get lost in my picture of West Texas bluebonnets on the wall.* 99

— **C. R. Oliver, President, Hydrocarbon Sector, Fluor Daniel, Inc.**

6

JUGGLING, JOGGING, AND JOKING:

Slotting Energy Breaks Into Your Work Day

66 *Fortunately, I am surrounded by people who know the value of taking joy breaks. Thus I don't have to justify a break to myself or my boss when I need one. It's fine to pick up an inspiring book or to do an imaging exercise using my weekend house in the country as the setting, taking a fifteen-minute break by walking to a small shopping area to buy a card for a friend or just window shop.* 99

— Glenda Benson, Executive Secretary, TU Electric

ow that you have considered an array of ways to have fun as an adult—especially fun that can be grabbed in short five- to sixty-minute increments—you are ready to start incorporating these fun breaks into your work day. And by experimenting with the ideas and suggestions in this chapter, we hope that you quickly feel the high-energy boost from achieving a better balance between work and play.

Four Energizing Daily Maintenance Times

First, focus on four times during the working day when most people either lose energy or overlook the possibility of putting fresh energy into their day: getting ready for work, commuting to work, eating lunch, and commuting from work. Most people devote from two and one-half hours to four hours per day to these activities. Think about how you use those four periods.

Do you review the day as you are getting ready for work in the mornings, worried about what might go wrong, or what you might forget or not get to, or how far behind you are already?

ACTION
I T E M

Answer the following questions and then add up the figures:

How long does it take you on most
working days between the time you
awaken and when you leave for work?   _____

How long does it take to commute to work?   _____

How long do you take for
lunch on a standard work day?   _____

How long does it take to commute home?   _____

Total Time

This daily time devoted to maintenance tasks can reap a dual value of
energy renewal by having fun in the process.

(Is this an energy drain?) Do you listen to the news and lose any
energy there? Driving to work, what do you think about? And as
you drive to work, do you allow traffic to drain your energy? Do
you rehearse what you will say to this person or that person? Is
it positive or negative? Are you gaining or losing energy?

Later, over lunch, how do you spend your time? Do you ever
plan a wonderful lunch with a special friend whom you really enjoy, then make the mistake of contaminating the time by focusing
on problems on the job or other energy-draining situations? Also,
do you often eat lunch in your office while continuing to work? Or
do you grab a fast-food lunch on the run while doing errands for
your household and family? And does the food you choose to eat
leave you feeling energized or sluggish an hour later?

The point to these questions is, how much of this time
do you consciously spend putting energy back into your own

system? If you do it for yourself, realize that your energy boost will be contagious—whomever you eat lunch with or work with later will feel it, too.

Now think of how you spend the time during the commute home in the evening. It is not unusual to focus on what you did wrong that day, what you failed to get to, or how much work is stacked up on your desk, waiting for you to get to it the next day. Note that all three of these are energy drains. When we are tired, we are least likely to be objective as we process our failures and mistakes of the day. Thus the commute home can easily turn into a critical review session where your best efforts never seem good enough. In addition, listening to the news or getting irritated by traffic can further deplete your energy.

Our purpose here is to help you systematically look at daily habits which may be energy-draining, to make you aware of how much time is wasted on these habits, and to help you discover some energy-producing alternatives to these habits to practice during these four maintenance periods each day.

When you answered the questions in the Action Item and added up the number of minutes you typically spend during these four time slots in your day, you probably came up with anywhere from two to four hours in which you can replace energy-sapping habits with energy-builders. Let's look at some options.

One method we suggest is *combining* an activity that produces low energy for you, such as rushing to get ready for work and driving through traffic to the office, with another activity or mental strategy that will boost your energy, such as positive mental imaging or listening to calming instrumental cassette music in the car. Then the sum of the combined activities will equal an energy gain, or at least will prevent your energy quotient from falling below par.

Many parents have instinctively known the value of combining pleasant activities with unpleasant ones for their children. Anna Marie Cwieka, manager of business development, Environmental Services Division, Fluor Daniel, Inc., recalls:

> *"My mother was an extremely creative, right-brained person who was always finding ways to turn a negative situation into the positive for us as children. Once we had to get flu shots. So she turned the whole day into a holiday, where we secretly played hookey from school. Although we still had to take the shots, we did many other wonderful things, such as seeing a ballet in a local theatre. I was truly mesmerized by it, became a ballet-lover from then on, and still appreciate how my mother turned a potential ordeal into a joyful experience. I wish that, as an adult, I had more of my mother's joyous attitude toward life . . . and would [reward myself by combining] more breaks with my daily work."*

Anna Marie is right when she says that many adults neglect to use this valuable lesson from childhood. But you can begin combining high- and low-energy activities by turning back to our list of five- to thirty-minute breaks in the last chapter. Can you find a variety of them that might be enjoyed during your morning routine, your commutes to and from the office, or your lunch break? Put a check by the ones that seem most energizing to you.

Do you also notice that some of these activities do not require dropping what you are doing to enjoy them? Although the word "break" implies stopping one activity and shifting to another, many of our energy-producing physical and mental activities can be done while you go about your business at hand. Thus, if right now you don't think you can spare the extra time in the morning to exercise for twenty minutes, then look instead at the positive mental techniques that you can do while taking a shower and commuting to work. Try the ideas that feel most comfortable and "do-able" to you now.

Morning Energy Maintenance

Immediately upon waking each morning, practice using the first two to five minutes by vividly picturing your upcoming day from start to finish in glowing positives. If it could turn out in the best possible way, what would it look like? This exercise is similar to making a very quick movie in your head. (A later chapter is devoted to this mental exercise, called "imaging.") If you find yourself falling back to sleep, do this instead as you get up and begin your morning routine of brushing your teeth and getting dressed.

Also plan something inspirational to enjoy in this initial, attitude-setting period of your day. Because your mind is very receptive to your feelings and ideas upon waking, whatever you focus on sets a dominant mood for the day. Try reading a favorite psalm or inspirational poem or enjoying music that creates a positive mood for you. In addition, your memory is keenest during this wake-up period. If you want to remember some new material, reviewing it then can be much more effective than reviewing it later.

> **Because your mind is very receptive to your feelings and ideas upon waking, whatever you focus on sets a dominant mood for the day.**

Enjoying an early brisk walk was not my life habit when I married Larry nine years ago. In fact, then I would say (and truly believed) that I was just not a "morning person." I wasn't mentally alert until 10:00 a.m. (even though I was always up and at the office early).

But my husband, who is a dentist, lived on a very different time schedule. If I didn't get up early with him, I missed seeing and talking with him until late afternoon. So partly to enjoy the special morning time with him and partly because I suspected that it might help my energy level and general health habits, I began to get up and run or walk with him. Now I am amazed at the changes this has brought me. I gain four or five extra hours each day when I am mentally alert. Furthermore, my metabolism is working much more effectively so my weight stays steady.

Next, can you make time to sit down and enjoy a healthy breakfast? Many professionals fall into the trap of gulping down their coffee and a meager slice of toast as they are dressing or driving to work. This manner of eating is not relaxing and may even provoke enough stress to interfere with digestion. Also, meals eaten on the run are rarely nutritious.

Chapter 19, "Getting Your Day Off with a Bang," provides a longer discussion about the best foods to eat for a high-energy morning. Turn to that section now if you suspect that your typical breakfast (or lack of breakfast) is causing an energy deficit in your day. But let us briefly state here that we believe, like many nutritionists, that breakfast is the most important meal of the day. Eating a high-fiber, low-sugar cereal and/or whole wheat item, fresh fruit, low-fat or skim milk, and no more than one cup of coffee or caffeinated tea is the best breakfast option for most adults. How does this compare with your normal breakfast fare?

A High-Energy Commute

Two factors can greatly enhance your energy maintenance during your daily commute to the office. First, leave home with plenty of time to spare. That means giving yourself at least fifteen minutes or more leeway in case you hit a traffic jam or miss your bus or train. Then if those problems do arise, you can face them calmly

ACTION
ITEM

Enter your own ideas for building and maintaining your energy in the morning:

Time	Activity

rather than fretting and chastising yourself about being late. Second, plan some restful, inspirational, or educational activity to do during your commute. Again, our final chapter provides some more detailed examples and ideas. But for now, consider listening to a tape of some favorite classical music. Hearing tapes of inspirational speakers or of books in your field of business are another suggestion.

A GOOD DOSE OF ENERGY DRAINERS NEEDS TO BE COUNTERACTED WITH ENERGY RENEWING STRATEGIES.

Your morning commute is also a great time to mentally rehearse any meetings or presentations you will be making during the day. Make your thoughts and images positive views of the events so that you are rehearsing not only your presentation but also a successful outcome (which often becomes a self-fulfilling prophecy!).

In addition, if you leave home with time to spare, chances are that you will also arrive a few minutes early at work. These extra fifteen to thirty minutes can feel like a luxury, offering you a high-energy opportunity to gather your thoughts, to plan both your work and joy break schedule, and to move comfortably into your day.

Maintaining Energy during Lunch

For lunch, we recommend planning at least twenty to thirty minutes of positive energy-building time. If we are meeting with someone else, we have learned to suggest some topics we would like to discuss over lunch. Then we rarely get caught listening to a long tale of their woes during our entire lunch break. It's fine to briefly focus on problems that concern either one of us, but this can easily dissolve into an energy-draining complaint session. To avoid this, quickly move the topic on to positive solutions or other positive thoughts.

Remember that worry and negative thoughts don't mix well with eating. The brain creates body chemicals that counteract effective digestion when we worry, fret, argue, or process negative thoughts. So focus on the positive during meal times. And teach others you share meals with to do the same for themselves and with you.

Before we leave the lunch-break period, let's also consider what you choose to eat for lunch. Do you ever struggle to stay alert for the two hours right after lunch?

If so, chances are you made some poor food choices. Heavy food, rich in fat and cholesterol, or foods high in salt, sugar, and caffeine are poor energy choices. Rich, high-fat foods cause most of your energy to be tied up digesting your lunch for the next two hours or so. Some studies indicate that after such a meal, the blood actually becomes more viscous with less oxygen in it. Or if you load up on sugar, you might be one of those people who feel the "sugar blues" for the next hour or so. As your glucose goes high to process all that sugar and then stays there, your energy will drop.

Remember that worry and negative thoughts don't mix well with eating. The brain creates body chemicals that counteract effective digestion when we worry, fret, argue, or process negative thoughts.

On the other hand, if you want to have optimum energy for the afternoon, choose fresh fruits and vegetables or steamed vegetables. A salad with a very light dressing or no dressing is great. Enjoy the crispness and pure flavor without all that gooey dressing. A vegetable soup, again low in salt and fat, is good. And skip the dessert.

We may have just shot holes in one of your favorite forms of fun—eating a good old American junk-food lunch—so be gentle with yourself. And rest assured that you don't have to change a thing until or unless you want to. In fact, if you feel pressured to change, you will resist. You can make permanent, lasting change only when it is your free and self-directed choice. So if right now you don't feel ready to change any of your eating habits, trust this inner feeling and move on to other areas where you are ready to change for the better. We have found that as we get other areas of our lives in balance with other sources of pleasure besides eating, it isn't so difficult to give up poor eating habits.

Rebuilding Energy during the Commute Home

If you have been able to enjoy two to three joy breaks during your afternoon (and possibly a short catnap), you have probably been able to sustain most of your energy. You can restore your energy even more, however, by making your commute home a restful and uplifting experience. Try making a ritual out of focusing strictly on what you did right or well that day. The commute home is a poor time to try to be objective and to harvest any negatives or failures. It is a great time, however, just to appreciate any and all affirmative efforts that you made that day. After practicing this exercise, you will be continually amazed at how many of your positive deeds and gestures you overlook unless you make a conscious effort to take time to review and appreciate yourself. This step will help you arrive home in a cheerful frame of mind, feeling entitled to an enjoyable evening spent with yourself or your family.

Another positive activity for the commute is to mentally remind yourself of all the possible ways you could choose to enjoy parts of your evening. By planning some purposeful fun into each evening, and by making a commitment to yourself to make it happen, you will arrive home ready to enjoy the evening.

And if your day has been stressful, it can feel great to take twenty minutes or more to enjoy a brisk walk, bike ride, or other aerobic exercise to get the stress toxins out of your system. If you sink into your big easy chair and doze off to sleep, you will often find that you wake up groggy, as tired or more tired than

when you went to sleep. This is because you have a buildup of toxins in your bloodstream that get trapped there. If you enjoy (and an important part of the process is the enjoyment) any form of aerobic exercise, the deep breathing and increased pumping of your heart will flush out the toxins and bring in lots of fresh, energizing oyxgen. And as a result, you will be revived and ready to enjoy a pleasant evening with a good energy level.

To close this section on the four energy-maintenance times, listen to how three executives boost their energy levels during their regular work travel. Imagine if your commute involved a ten- or twelve-hour transatlantic jet flight. That's the regular "office commute" that Hugh Coble, group president of operations for Fluor Daniel, Inc., dealt with for six months while he flew back and forth between England and Fluor Daniel's various sites in the United States. Yet by incorporating relaxation techniques, high-energy eating habits, and a positive attitude into what many would term "an ordeal," he was able to hop off the plane with energy to spare:

> *"For nearly a year, I tallied up some 400,000 air miles flying back and forth between England and California. It would have been easy to run out of gas during that period. But I used energy-building techniques I learned in Perspective III (a whole-brained executive development program taught by Ann's team) to turn a potential negative into a positive. During each flight, I usually listened to motivational tapes or to soothing music. While the music played, I would visualize all the positives about my upcoming day at work—how great the first four hours would be, whom I wanted to see, and so on. Eventually I would become so relaxed that I would fall asleep. Then when I arrived in a new time zone, I would feel totally reoriented, totally relaxed. I also made a point of not drinking any alcohol. I mainly had water, and I always ordered either the low-calorie meals, the seafood selection, or occasionally the vegetarian meals. Using all these strategies was critical; I don't think I would have survived that year without them."*

Vince Kontny, president of Fluor Corporation and president and CEO of Fluor Daniel, Inc., has another excellent suggestion to help you refuel your energy after work. He says:

"My biggest problem has been getting myself to unwind after work. I found that one thing I need to do is change out of my work suit into something comfortable. During those times when I've had to go straight to dinner without changing, I don't get completely revitalized. My other strategy is to lie down for five minutes or longer as soon as I get home. I'll lie down either on the bed or on the floor, close my eyes, and feel the tiredness drain away. Then I'm completely renewed for the evening."

Dallas executive Tom Baker of Texas Utilities Company tells how he uses his commute home to help him renew his energy and leave his work behind at the office:

"I used to arrive home feeling uptight and nervous after a long day at work. And I found it difficult to get my mind off work, even after I had been home for a while. But I found two things that have helped me break out of that habit. First, the dashboard on my car has a yellow note stuck on it on which I have drawn a big plus sign. And every time I glance down at it, the sign reminds me to think about at least one good thing I did that day. I'll remind myself, 'By golly, I accomplished that today,' rather than worrying about something that didn't get done. And whenever someone else is in the car with me, that person invariably asks me the story behind the note. This gives me a chance to teach someone else about the idea, which reinforces the concept for me, too.

Another thing that helps me relax is to stop by my neighborhood recreation center on the way home. I like to walk thirty minutes, followed by a few laps in the pool. I use this as my transition point between work and home."

Building Breaks into your Work Schedule

Our team has learned the long-term benefits of planning energy breaks as carefully as we plan work assignments. Once we discovered the intrinsic link between energy-reviving breaks and overall productivity and creativity, we stopped thinking of work and breaks as separate entities. Now we define them as basically one and the same—*a continuum of activities all geared toward accomplishing whatever goals we have set for ourselves that day.* Once you discover this for yourself, you will no longer think of breaks as being an indulgence or a gap in your work schedule. Nor will you feel guilty about taking time off to relax, because these short breaks will contribute as much to your efficient completion of a project as, say, arriving at work on time, having clear-cut objectives for the project, or having the proper skills to accomplish the task.

Even if you have been working quite successfully without taking breaks, you probably have not experienced the optimum level of creativity, motivation, and sustained energy that you can achieve. We feel confident in making this claim to our clients and seminar participants because few people can maintain a high energy level throughout the work day without stopping from time to time to

- switch brain hemispheres (helping to promote brain synergy and creativity),
- release tension and fatigue,
- rebuild the oxygen supply,

ACTION
I T E M
▼

Make a list of positive, enjoyable things to think about and do during your commute home and upon arriving home.

Time	Activity

- recharge the neurotransmitters in the brain, and
- replenish energy reserves.

The best way to achieve these five vital benefits is to take a number of short, five- to fifteen-minute breaks throughout the day. In addition, a for-pleasure-only lunch break away from your desk will work wonders to restore your momentum and enthusiasm for the second half of your day, especially when you are faced with a difficult or tedious project.

Another general tip when deciding what type of break to take at a given moment is to choose an activity, and possibly a location, that is different from your current task and site. For example,

1. If you have been sitting still, hunched over papers at your desk or glued to your phone, then stand up and stretch, take a walk down the hall and up a flight of stairs, and get your circulation going again. You could even grab a jump rope and get in a few minutes of fun, invigorating exercise.

2. If you have been doing close work, such as staring at figures or reading legal documents, stop and look out the window. Observe the sky, the cloud patterns, the city's skyline, and so forth. You might also relax your eyes by closing them and doing an imaging exercise.

3. If you have been doing something that requires lots of concentration and accuracy, switch to a playful activity such as reading the comics, reading a humor column, juggling, playing with jacks or some wind-up toys, drawing a picture with crayons, or playing a game on the computer.

4. When you've been doing a task demanding creative thinking, such as brainstorming, illustrating, writing advertising copy, or teaching, an opposite type of break would be shifting to a less taxing activity for a while, such as filing, unpacking your briefcase, or distributing files to personnel.

5. And, finally, if you have been working alone for many hours, interact with someone else. Talking, laughing, and responding to others' reactions is an energy lift. Conversely, if you've been engaged in meetings all day, having ten minutes to yourself will be very relaxing.

In a later section, the testimonies of top professionals about their favorite types of breaks and the benefits they derive will perhaps convince you of the value of breaks and inspire you to try a variety of activities. And once you realize their power to enhance overall productivity, accuracy, motivation, creativity, and problem-solving ability, you may want to promote breaks—on both an individualized and a group basis—for your entire staff. Some of these examples address this idea as well. The end of the chapter will discuss the best times to schedule breaks.

Expanding Your List of Office Breaks

In the last chapter, we asked you to think of numerous five- to ten-minute breaks you could take at the office, plus fifteen longer breaks that could be incorporated into a lunch hour. Were you able to come up with ten to fifteen ideas that truly sounded fun and relaxing to you? Or were you stumped after three or four ideas, as some of us were when we first attempted the exercise a few years ago?

One tip that might help you add to your list of short breaks is to name activities you enjoy doing that require two or more hours. As we commented earlier, when most adults name what they consider to be their personal "play," they are activities like tennis, golf, bridge, movies, dancing, sightseeing, going to the beach, visiting a museum, and so on.

Since the two-hour activities you listed in the Action Item represent established interests, they are good sources from which to create related but shorter breaks. For example, let's say your list includes playing tennis and golf, going to antique sales and auctions, and touring museums. Then you could bring your copies of *Tennis* or *Golf Digest* to work and spend a number of short breaks by reading the articles in them. Or bring your putter and a few golf balls to enjoy when you have ten minutes during a lunch or afternoon break to practice.

In addition, you could bring to work a variety of books and magazines devoted to antique collecting, then leaf through them as you help yourself to a cup of herbal tea. You could also do an imaging exercise based on a past or future visit to an auction, or call up a friend and plan an antique-hunting expedition for an

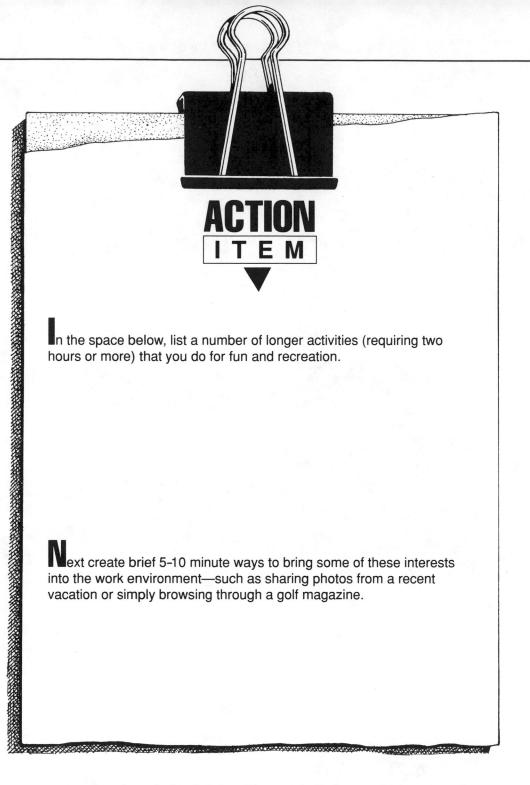

ACTION
ITEM

▼

In the space below, list a number of longer activities (requiring two hours or more) that you do for fun and recreation.

Next create brief 5-10 minute ways to bring some of these interests into the work environment—such as sharing photos from a recent vacation or simply browsing through a golf magazine.

upcoming weekend. And to build energy based on your passion for art shows, try bringing colorful art books to work, brochures and catalogs from exhibits you have toured, biographies of your favorite artists, and articles on upcoming exhibits. If you work near a gallery or museum, you could take a special lunch break by packing a sack lunch and visiting a new exhibit.

Do you see how easy it is to bring your weekend recreation and play time into the office with you? Yet other types of breaks, such as imaging, taking a coffee break with a friend at the office, calling a friend on the phone, or sending a quick note to an out-of-town friend, require no extra supplies. Since we're strong advocates of variety, though, we suggest that you have an array of break-taking possibilities handy at the office.

Peak Performers' Favorite Breaks

Hearing how other peak performers, many of whom participated in our field research, spend their break times will also give you some novel suggestions for breaks. Some of these professionals had been taking breaks for years before we met them—they intuitively understood the need for refueling their energy reserves throughout the day and evening. Other managers and CEOs began after hearing our strong sales pitch on the value of energy breaks. Most of them have shared their new, high-energy routine with their staff, making breaks and toys in the office an established habit within their organization.

Vince Kontny, president of Fluor Daniel, Inc., has this to say about breaks:

> *"My main form of break-taking is merely allowing myself to day-dream, letting my mind flow on to some other topic. I also enjoy looking out my window; it has a great vista of the green hills of Southern California. I have always intuitively done this, but before Ann explained the benefits of breaks, I used to feel guilty. Now I don't. My general philosophy is to approach business as a bit of a game. People frequently take things too seriously at work, so I try at times to put things in a more informal setting, such as breaking people up into teams for discussing ideas. I also try to tell some jokes during our meetings. In fact, humor is the last thing I would like to lose in my life."*

Patsy Fulton, president of Brookhaven College, shares these ideas:

> *"I have a toybox with an assortment of energy toys in my office—a bola paddle [ball on a string], a dart board, sunglasses with pop-out eyes, and a kazoo. My collection began several years ago when my staff organized a group picnic. We decided*

to add extra fun to the event by bringing toys to hand out. I received the bola paddle. We organized a kazoo band and bola competitions. Now, whenever I finish with a frustrating meeting or situation, I close my door and get out that paddle to relieve stress and recover my energy.

I also believe in spreading playfulness and creative thinking throughout the office. For example, I have given all my staff a kaleidoscope, asking them to shake it up . . . whenever they feel stuck . . . and to see the world and their problems differently. My staff also has a Fun and Games Committee that organizes an appreciation day each semester when we hand out ribbons and balloons and have special events together. You have to remember to have fun together, to break the tension . . . and enjoy that other side of each other's personality."

Paul Varello, president of Process Sector, Fluor Daniel, Inc., says,

"If I'm working on a tough, left-brained job and my mental energy is draining, I shift for a while into thinking about one of my creative projects at home. I will doodle out my ideas for the next step on the project and consider different options I might have. Then I can go back to my left-brained project fully charged with energy. It works every time.

If I have a whole Saturday at home (not often the case), I'll spend half an hour just walking around [my workshop and house] finding the jobs I think I'd like to do that day, such as building a clock, fixing a faucet, adding a planter, painting a bird feeder, etc. Then that's what I do. And by the end of the weekend I'm fully recharged and ready for my left-brained working world!"

C. R. Oliver, president of Hydrocarbon Sector, Fluor Daniel, Inc., explains:

"I truly enjoy people, laughing with them and about myself. So I seem to get natural energy simply being with others. Otherwise, I have learned to take short breaks by mentally shifting gears and focusing on simple things like the greenness of the landscape, the clear sky, or simply the rabbits outside my window here in Irvine. I also daydream quite a bit, dreaming the 'impossible dream.'"

Angela Ozymy, an administrative assistant with Benson Insurance Agency, describes a successful break at her company:

"Last spring the people in our office decided to take a group break together, a picnic during the lunch hour. We also decided it would be fun to relive some of our childhood days. First of all, we dressed in the garb we enjoyed wearing in school, then did things that were popular back then, such as jacks, jump-rope, bubble-blowing, and frisbee-throwing. We also played 'do you remember when?' There was 100% participation in all activities. At the end of the picnic, everyone's energy level had increased, people had smiles on their faces, and there was very little friction between people for the rest of the afternoon regardless of the problems we were involved in. This extended joy break worked!"

Diane Carpenter, manager of External Reports and Regulatory Accounting, Texas Utilities, explains the benefits of breaks:

"My breaks range from stopping to take three slow, deep breaths when I'm under tension—it's amazing how helpful that is—to enjoying my assortment of personal energy toys. Scattered all over my office are some traditional Japanese origamis, which are delicate paper figures made by a friend of mine. I also have a structure with a metal magnet and swing that produces a soothing motion, a wind-up frog, a little doll from a close friend, a shelf with my collection of shells and a miniature house, and some trophies that I've won over the years. All these homey objects give enjoyment to people visiting my office, allowing them to

feel more informal with me than they might otherwise feel. Also, I've given myself permission to take a real coffee break now and then, though I used to feel too busy to take them. Or sometimes I'll start talking business with one of our managers, then I'll stop and say, 'Hey, let's do this over coffee instead.' I also use these breaks to have a pleasant conversation with a friend or to reflect upon the past weekend. In general, I have a more relaxed style of doing business now. Yet I'm just as or more productive than before."

As you can see, breaks come in a variety of shapes and forms for different peak performers. Virtually anything that diverts your mind from the work at hand and that gives you a few minutes of humor, relaxation, pleasure, sensory stimulation, exercise, and just plain fun will give you an energy boost. In addition, many professionals use a wooden foot roller, a hand exerciser, or a tactile toy like a koosh ball to ease fatigue as they talk business on the phone.

But let me interject here that, just as children frequently grow bored with their toys, adults can be expected to feel the same way. Remember that change, novelty, and surprise are all powerful suppliers of mental energy. So switch your energy toys and routines from time to time. Every few months, take yourself to a novelty shop or all-ages toy store and see what piques your fancy. Then put that dartboard away for a few months and replace it with a game of ring toss or a beautiful puzzle that you enjoy for five minutes between tasks.

How Our Team Takes Breaks

As you can imagine, our office is highly conducive to taking breaks. In addition to being filled with colorful, right-brain-stimulating supplies, decorations, toys, musical instruments, art supplies, and exercise equipment, plenty of space for group and private breaks abounds in our tri-level office. However, we don't want to paint a picture of only breaks and play. Providing state-of-the-art technology and having well-organized work spaces are other keys to high energy and working excellence.

One factor that promotes breaks and a relaxed, playful atmosphere is our attitude that work should not be divorced from fun. In fact, we don't necessarily wait for energy boosts to happen at appointed times each day but instead try to do many things that will enhance our enthusiasm and momentum during the day. Here are more examples of breaks—and fun, informal attitudes—that build energy at our office.

Three favorite energy-building habits of Georgia, our research specialist, are

- bringing a good joke to work each day,

- finding someone to laugh along with you when you've made a mistake, and

- doing a favor for one work partner each week (your satisfaction and their gratitude will give you energy all that day).

For both Jonnie (our seminar coordinator) and Rayo (our production director), music is another powerful energy-charger. Thus, Rayo puts on one of his favorite tapes when he is about to start a task he is not looking forward to. Jonnie listens to soothing music such as "Largo" when she feels "under pressure to rush through a project." And since computers are still "somewhat like a toy" to Rayo, he finds that converting a project to computer gives him more energy than doing the same task on paper. He also alternates computer-oriented projects with his more routine on-paper projects, using the computer tasks as frequent energy renewals.

Billie (our chief word processor) suggests a way to energize coffee breaks, particularly if they are turning into complaint sessions at your office: "I know one office where the staff decided to apply the concept of recess to their morning group break. People were encouraged to do something fun or positive for ten minutes instead of just drinking coffee and groaning."

Stevie (our anchor person) enjoys

- using colored self-adhesive notes for sending messages to people;

- reviewing thank-you notes from her co-workers whenever she is feeling down about making a mistake; and

- reviewing her "to-do" list at the close of the day, celebrating her accomplishments, and prioritizing what she will schedule for the next day.

Kay (our targeting coach) realizes the importance of using breaks to put your mind in the proper mental set for work. Here's her story of how she turned around an almost-lost day into a successful one:

"Recently I came to the office with a pressing problem from home. I found myself basically hovering over my work but not getting anything done. I told myself that I was too busy to take a break, but my anxiety and distractions kept building. Finally I drove to a nearby trail and spent thirty minutes walking and releasing my stress. When I returned, I couldn't believe how much better I felt. I was able to dive into the work and get lots accomplished. This once again convinced me how effective aerobic exercise is for reducing stress."

Duane enjoys short weekend get-away trips. One of his favorite joy breaks is to flip through weekend guides or airline magazines and discover a hotel chain offering a special package

plan. A five-minute call to the company travel agency completes the joy break by learning about Super-Saver air fares.

Another one of Duane's hobbies is cooking and entertaining. On a day that he knows is going to require an extra effort from the staff, he will put a blender, some bananas and strawberries, a jug of low-fat milk, and other flavorings in a shopping bag and take it to work with his briefcase. At 3:00 p.m., everyone will take a fifteen-minute break and have fresh-fruit smoothies.

Another fun mid-afternoon joy break for Duane is to call up three or four friends to come over for a spur-of-the-moment-no-special-occasion-nothing-fancy midweek supper. Stopping by the pasta shop on the way home from work makes this an effortless but energizing evening.

Since Barbara spends much of her work day in her private office alone, her way of restoring her energy is a bit different from ours. She explains:

"Since I don't get to have an energy charge from others working around me, I have to arrange for that to happen by periodically calling a friend on the phone and having lunch with business associates and friends. In addition, walking outside and feeling the sun on my face is a great energy boost, as is listening to music while I do certain tasks. Also, when my mind gets sluggish and my body feels restless, I get up from the computer and do anything that is not work-related—open my personal mail, look at favorite photos, flip through a magazine, get some tea or juice, even brush my hair and put some lipstick on. Usually when I return to my writing, just five minutes later, my mind pours out the next paragraphs I need to write, and I'm back to writing quickly again. Also, whenever possible, I take a fifteen- to twenty-minute nap in the early afternoon. It revives me completely; without it, I end up fighting sleepiness and sluggishness all afternoon."

Tips on Scheduling Breaks

Now that you have a multitude of suggestions for types of breaks to take, let's consider when to schedule those energy lifts. Some days, due to your work load, your mental set, or your physical condition, you may feel the need to take a short break every hour or so. Other days you may have enough momentum to concentrate on a project for two to three hours before feeling the need for a break. Other days, your agenda may be so tightly packed that your break time may merely consist of taking a series of deep, slow breaths between appointments.

In general, we encourage taking an average of two short breaks in the morning and two in the afternoon. But if you are a "morning person" and naturally have much more energy before noon than after, you may prefer to take just one break in the morning and three to four in the afternoon. If you are an "evening person," then just the opposite may be true for you. Obviously, scheduling breaks is a highly individualistic thing, and you will probably want to experiment to find out when, and under what circumstances, you will benefit most by taking a cleansing, energy-reviving break.

In addition, asking yourself a few questions about your natural energy highs and lows will help you determine other times when a break is in order. First, notice which of your regular projects make you feel least motivated and which tend to drain your energy. Slotting a break at the start and finish of these tasks can balance a low-energy task with two high-energy activities. Furthermore, as mentioned above, you may feel the need to take more breaks during your low-energy periods when your energy tends to sag (such as after lunch).

Another time to schedule a break is after dealing with an energy-sapping personality. Simply being in the presence of these pessimistic, gloom-and-doom types can drain your energy. On the other hand, having a visit with an optimistic, motivated person will give you an energy boost. You can use these people as sources of breaks for you—be it a phone conversation, a coffee break, a lunch date, or a shared work project with them. In fact, talking to a high-energy person after experiencing a low-energy personality is another good energy strategy.

We also encourage taking breaks connected with six fairly common conditions: lack of motivation, tension, high-concentration work, procrastination, complex work, and mental blocks.

1. **Lack of motivation.** When your motivation is waning or when you can no longer make a decision on something mundane, it's time for a short break. Granted, sometimes you are working under such a tight deadline that you feel unable to spare even five minutes. However, when you notice yourself

   ■ having to reread the same material twice because nothing sank in the first time;

   ■ daydreaming and staring out the window;

   ■ feeling so restless that you want to climb out the window; and

   ■ making careless errors,

   you are not working up to speed anyway and are already squandering your time by working very inefficiently. It is much better to simply put down your work for a moment and recharge your batteries. We suggest that you get up from wherever you are, stretch, take some deep breaths, and immerse yourself in a totally different activity that will engage your other brain hemisphere and bring you some instant pleasure. If you are feeling sleepy, a brisk walk around the block (or up several flights of stairs) will help to jump-start your metabolism and fill your brain with oxygen. Doing something that piques your emotions—that makes you chuckle or feel happy—will also give you an emotional energy boost. You might try something that will build both physical and mental energy, such as juggling, playing with a yo-yo, or waltzing around the office to some music.

2. **Tension.** Whenever you feel tense, frustrated, or angry, it's also time for a break. Of course, heading for the gym for a good workout is the most thorough way to release stress and the toxins it produces in your body. But short of that, taking any kind of break that refocuses your attention on something positive will help. Doing several minutes of deep breathing and positive imaging is one effective type of stress-breaker. During your imaging, take yourself to a place that connotes utter peace and sensual pleasure to you. During this exercise, you can physically unwind by contracting all your muscles, starting from your toes and working up to your face, then releasing them.

   Laughter is another powerful tension-breaker, much better than complaining about the cause of your tension. Call a friend or find a colleague, and, instead of sharing your frustrations, get away from the situation by sharing some laughs.

3. **High-concentration work.** Are you engaged in work that requires memorization or the analysis of new information? Some studies indicate that memory is highest at the beginning and end of each work period. So several shorter work or study periods can be far more effective than one long, unbroken period. For most folks, an hour is the maximum amount of time that the brain can take in new data before needing time to stop and process it. By shifting your attention to an entirely different activity—preferably one that stimulates your opposite brain hemisphere—the brain can then process and store this collection of new information.

4. **Procrastination.** We advise using breaks as a reward for completing a project. For example, having a special lunch or coffee break to look forward to will help sustain your momentum as you work on your assignment. Or if it is an unpleasant but necessary task for which you can drum up

almost no enthusiasm, use a reward at the close of the project to serve as your source of motivation.

5. **Complex work.** Breaks can help you to separate a long, complex assignment into a series of "do-able" steps. For example, if you are asked to create a three-year projected budget for your division, the task at first may seem so laborious and time-consuming that the mere thought of beginning makes you tired. Rather than procrastinating until the last minute, try to break the job down into ten one-hour steps that you schedule over several days and that are followed up by ten fun, rewarding breaks—the assignment will feel less overwhelming.

6. **Mental blocks.** Whenever you feel stumped, unable to come up with the answer to a question you've been trying to solve, that's another clear-cut signal that a break is needed. In this case, a longer break is usually necessary. Sometimes your subconscious mind needs a night's sleep to dwell on the problem and come up with the creative breakthrough. Sometimes an activity that will clear your mind of all work-related data, such as a game of tennis, a movie, or time spent with your kids, will enable your mind to hit upon the answer you are seeking. On the contrary, staying at your desk, trying to browbeat yourself into coming up with the solution, will rarely bring you the desired results. Your time will be much better spent by taking a break to switch gears, then refocusing on another assignment for the rest of the day.

The few minutes you put your work aside to take a break will pay off in the extra productivity you will gain by not letting your energy dwindle as the afternoon and evening go by. Just think of how much time it takes to reread several pages of a report that you daydreamed through, to rewrite a poorly composed letter, to refigure a column of expenses that you miscalculated, to apologize to an employee you snapped at because you were tired and frustrated, and so forth. Our list of examples could go on and on simply by taking them from our own lives during the times we functioned below average because we allowed our energy reserves to run low. So whenever you think that you don't have time for a break, weigh the probable consequences and the time required to correct them.

Summary

1. You can turn your four daily maintenance times (your morning routine, commute to work, lunch, and commute home) into energy-building periods by filling them with high-energy breaks and positive thinking.

2. Rather than think of work tasks and break times as separate entities, consider them as two combined activities that will help you meet your productivity goals and enjoy life.

3. When choosing what type of break to take, consider an activity that is very different from the task you have been doing. For example, take a break that involves moving if you've been sitting for a long stretch, or look at pictures rather than words if you've been reading or working with figures.

4. Think of ways to turn your interests into short breaks, such as reading articles in a tennis magazine if you play tennis, or scanning recipes in a specialty cookbook if you love gourmet cooking.

5. It is especially important to take a break before and after an energy-draining activity. Use breaks as rewards for completion of a task, too.

Taking a variety of short breaks is the key to enhancing my work day. It's easy to get so involved in your work that you hunker down over your desk for hours. But I find that it takes just a few minutes to cleanse your mind of 'paperwork pollution.' I feel the need to do that about five to six times a day. Sometimes all it takes is getting up and walking around the room or pushing against a wall, doing isometrics. In fact, often when I talk on the phone, I'm standing up, moving around. So I don't necessarily stop working every time I take a break. I also get an energy lift by looking out my window at the ever-changing scenery or by calling my wife and having a quick talk with her. I feel free to take these breaks whenever I sense that my energy is diminishing.

—Hugh Coble, Group President, Operations, Fluor Daniel, Inc.

P A R T
THREE

Hemisphericity:
Two Opposite Paths to Energy

7

**Brain Dominance and Energy:
What's Good about Your Messy Desk?**

8

**"Half-Brained" Duality versus Whole-Brained Integration:
Resolving Your Mental Civil War**

7

BRAIN DOMINANCE AND ENERGY:

What's Good about Your Messy Desk?

66 *I now do energizing hobbies during the time after work that I used to spend just being tired.* 99

— **Ed Platt, Manager of Generation, Eastern Gas Plants, TU Electric**

66 *I'm right-brain dominant . . . I've never done well at setting out a schedule in advance. But my mind is great at delivering solutions just when I need them. I never write my radio spots in advance, for example. I can always count on the idea popping out during my drive to the studio.* 99

— **Don Frick, writer and producer, Indianapolis**

n Chapter 3 you learned about fifteen behavior traits that produce high energy levels in children and you observed these tendencies in the outstanding role models for high energy that were profiled. We have also found and studied these same behavioral traits among highly accomplished men and women with whom we have taught and worked. Thus we are convinced of the link between these actions and high energy output.

Yet these behavior traits are not the most fundamental source of energy stimulation and maintenance. Underlying the external actions are four integral mental principles that are the real basis of ongoing Energy Engineering. They are

- working and living in sync with your brain dominance;

- balancing both brain hemispheres through brain integration rather than mental duality;

- creating and experiencing a balanced blend of work and play throughout the day and the week; and

- experiencing a stimulating, pleasing work environment that supports your brain dominance.

By practicing these four energy-building principles, you will greatly reduce your daily energy exertion, or loss, and will provide many opportunities to gain fresh energy.

For most of us adults, the ability to continually rebuild our energy reserves—doing it so naturally and efficiently that we rarely suffer a major energy setback unless an illness sets in—requires a fine-tuned balancing act. And like learning to ski or ride a bike, balancing energy loss and gain requires practice and foresight. Mastering these four mental principles is well worth the effort, however, because they can produce the kind of drive, vitality, and achievement levels that you observed in the six high-energy role models profiled in Chapter 3. These four principles can also make burnout and most illness a thing of the past, for most illnesses occur when we have blocked our immune system by living out of balance for long periods.

This chapter will discuss how and why these four principles build energy.

Discovering Your Brain Dominance and Its Link to Energy

One of the most effective steps you can take to quickly increase your energy is to discover your natural brain dominance, then to develop a work style that is in sync with it. The term "brain dominance" refers to a person's tendency to think and act according to the characteristics of one side, or hemisphere, of the brain cortex rather than the other side. Over the past thirty years, Roger Sperry, Robert Ornstein, and other scientists have learned a great deal about the individual traits of the brain's two frontal hemispheres. We are beginning to understand how brain dominances affect our behavior, our learning and work styles, and our personalities.

One of the first indications of the separate functioning of the brain's two hemispheres occurred when physicians discovered that an injury to the left side produced very different results from injury to the right

> **One of the first indications of the separate functioning of the brain's two hemispheres occurred when physicians discovered that an injury to the left side produced very different results from injury to the right side.**

side. The left side of the brain appears to govern the ability to use language, writing, and mathematics, to perform logical deductions and other types of analysis, and to be disciplined. The right side of the brain appears to govern visual, spatial, artistic, and intuitive concepts, plus be the source of imagination and spontaneous play. Persons who have suffered either a stroke or a damaging blow to the left side of their brain, for example, often are unable to put their thoughts into words (speech and writing). Yet they are able to draw pictures to convey their ideas.

In the early 1960s Roger Sperry began research that confirmed the two hemispheres' separate functions, earning him a Nobel Prize in 1983. In one experiment he studied the brains of epileptic patients where the connection between left and right hemispheres had been severed in order to decrease the symptoms of their disease. In one experiment a split-brain patient held a pencil in his right hand but was not allowed to see it. Because the right hand is connected to the left brain hemisphere, the patient could describe it in words. But when he held a pencil in the opposite hand, which stimulated the right brain hemisphere, he could not identify it by speech but instead by pointing to a picture of it.

Despite some controversy on the matter, the latest research conducted on brain hemispheres firmly acknowledges the differences between the two sides and their functions. The March 1989 issue of *Discover* describes hemisphericity research being conducted at the Washington School of Medicine. At the Mallinckrodt Institute of Radiology, neurology researchers can create images of the brain engaged in various tasks by using PET (position emission tomography) technology, which can actually map the biological topography as the brain does its work. Experiments indicate that several areas of the left brain are engaged in reading language. With the PET technology, we can now be more specific and pinpoint where the left brain processes rhyming words, the meaning of words, and familiar words. Through this and similar research, it is now possible to track any task being performed by the brain and know its location.

Before we describe some of the separate characteristics of the two sides, first realize that there is a constant give and take between the right and left hemispheres of a normal brain. The two hemispheres are connected by a bundle of nerve fibers called the corpus callosum, which serves as an instant message pathway. Therefore, the two sides are constantly "in touch" with

each other. In addition, many abilities such as writing a poem or performing in a play require the co-workings and continual cooperation of both sides of the brain, because both activities need an emotional and aesthetic response as well as logic, analysis, and language skills.

However, certain tasks and responses are thought to primarily require the work of one side of the brain versus the other. In addition, most of us develop a preferred, or dominant, side of the brain. And the more that we call on, and thus stimulate, this preferred hemisphere, the better it performs for us. Furthermore, the more we use it, the more we depend upon it. In this way, developing a brain dominance is similar to being left- or right-handed and choosing to do things like write, throw, and eat with the dominant hand. The more skilled we become with our dominant hand, the more clumsy and unacceptable becomes the performance of the other hand. We grow dependent on one hand and stop developing certain skills with the other. In the same way we seem to develop a brain hemisphere dominance.

The exercise entitled "Self-Assessment of Brain Dominance and Energy" will help you identify your natural brain dominance as it links to ways you gain or lose energy.

Self-Assessment of Brain Dominance and Energy*

Read through the following list of statements and quickly decide which tasks give you energy and which drain your energy. Circle the number that best represents your energy response to the task. The scale ranges from "5" (for a task or behavior that highly energizes you) to "–5" (for a task that leaves you energy-depleted).

   If you find that on some statements you have both responses (sometimes you get energy from this situation and sometimes it drains your energy), then score twice on that line, once for the degree of energy gain and once for the degree of energy drain.

1. I enjoy and get energy from creating options such as making "to-do" lists, brainstorming many possible places to go on vacation, thinking of lots of possible ways to do a project. In meetings, I can get interested in a new idea and get energy by adding lots of ideas to it.

Energy Gain						Energy Drain				
5	4	3	2	1	0	–1	–2	–3	–4	–5
					(neutral)					

(Remember to score on both sides if you sometimes gain energy and sometimes lose energy from the same activity.)

2. I get energy from creating order and organizing. I enjoy going through piles of stuff and eliminating the unnecessary. In meetings, I get energy by bringing agenda items to closure and knowing specific tasks are assigned and will be followed up.

Energy Gain						Energy Drain				
5	4	3	2	1	0	–1	–2	–3	–4	–5
					(neutral)					

3. I get my creative juices going by having lots of materials out to work with. Typically I have lots of stuff around me in my work area.

Energy Gain						Energy Drain				
5	4	3	2	1	0	–1	–2	–3	–4	–5
					(neutral)					

4. I typically leave my desk and work area straight and clean primarily because I get energy from putting things back in their place and like to work in a clean, neat area. This seems to apply equally to projects at home such as yard work.

Energy Gain						Energy Drain				
5	4	3	2	1	0	–1	–2	–3	–4	–5
					(neutral)					

5. I enjoy and get energized by juggling several tasks at once and by moving from one to the other intuitively. As I tire of one job or get blocked on how to proceed, I shift and work awhile on another task. This is energizing for me and I often get ideas for one project by putting it out of my mind and working on something completely different.

Energy Gain						Energy Drain				
5	4	3	2	1	0	−1	−2	−3	−4	−5
					(neutral)					

6. I get energy by finishing one thing before I move on to the next. I prefer to create and follow an orderly process in my work. I accomplish the high-priority tasks first and then move on to lower priorities.

Energy Gain						Energy Drain				
5	4	3	2	1	0	−1	−2	−3	−4	−5
					(neutral)					

7. I seem to get energy from being unpredictable. I like to keep all my options open and find being flexible and spontaneous easy and energizing.

Energy Gain						Energy Drain				
5	4	3	2	1	0	−1	−2	−3	−4	−5
					(neutral)					

8. I get energy from being predictable and want others to do the same for me. I enjoy planning and keeping on schedule. I like to plan ahead and know well in advance what is coming.

Energy Gain						Energy Drain				
5	4	3	2	1	0	−1	−2	−3	−4	−5
					(neutral)					

9. I get energy from breaking old rules and policies and finding new ways to get things done. I frequently find rules and policies limiting.

Energy Gain						Energy Drain				
5	4	3	2	1	0	−1	−2	−3	−4	−5
					(neutral)					

10. I prefer to follow the rules and wish others would as well. For me, policies and structure help things to run consistently smoothly. I get energy by providing a positive role model for "going by the book."

Energy Gain						Energy Drain				
5	4	3	2	1	0	−1	−2	−3	−4	−5
					(neutral)					

11. I get energy by risking. I seem to leave things until the last minute and frequently race to meet an important deadline or have to rush in traffic to get places on time. Racing in just at the eleventh hour seems to give me a rush of adrenaline. I perform well under pressure so I don't worry about this part of my profile.

Energy Gain   Energy Drain

5   4   3   2   1   0   −1   −2   −3   −4   −5
                               (neutral)

12. I get energy by planning ahead in detail and allowing a safety "cushion" of time so that I won't lose energy by getting pressured into a mad rush at the last minute. I pride myself on being prompt and usually am early to most appointments and meetings.

Energy Gain   Energy Drain

5   4   3   2   1   0   −1   −2   −3   −4   −5
                               (neutral)

13. I get energy by "flying by the seat of my pants" on projects and other assignments. When specifications are too detailed, there is not as much opportunity for me to get into it and innovate. I prefer a wide-open assignment and enjoy the challenge of a spur-of-the-moment need to respond without lots of planning or rehearsal.

Energy Gain   Energy Drain

5   4   3   2   1   0   −1   −2   −3   −4   −5
                               (neutral)

14. I prefer to plan and rehearse. I want to have a clear idea of what I am going to do and what is expected of me well before the deadline. "Flying by the seat of my pants" is not my best style. I get energy by having the time to coordinate my plans with others.

Energy Gain   Energy Drain

5   4   3   2   1   0   −1   −2   −3   −4   −5
                               (neutral)

15. I get energy by tackling the impossible. The bigger the challenge, the more I like it. In fact, when things get too easy I may even subconsciously cause a little crisis just to keep things stirred up.

Energy Gain   Energy Drain

5   4   3   2   1   0   −1   −2   −3   −4   −5
                               (neutral)

16. I get energy by implementing solutions. Once a new project has been conceptualized, my strong suit is to manage the project to completion.

Energy Gain   Energy Drain

5   4   3   2   1   0   −1   −2   −3   −4   −5
                               (neutral)

17. I do my research, but I trust my intuition and get energy by leaving things a bit open. I like to go into a situation without too much preconditioning so my intuition can work. For example, in a sales call or project negotiation, I trust my ability to listen to and read the client and respond in the moment, so I don't do a lot of rehearsal and tight planning prior to the event.

Energy Gain   Energy Drain
5   4   3   2   1   0   −1   −2   −3   −4   −5
                            (neutral)

18. I get energy by researching all the options before starting. I probably put more time than most into planning and research, but this is my strong suit and I enjoy this part of the job.

Energy Gain   Energy Drain
5   4   3   2   1   0   −1   −2   −3   −4   −5
                            (neutral)

19. I get energy with a new challenge. I find myself more challenged if I move on to a new job or position every three years or so. For me the big energy comes at the beginning when I am trying to get on top of the assignment and see the big picture. Once I have the job in hand, I begin to lose energy and interest. Then I find myself looking for a new challenge.

Energy Gain   Energy Drain
5   4   3   2   1   0   −1   −2   −3   −4   −5
                            (neutral)

20. I get energy when I've been at a job for long enough to reach mastery. I like to stay with a job five to seven years at least. I feel that I do my best work in a new assignment after I've learned all the ropes.

Energy Gain   Energy Drain
5   4   3   2   1   0   −1   −2   −3   −4   −5
                            (neutral)

Now go back and total your scores on the odd-numbered questions (1, 3, 5, 7, 9, etc.) for energy gains _____ and energy drains_____. These questions describe more right-brained processes, so if you have a high energy gain score here (and a low energy drain score), most likely you are a dominant right-brained person. Next, total your scores on the even-numbered questions (2, 4, 6, 8, etc.) for energy gains _____ and energy drains _____. These describe a classic left-brained preference. Thus, if you have high energy gain scores for these questions and low energy drains, very likely your mental processing is dominant left-brain. And what if your scores seem balanced with energy gains from both odd- and even-numbered answers? If your energy gain scores are high on the majority, you probably have already discovered your own ways of using your two hemispheres as supportive partners. We call this profile *brain integration*. However, if you use both systems represented by the twenty questions but still end most days feeling drained or wiped out, then you may be using both hemispheres but one against the other—a process called *duality*.

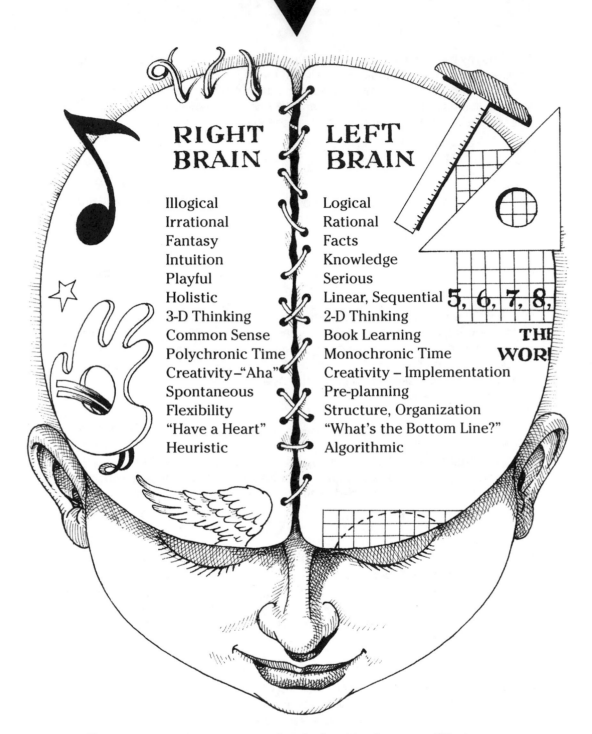

RIGHT BRAIN

Illogical
Irrational
Fantasy
Intuition
Playful
Holistic
3-D Thinking
Common Sense
Polychronic Time
Creativity – "Aha"
Spontaneous
Flexibility
"Have a Heart"
Heuristic

LEFT BRAIN

Logical
Rational
Facts
Knowledge
Serious
Linear, Sequential
2-D Thinking
Book Learning
Monochronic Time
Creativity – Implementation
Pre-planning
Structure, Organization
"What's the Bottom Line?"
Algorithmic

Recognizing your current brain hemisphere profile is a great opportunity for you to make major energy gains. Duality and integration will be described in the next chapter. Unlimited energy comes from learning to call on both hemispheres in balance as supportive partners. This is a basic key to high energy.

Brain Dominance and Work Styles

If you behave one way at work and another way at home, this may mean that your behavior at home is the most natural way for you to act because you are freer to act more according to your feelings than you probably are at work. Thus your home behavior is the most likely indicator of your real brain dominance. Many people at our seminars who initially thought they were left-brained because of the work habits they followed at the office discovered that they exhibited strong right-brained tendencies once they were away from work. In these cases they are probably either right-brain dominant or, if they feel fairly comfortable both at home and at work, they have learned to balance both sides of their brain and thus are whole-brained.

To begin to analyze what these results can tell you about your natural—rather than imposed—work style, briefly review the key characteristics of your brain dominance found in the two lists. People with left-brained preferences usually process information in a manner that is sequential and logical. They prefer to deal with concrete data (rather than nebulous or unstructured information), rules, systems, linear processes, and mathematical and written problems. They also like to work in a step-by-step fashion and to complete one project before going on to another. They thrive on consistency; thus they often get frustrated if their plans and daily schedules are changed or interrupted. They dislike clutter and prefer keeping their work in neat, organized areas or filed away when not in use. In addition, they usually prefer to work alone in a quiet setting. Traditional time management principles are suited for left-brained folks who are good at planning, establishing priorities, scheduling their daily tasks, then staying focused on their agenda.

Conversely, right-brain-oriented people are energized by a different set of conditions. They usually find inflexible routines to be boring or stifling. Thus they enjoy change, flexible schedules, working spontaneously and intuitively, taking on new challenges, and working on several projects during the day. They usually work well under a deadline (which is why many of them let projects go until the last minute) and get energized by challenging or unconventional situations. Most like to have lots of sensory stimulation within their work area, including bright colors, posters, and other kinds of artwork and music. They also like to have their work within view of them, which accounts for the large stacks of folders, papers, and equipment that is found in most right-brain-oriented work spaces. In fact, having these constant visual cues about what they are working on now, and what they intend to get to next week, reminds them to keep incubating ideas and makes them feel much more comfortable and secure than filing their work away out of view. Furthermore, many right-brained folks complain that when they file their work, often they can't recall which heading they filed it under, then end up with several file folders for the same project and all under different headings.

Right-brained people also tend to be very inventive and imaginative folks who need time to dwell upon their formative ideas and work plans. Many are adroit problem solvers who can come up with a variety of alternatives to a situation. They are better at conceptualizing the whole picture rather than remembering to attend to all the details involved. They approach projects intuitively and may be more open about and influenced by their emotions than left-brained people.

Professions that are mainly suited to right-brained people include the arts and entertaining, teaching, writing, decorating, architecture, counseling, motivational speaking, advertising and marketing, sales, and the ministry. Professions that primarily (but certainly not exclusively) attract left-brained people are engineering, accounting, research, law, computer technology, and science.

However, there are many exceptions to the description above. In working with a large majority of engineers as clients (almost all men), our team has discovered that there are a significant number who are what we call "closet right-brain dominant." We playfully gave them this name because, although they have learned to give the impression through their work methods and behaviors that they are dominant left-brained, in truth it is their right-brained skills and traits that work the best for them. Typically they have kept this secret from others and often even from themselves. As they learn more about brain dominance, they begin to suspect and worry a bit about this pattern. When we show them what a benefit it can be for them to be strong and effective in a left-brained career but confident and comfortable with right-brained behaviors, they relax and begin to blossom.

Typically these engineers are strongly visual (which means they usually have stacks of work in progress out on their desk

and other work areas). They typically work on several projects at once, moving from one to another as needed. They are strongly intuitive, but can mask their decisions in enough data to convince others that they get their answers analytically (when actually they are working backwards—intuitively deciding what needs to happen and then collecting the facts to support their intuition). Meetings are often a problem for them in that they can construct an agenda, but are much more sensitive to polychronic time than monochronic time.

The right-brained polychronic person is more apt to focus on people's feelings, a lack of group consensus, and side issues that are obstructing a cooperative spirit. These complex issues are unpredictable in advance, so polychronic people frequently go beyond preset deadlines.

In contrast, left-brained monochronic people focus on preset agendas, schedules, and deadlines. People issues and in-the-moment new ideas are more apt to be seen as interruptions and unnecessary tangents. Their priority is to stay on schedule and to be punctual.

Here's how Don Frick, an Indianapolis writer and video producer, describes his strongly right-brain-dominant work habits:

"Although I am capable of doing left-brain-oriented linear thinking, I have a right-brain profile and have never done well with setting a schedule in advance and sticking rigidly to it. Also, the nature of my work demands flexibility, jumping from project to project, then putting in intense work periods to reach deadlines.

My style of diving into a script I'm assigned to write is to read the material in full, then totally walk away from it—sometimes taking up to four days for this gestation period. Then something clicks in my brain to tell me I'm ready to tackle it. Those times when I've tried to work on the script right away, it usually comes out shallow. I also trust my mind to come up with solutions when I need them. For instance, I wait to write my weekly radio script until I am in the car driving to the studio. The lines always pop into my mind before I arrive.

Another work habit of mine is to have intense bursts of energy with long work periods. But I always find myself walking away from my work every fifty minutes or so to wander about the house for a few minutes, looking at picture books, getting a glass of tea, listening to a short piece of music before returning to work."

Of course, both types of brain dominance are equally valuable and necessary in this world. What matters is that you learn to work in sync with your natural dominance—which is the most productive and energy-efficient way for each individual to work. Learning how to be whole-brained—how to integrate both hemispheres into a harmonious working relationship—is the next high-energy building block. This step necessitates learning to respect your less dominant hemisphere and allowing it to affect your ideas and behavior. In addition to increasing your energy, you will become a more well-rounded person, able to meet a wider range of challenges in your job and life.

Stimulants and "Tools" for Both Brain Hemispheres

Another way to understand what produces and drains your energy is to think about stimulants and/or "tools" for each brain hemisphere. We've listed some on the following pages.

Right-Brained Preferences

- new objects and things to explore
- sensory stimuli: beautiful objects, pleasing sounds and smells, interesting colors, shapes, and, textures
- fun activities: toys, games, fanciful objects
- free emotional expression (feelings of joy, excitement, fear, anger, caring, etc.)
- interactions with others
- an environment that surrounds you with your work (or hobbies); having things in view
- things that make you laugh

Left-Brained Preferences

- familiar objects and procedures
- tools, equipment, and other things that are considered useful
- logical progression of facts
- rules, systems
- approaching things rationally; being in control of your feelings
- quiet and solitude
- neat, organized; work filed away
- activities construed as productive and serious

Working and Thinking Styles

In addition to having a preference for different stimulants and objects, the two hemispheres prefer very different ways of thinking, learning, working, and being.

Right-Brained Preferences

- "cluttered" desk and office, things out in view
- enjoying new challenges and risks
- often jumping from project to project or juggling several things at once before going on to the next
- considering or experimenting with many options (may seem disorderly or

Left-Brained Preferences

- tidy and organized
- prefers predictable situations and knowing what's coming
- working in a step-by-step style, finishing one project before starting the next
- sticking to one plan (creating "order")
- following set procedure; predictable, dependable

indecisive to a left-brained person)

- being flexible and sometimes unpredictable
- good at last-minute projects and "flying by the seat of the pants"; often puts off finishing something, incubating options and ideas, until the final deadline
- best at conceptualizing something
- frequently acting playful or emotional; may be a somewhat sporadic worker rather than a methodical worker
- breaking or bending rules
- divergent thinking

- detailed planner who sticks to a schedule; dislikes the risk of leaving things to the last minute
- best at following plans, sticking to details, and completing projects
- more often a serious, methodical, steady worker
- following rules
- convergent thinking

The preceding, however, are not either-or lists. You probably noticed that some people's work styles and personalities reflect a blend of both right- and left-brain characteristics. In fact, this may be true of yourself. Furthermore, some folks tend to act in a left-brained manner at work, then they switch to a right-brained style at home and during the weekends. Yet most of us have a definite predilection toward relying on one side of the brain (and its accompanying behavior traits), and it is important to know which tendency you have.

Actually, striking a *balance* between the two hemispheres is the most productive and creative way to live. That way, you can benefit from the capabilities of both sides of your brain. Integrating both sides is also the most beneficial and energy-efficient way to process, as we will explain in the next chapter. We call this being "whole-brained" rather than "half-brained." If you will turn back to the profiles in Chapter 3, you will see that Mead's, Schweitzer's, Edison's, O'Keeffe's, Churchill's, and Claiborne's work styles and personalities reflected both right- and left-brained tendencies. In fact, if we had to pick one other factor (in addition to extraordinary imagination and intelligence) that appears to have accounted for their accomplishments, it would be their ability to call upon and bring into play a much broader range of hemisphere skills than the average person.

Discovering your initial brain dominance (if you do not yet have a balanced, "whole-brained" orientation) is the first step toward creating a harmonious interchange between your two hemispheres. The next step is understanding how this dominance affects your organizational, learning, and overall work patterns and then creating a comfortable and energy-efficient work style for yourself. This step is crucial, because working out of sync with your natural brain dominance is like trying to walk with your shoes on the wrong feet or trying to write with the opposite hand from the one you are used to. In other words, it feels uncomfortable, jarring, frustrating, and tiring. And it requires a much greater expenditure of energy.

For example, a left-brained person most likely would feel uncomfortable if she were suddenly transferred into an office space occupied by two right-brained work partners. The left-brained worker probably would prefer to work in silence at a neat work area. She would feel best starting each project well in advance of deadline and scheduling each step of every project. But it's likely that her right-brained partners would prefer working in a different manner and environment. They would talk back and forth as they work, would tend to finish up their projects at the last minute, and would change things in mid-stream. And since they would be jumping from one project to another throughout the day, their desks would be cluttered with stacks of materials and equipment. This appearance of disarray would bother the left-brained worker and possibly make her feel nervous and disorganized in that environment.

Can you see how much tension and exhaustion the left-brained worker might experience if she could not carve out a quiet, neat, and structured niche for herself amid the seemingly chaotic work environment and style of her two right-brained partners? Have you ever experienced a situation similar to this?

But a right-brained employee can feel equally uncomfortable when working in a highly structured, sterile-feeling environment. And since most of the American work world reflects a left-brained orientation, right-brained people are more often the ones being forced to function out of sync with their brain dominance. As the previous lists show, our right hemisphere does not prefer the type of set, step-by-step methods promoted by the standard time management courses (such as following "to-do" lists, prioritizing all assignments, sticking to a schedule, finishing one project before moving to another, etc.). Instead, the right brain thrives under a much more flexible, spontaneous, and intuitive work style. Forcing someone with a strong right-brain dominance to adhere to all these rules, day in and day out, could create a very unproductive scenario. Yet some of the time management principles can be restructured for right-brained people—as you will discover later. In fact, if they are adapted to a right-brained working style, they can energize and enhance the right brain by adding support, organization, and balance.

Brain Dominance, Personality, and Relationships

The effect of brain dominance can be felt in many relationships outside of work, too. When choosing a mate, for instance, most of us are drawn toward someone of the opposite brain dominance. Then we make the mistake of assuming that what works well for us should work equally well for them. And nothing could be farther from true.

Remember, what energizes one hemisphere (and one brain dominance) tends to tire and frustrate the opposite one. Hence, can you understand what happens in our relationships when we make the mistake of trying to force our partners to use our own system of thinking and doing things?

The same conflict can arise at work if we are paired on a project with people having an opposite dominance from ours. Left-brain-dominant people will probably want to set a detailed schedule in advance and stick with it. But the right-brained folks appear to keep wandering off in all directions with no apparent focus—much to the dismay and consternation of their left-brained counterparts. Then in a break-neck fit of speed, the right-brained workers will make the final deadline by the skin of their teeth.

As you may have already witnessed in your own job, these disparate work styles can sabotage each other and be the cause of tremendous friction and ill will. But if all team members have

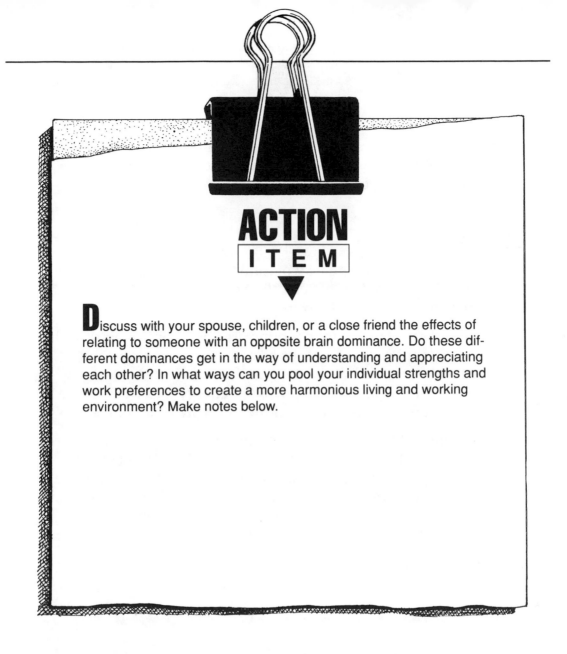

ACTION ITEM ▼

Discuss with your spouse, children, or a close friend the effects of relating to someone with an opposite brain dominance. Do these different dominances get in the way of understanding and appreciating each other? In what ways can you pool your individual strengths and work preferences to create a more harmonious living and working environment? Make notes below.

an understanding of the strengths of both brain dominances, a team comprised of both types of workers who support each other's needs can be the best possible match. Where one style is weak and less motivated toward a particular task, the other style may be strong and well suited for it.

In the realm of parenting, we adults almost always parent from our left hemispheres, enforcing rules, setting limits, voicing expectations, and so forth. Yet most children function primarily from their right hemispheres—creating clutter everywhere, breaking rules, and resisting structure—until they are in their late teens and early twenties. Can you see the possibilities for clashes and misunderstandings? Remember, both brain styles can get to the same end, but each will take an almost opposite route to do so. This makes for some interesting insights that can have a major influence not only on your energy, but also in your ability to be an effective parent, partner, leader, and team member.

Summary

1. We all have a favorite way of thinking, behaving, and working based on brain dominance. What energizes one hemisphere tires and frustrates the other.

2. Whereas we tend to marry opposites, we want to work with those people who share our same brain dominance and "think like we do." Since there are as many left-brained as right-brained people, we can avoid energy loss by learning to appreciate the work styles of the opposite dominance.

3. It is natural to parent and manage from the left hemisphere, which creates a tendency to distrust and want to control others. This sets up a huge energy loss for both parties. By bringing in right-brain flexibility, trust, and openness to parenting and managing, we can create brain integration and thereby increase everybody's energy.

"HALF-BRAINED" DUALITY VERSUS WHOLE-BRAINED INTEGRATION:

Resolving Your Mental Civil War

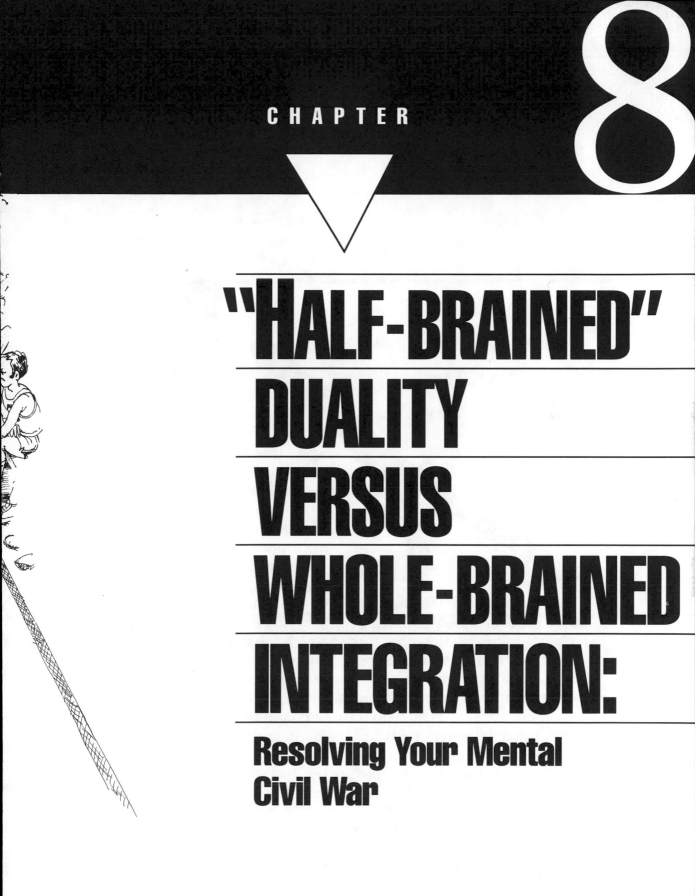

magine that you are a spectator at a very unusual basketball game. One team runs up and down the court with great agility and speed, dodging and leaving the other team behind. The second team is much slower, providing no competition for the first team. As you look more closely, you notice that each player on the second team is playing primarily on one leg, only occasionally allowing the other foot to touch the floor. As you can imagine, the first team has more than a double advantage over the second, for hopping on only one foot allows much less potential and is far more tiring than running and dodging on both feet.

This metaphor can help us understand how most of us overlook the unlimited potential of brain integration. Even though we all have two hemispheres and we all draw from both throughout the day, most of us spend most of our time drawing from our favorite or most skilled hemisphere and only call on the other here and there. An even bigger loss is to play the mental game of trying to decide which hemisphere is better and pitting one brain against the other. If we stick with the basketball metaphor, it would be like having all the players decide it is more important and rewarding to play offense only, so each of them would stop playing defense and would only wait for opportunities to make points. You can imagine that without any of them playing defense, there would be no one down court to stop the other team from scoring and to bring the ball back up court. Now there might be lots of angry blaming and finger-pointing as to who should be playing defense. This often happens if one player becomes a "hot dog" and, instead of working with his other team members, just looks for every opportunity to score on his own. Soon the other players resent his grandstanding and taking praise at their expense. So they become less and less willing to set picks for him or pass the ball to him.

This is a powerful example of duality, which is breaking something into two distinct parts and then struggling over which has value or is more important. In this process, respect and trust are lost and replaced by discounting and mistrust. The very partners who have the potential to create an effective, powerful, and synergistic team use their energy and resources to defeat and thwart each other.

Now let's apply this metaphor to understand how we might use our two brain hemispheres.

Recognizing Duality

Duality occurs when each hemisphere of the brain distrusts and discounts the other. Duality is so much a part of our lives and is so ingrained in our institutions that it will be difficult to see at first. It's like pulling a big heavy door open with one hand while holding it closed with the other. Lots of energy gets spent with little gain!

Here are some examples of duality which may be familiar to you. Sales personnel are out scrambling to get new business, frustrated because the estimating department refuses to be rushed on getting bids out. The estimating department wants to be sure the figures quoted are absolutely accurate instead of "shooting from the hip." The estimators cringe at the ball-park guesses some of the sales reps give out. From their view, sales reps should say nothing until

Duality occurs when each hemisphere of the brain distrusts and discounts the other.

they are absolutely sure of a correct bid. From the sales reps' point of view, waiting several days or weeks could mean losing all possibility of staying competitive. Quick response is key to keeping clients interested, and new clients are hard to find.

Can you see the right-brained values of sales (speed, spontaneity, big-picture thinking, such as ball-park guesses, a willingness to make up the rules as they go) flying in the face of the left-brained values of the estimating department (accuracy, sticking to the rules, planning ahead, unwillingness to release figures until they have been carefully checked and double-checked)? For a company to be successful, both these groups need to appreciate the unique problems and values of the differences they represent. By working together and seeking whole-brained, cooperative solutions, a *synergy* of brain integration can be achieved.

SYNERGY means the whole is worth more than the sum of the parts (2 + 2 = 7 or more). You might also think of synergy as the "over and above" energy you experience when these two opposite brain processes team up as supportive, nurturing partners.

A second example of duality might be a person who is very creative and loves to generate ideas. Being a right-brained, highly visual person, her desk is stacked with work in progress, data from phone calls, files with research information, etc. If the person rarely devotes time and energy to filing away work and resists allowing others to file work, then soon she can get buried in the prolific generation of good ideas and have a breakdown in following up on them. I know this painfully from my own patterns of duality. My right brain becomes like a rebellious kid, as I "creatively" stay too busy to attend to the chores I don't enjoy. Meanwhile my left brain becomes very critical and judgmental, nagging me for the "awful mess" I work in and creating great internal anxiety, imagining all the terrible things that might result from my out-of-balance and out-of-control state. Does any of this sound familiar?

And if you are smugly thinking you would never fall into such a state of disorganization, let's consider the duality from

the left brain. This might be the person who rarely if ever risks trying something totally new. He insists on the comfort of staying close to the "standard" way of doing things and demands perfection even when he knows it is no longer working. He is big on accuracy and the tried-and-true ways of doing things, insisting "if it ain't broke, don't fix it." When presented with ideas for innovative improvements, he may quickly find fault and resist. His strengths are in details, order, and sticking to the agreed-upon way of getting things done. Typically his blind spots are shifting into whole new ways of thinking. His desk will be clean, but his mind will be resistant or closed to innovation or new ways to solve old problems.

The following, from *The Experts Speak: The Definitive Compendium of Authoritative Misinformation*, are classic examples of this kind of duality whereby the so-called experts were the most resistant to change and the most blind to new ways of thinking:

"Everything that can be invented has been invented."

(Charles H. Duell, commissioner of U.S.Office of Patents, urging President William McKinley to abolish his office in 1899)

"When the Paris Exhibition closes, electric light will close with it and no more will be heard of it."

(Erasmus Wilson, professor at Oxford University, 1878)

"I think there is a world market for about five computers."
(attributed to Thomas J. Watson, chairman of the board of International Business Machines, 1943)

Recognizing Duality in Yourself and Others

If you think of duality as one side of your brain wanting one thing while the other side pushes for the opposite, you have a good picture of what is taking place. For example, when you awaken to your alarm clock, one side of your brain expects you to get up promptly and begin getting dressed for your day. The other side of your brain may wish to stay snuggled warmly under the covers, peacefully dozing for just a bit longer. Next you may feel guilt and judgment coming from your impatient left brain while the rebellious right brain invents a reason to stay snug for just a bit longer. It becomes hard to enjoy those last few minutes with the left brain nagging and blaming, reminding you of all the other times you wasted precious minutes sleeping your life away when you could have been getting that all-important early start!

Does this sound familiar? Can you remember any mornings like this? When we slip into duality, we experience this mental civil war with each hemisphere out to punish and sabotage the other as an adversary rather than out to team with the other as a partner. Our language can signal duality and an opportunity to shift into brain integration. The following phrases are a tip-off to duality in our thinking:

"I've got to . . ."		"You've got to . . ."
"I have to . . ."		"You have to . . ."
"I must . . ."	or	"You must . . ."
"I should . . ."		"You should . . ."
"I ought to . . ."		"You ought to . . ."

The issue is *control*. You feel pressured by yourself or whoever is saying you must or should do something. There is no trust that you will follow through without coaxing or nagging. You can think of this as the left brain pressuring and attempting to control the right brain. In response, notice that your right brain typically becomes resistant and defensive. You might find yourself thinking of why you don't want to do whatever you "should" do. You may behave much like a rebellious child, thinking of ways to put off or resist the pressure to perform.

In these examples you can see the two aspects of duality: the discounting and the distrust of each hemisphere for the other met with resistance, defensive blocked thinking, and often rebellion. Can you see why this mental tug of war drains so much energy? One part of you is literally nagging and cajoling, much as a bossy parent might, while the other part of you becomes the rebellious child, resenting advice and instruction even if it is in your best interest.

Choosing Brain Integration over Duality

To shift yourself out of duality, think of these two parts of yourself working as a cooperative team. If you decided with your logical left brain to get up early and get on the road ahead of the traffic, your left brain might gently remind your right brain of how good it will feel to miss the traffic and get to the office early. Remember that the right brain responds much as a kid might, so think of reasoning with a child. Rewarding the child in you with something appealing may be a successful strategy. As you lie in bed, visualize your day quickly, imaging how well you will perform and how much you will be respected by being early and well prepared. Then plan something special as a reward, such as listening to a tape you enjoy while on the toll road or meeting your spouse at a special restaurant for dinner after a busy day. These images invite your right brain to join the left in choosing wholeheartedly to get up early.

This choice clearly indicates brain integration. When all of you chooses wholeheartedly to do something, both of your hemispheres are cooperating and in agreement. When you feel like part of you wants to do something and part of you doesn't, you are in duality. And it is this push/pull argument between the two parts that erodes your precious energy. Thus, integration is *drawing on the benefits of both sides of the brain.* Each hemisphere is called upon as needed. There is high trust, cooperation, and appreciation between and for both hemispheres.

The Language of Integration

A quick way to shift yourself into brain integration is simply to use such phrases as these:

"I *choose* to . . ."

"I *get* to . . ."

"I *look forward* to . . ."

"I *want* to . . ."

These indicate that both your logical left brain and your emotional right brain are together on each decision. As a result, your logic joins your enthusiasm in entering into these commitments. The problem with "have tos" is that they make us feel controlled, and we have a natural tendency to resist control. This resistance we set up for ourselves drains our personal energy. Can you feel the difference, as you think of real choices in your immediate life, in shifting from a "have to" to a "choose to"?

For example, let's consider paying income taxes. You may think of that as a "have to" job and feel you have no choice in the matter. Certainly nobody wants to pay taxes. Let's test this assumption.

"If you don't want to pay your taxes, then don't."

"But if I don't, I will go to jail."

"Then go to jail."

"But I don't want to go to jail."

"Then it sounds like you may want to pay your taxes."

You may not like your choices, but you do have a choice. Of even greater importance is the freedom to choose your attitude and the energy drain or gain that goes with it. The first group of executives to go through our whole-brained program (Perspective III) took this a step further. Since one can get more energy by changing a "have to" task to a "choose to" or "want to" task, you can take this idea a step further and add more energy by saying, "I *get* to pay my taxes." You may discover not only new energy but new reasons why there really is a "get to" in the situation. For example, with taxes we get to live in a free country, we get to help fund well-built highways, hospitals, parks, social programs, etc. We can easily find as many reasons to feel good about "getting" to pay our share of the taxes as we previously found reasons for feeling bad about "having" to pay them. It's all a matter of perspective—and integrated thinking.

Duality:
Splitting Our Brain into the Rebellious Child versus the Merciless Master

We have named the personalities of our two hemispheres the Rebellious Child (right brain) and the Merciless Master (left brain). When you are in duality, your right hemisphere behaves much as a rebellious child, sulking, feeling guilty, and feeling like a victim with no options but to blame others and to feel self-pity. In this "poor me" mood, a person is hard to deal with. This is the defensive self, full of excuses and unwilling to be held accountable for any actions. Attempts to get the person to be more objective and solution-oriented will feel like unsupportive attacks.

Duality Self-Talk

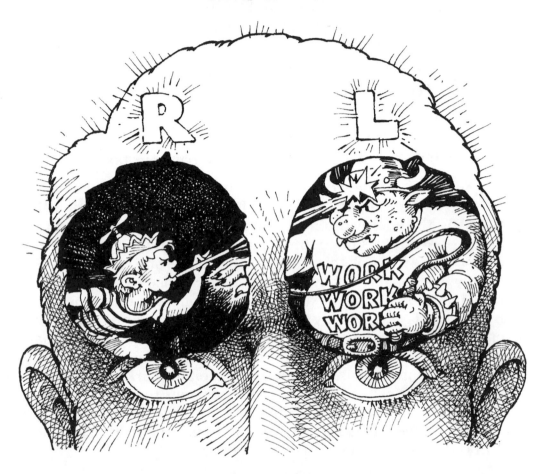

Rebellious Child vs. Merciless Master

The left hemisphere is the Merciless Master. When in a state of duality, this part is never satisfied with the individual's performance, is constantly critical, and demands more and more. The Merciless Master fears play and celebrations as a threat and condemns such behavior as wasting time and being complacent instead of constantly forging ahead. When the Rebellious Child becomes more active, the Merciless Master becomes more aggressive, feeling justified in lowering the boom. It becomes a self-perpetuating, negative spiral, endlessly draining energy and self-image.

You can also project these two parts of the personality onto other people. When you are in duality, you perceive others in duality as well. They are either good or bad, black or white. You fear the playfulness in others because you can't control your own playfulness (in the form of your rebellious child).

Brain Integration:
Teaming the Free Child with the Supportive Coach

Now let's look at how these two hemispheres can become transformed into two cooperative, interdependent partners. We call them the Free Child (right brain) and the Supportive Coach (left brain). Notice how the very same parts of us that were operating like a Rebellious Child and a Merciless Master can become totally positive. As the Free Child, our right brain becomes

- eager,
- playful,
- cooperative,
- enthusiastic,
- energetic, and
- creative

in response to our Supportive Coach, who nurtures, guides, protects, and encourages the positive growth of the Free Child. The Supportive Coach is the analytical, measuring, strategic side of the brain. But in a state of integration, this part of us totally supports and values all the counter qualities of the right brain. It knows that curiosity, innovation, and spontaneity are essential for creative breakthroughs. So it helps in honing and evaluating, but always from a positive position. This part of your brain

- knows when to nurture and when to discipline;
- encourages dreams of excellence as well as outrageous dreams;
- provides structure and discipline;
- is firm but fair;
- uses positive affirmations;
- helps you move past fears;
- helps you harvest mistakes;
- helps you reframe problems as opportunities; and
- can admit failures and ask for help.

Integration Self-Talk

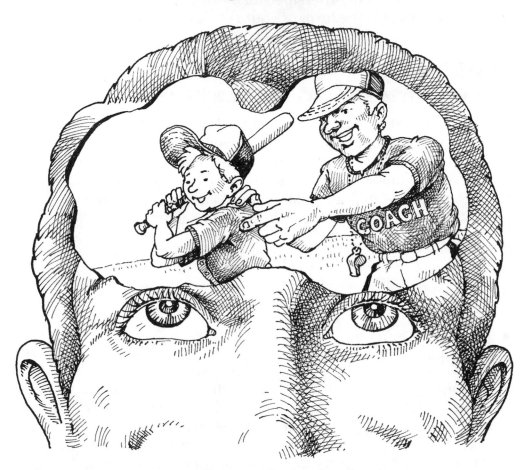

Free Child and Supportive Coach

There is high trust and cooperation between these two opposite but mutually supportive partners, with each drawing energy and insight from the other.

One clear example of the effectiveness of brain integration is my own experience of working on a typewriter versus a word processor. I once worked for a bank president who insisted that everything be typed perfectly the first time. No erasures or corrections were allowed! (Can you hear the Merciless Master in this?) As I would get to the bottom of a complex page of typing, I would feel more and more tense, fearing that one small error would cause me to have to begin again. And, like a self-fulfilling prophecy, this frequently happened.

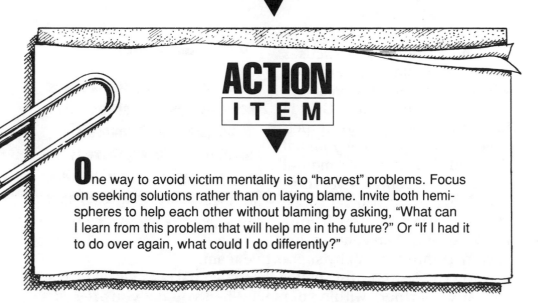

ACTION
I T E M

One way to avoid victim mentality is to "harvest" problems. Focus on seeking solutions rather than on laying blame. Invite both hemispheres to help each other without blaming by asking, "What can I learn from this problem that will help me in the future?" Or "If I had it to do over again, what could I do differently?"

Working on a word processor now, I notice that both my typing speed and accuracy have increased tremendously, primarily because any error can be corrected easily with no fear of punishment or embarrassment. The word processor is like a Supportive Coach, giving me ways to make my work better and even coaching me through the spell check. I look forward to and get energy from writing on a word processor, whereas I used to experience writer's block and dreaded "having" to write on a typewriter.

Self-Directed or Proactive versus Victim Mentality

One final tip for catching yourself when you have slipped into duality is to observe your level of motivation. When you are in duality, you will feel like you are having to force yourself to do things. A part of you will be pushing yourself forward and another part will be dragging your heels. You may drag yourself to the office and then sit there limply, without the enthusiasm or motivation to plunge into the day. This is classic duality. It also describes burnout, which results from living in duality. In this mental state we operate out of victim mentality, not seeing the many opportunities to make our lives positive and satisfying but instead blaming others for why we are unsatisfied and unsuccessful:

"My boss doesn't . . ."

"My parents didn't . . ."

"When I was in college, they didn't teach me . . ."

There are endless excuses and ways to blame others. And when we blame ourselves, it is in lieu of taking action. Or it is just another excuse not to persevere. When you feel yourself dragged down by this mental struggle, be gentle with yourself. Start by nurturing those two battered parts of your thinking, and then gently bring each part into a mutually supportive team.

When you feel yourself dragged down by this mental struggle, be gentle with yourself. Start by nurturing those two battered parts of your thinking, and then gently bring each part into a mutually supportive team.

You can see how this unites these two parts as working, co-operative partners within yourself. When you do, you are self-directed rather than dependent on others to "make" you do whatever needs to be done. This cooperation is also called pro-active rather than reactive. It means planning ahead and deciding in advance what you want as a total picture of your day and week instead of reactively just taking one thing at a time.

When you invite your two hemispheres to become partners in living your life, you will reap the benefits of long-term planning (which will keep you from suffering from last-minute crises) and also the joy of living in the moment, being totally present to each event and person in your life. There is a wonderful synergy which comes from this union.

Duality Attitudes (Half-Brained)	**Integration Attitudes (Whole-Brained)**
1. Play is frivolous (left brain).	1. Playfulness can enhance my work.
2. Keep playfulness out of the office (left brain).	2. I enjoy breaks AND the opportunity to work.
3. I and others have to be frightened, coerced, or forced into work (left brain).	3. I and others work better when motivated through positive support, trust, and challenge.
4. Anything I want to do at any time is okay regardless of the rights of others (right brain).	4. I value my freedom but equally value the rights and freedom of others.

5. I put things off to create a crisis because I do my best work under pressure (right brain).

6. If I stop to play, I can't trust myself or others to get back to work (left brain).

5. I replace last-minute crises with planning for challenges in advance.

6. Trust and intrinsic motivation are the foundation for personal and team productivity.

Duality Behaviors

1. Every situation is win/lose, a battle or competition to be won.

2. Life is seen only in absolutes—black or white, my way vs. your way, right way vs. wrong way.

3. The doer is dependent and/or independent, unwilling to delegate or delegating only with elaborate, resistive instructions: "I'd rather do it myself and be sure it gets done right!"

Integration Behaviors

1. The doer sees every situation as an opportunity for teaming; wants things to work out as well for others as for self—win/win/win; doesn't demand credit or spotlight; emphasizes cooperation. Therefore, synergy occurs.

2. The doer realizes there is more than one right answer.

3. The doer is interdependent, not only delegating the job, but also trusting the other person to decide how to get it done.

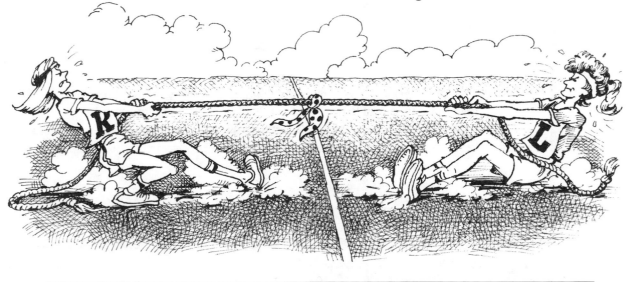

How do you know if you are becoming more whole-brained? This is a beginning list to help those interested in brain transformation continue personal growth. As you read down the list, you might look for opportunities to expand your frame of reference and appreciation. After reading each question, rate your current behavior patterns on the scale ("1" means seldom or not a part of your behavior and "10" means consistently a part of your behavior).

1. I am open to and interested in ways of thinking not like my own. When others differ with me, I am curious and open to learning a new way of seeing and thinking rather than assuming that they are wrong or even thinking that one of us has to be wrong.

1	2	3	4	5	6	7	8	9	10

2. I am learning to be equally interested in strongly left-brained ways of thinking and working as well as strongly right-brained ways.

1	2	3	4	5	6	7	8	9	10

3. When my spouse or children disagree or differ with me, I am able to listen to and learn from their point of view. I am learning from others that having one right answer to everything is too narrow.

1	2	3	4	5	6	7	8	9	10

4. I am learning to have fun doing things that I used to think were silly or not my cup of tea. I purposely seek out some of these new experiences to broaden my perspective.

| 1 | 2 | 3 | 4 | 5 | 6 | 7 | 8 | 9 | 10 |

5. I seek ways to play that are not competitive. I am able to enjoy being curious and full of wonder rather than having to compete or win to be entertained. (Or, if your fun is typically noncompetitive, you might seek out more competitive fun as a means to balance. You will be the best judge of your needs and balance point.)

| 1 | 2 | 3 | 4 | 5 | 6 | 7 | 8 | 9 | 10 |

6. My work is fun, satisfying, and fulfilling to me. Even parts of my work that could be considered routine or a drudgery, I am able to enjoy in the fuller context of my mission. I am also very creative in finding ways to enjoy even the unenjoyable.

| 1 | 2 | 3 | 4 | 5 | 6 | 7 | 8 | 9 | 10 |

7. I have an equal dedication to my play and to my work. I take time to refresh myself and relax regularly, so I can work with more creativity and energy.

| 1 | 2 | 3 | 4 | 5 | 6 | 7 | 8 | 9 | 10 |

8. I am able to admit my mistakes openly and learn from them with little or no self-punishment or guilt. I talk about my mistakes openly to encourage others to feel equally comfortable about their mistakes. I see them as opportunities to learn and necessary steps toward innovation and growth.

1	2	3	4	5	6	7	8	9	10

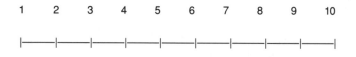

9. I take good care of myself—my body as well as my mental and spiritual self. I enjoy eating healthy food most of the time and enjoy healthy aerobic exercise on a regular basis.

1	2	3	4	5	6	7	8	9	10

10. I typically choose to view problems as opportunities. I spend very little time overwhelmed and discouraged. I am aware of a wide range of resources personally, socially, and professionally. I am convinced that creative people look for innovative new ways to view the situation and make breakthroughs where others choose to be stumped by the "impossible." I enjoy brainstorming new ideas as well as following through on the details to project completion.

1	2	3	4	5	6	7	8	9	10

11. I am consistent with my attitudes and behaviors; my team and family know that they can come to me almost anytime about anything and I will be open and supportive.

```
1    2    3    4    5    6    7    8    9    10
|————|————|————|————|————|————|————|————|————|
```

12. I stay in touch with my feelings and am comfortable expressing anger, grief, joy, love, and other emotions. I can give clear messages without blaming or accusing.

```
1    2    3    4    5    6    7    8    9    10
|————|————|————|————|————|————|————|————|————|
```

13. I recognize the principle of "in order to keep, I must give away." As I come into more balance and brain integration, I value sharing with others (i.e., role modeling, teaching, listening) FOR MY BENEFIT.

```
1    2    3    4    5    6    7    8    9    10
|————|————|————|————|————|————|————|————|————|
```

Note: If you found yourself frustrated and confused by being asked to arbitrarily rate yourself with no clear, measurable criteria, gently be aware that this indicates your strengths in left-brained processing. Realize that to become truly whole-brained, *intangibles* must become as obvious, measured, and valued as *tangibles.* To grow toward whole-brain synthesis, you may want to risk making some "guesstimates" or inviting others who know you well to give you feedback. Or you may want to just skip over the rating scale, but reflect on where and how you can grow.

Summary

1. We experience a huge energy loss when we play the mental game of trying to decide which hemisphere's way of processing is better.

2. Duality is when we value only one hemisphere and spend most of our energy trying to define it while attacking the opposite way of thinking or behaving.

3. Duality happens when people of opposite thinking styles are in conflict, but duality also happens when our own two hemispheres are in conflict about an issue.

4. You can recognize duality by listening to language. Phrases like "I have to," "You must," "I should," and "I ought to" represent a victim mentality. Worry and guilt also signal unhealthy duality. Conversely, phrases such as "I choose to," "I want to," and "I get to" show positive, integrated thinking.

5. To maintain high energy, you must shift out of duality into brain integration—using the two opposite sides of your thinking as a cooperative team.

6. The key to brain integration is learning to be self-directed, or "proactive." Valuing each part of your thinking and using each when appropriate will increase your personal energy. Cooperating and supporting opposite thinking styles in others will result in increased team energy as well.

P A R T
FOUR

Energy Traps and Solutions

9

BURNOUT SYMPTOMS:

Avoiding Traps That Drain Your Energy

How do we know when we are in duality? Typically it results in burnout, so let's examine the symptoms and see what we can learn:

> *I wake up tired, I go to sleep tired, I just don't seem to have the energy to do much of anything anymore.*

> *Even a vacation sounds like too much of an effort to be worth it. Nothing I can think of sounds like fun to me.*

> *I have an overwhelming case of the I-don't-want-tos.*

> *I feel a lot like I'm on a treadmill, going nowhere fast.*

All of these comments on the preceding page are the all too familiar symptoms of burnout. You can get a minor case after a few weeks of pushing too hard without relief, or you can fall into a major case of burnout after a few years of living out of balance. Like the flu, it can be a temporary setback and leave you drained and out of sorts. Or you can experience a terminal case with major depression leading to suicide, and like the flu, burnout is something to which you are never immune! You can get it again every year or more often. So burnout is something to become aware of and to know how to avoid.

The symptoms are all basically "lack of" symptoms, lack of

- energy,
- enthusiasm,
- motivation,
- zest,
- ideas,
- permission to play,
- humor,
- joy,
- satisfaction,
- interest,
- dreams for life,
- concentration, or
- self-confidence.

Then there are at least three symptoms of burnout that can be called dysfunctional:

1. **Sexuality.** (You may temporarily lose interest in sex or have a strong sex drive but find yourself unfulfilled no matter how much you experience.)

2. **Appetite.** (You may lose your interest in eating or want to eat everything in sight—primarily junk food. Again you seem to be eating without feeling fulfilled.)

3. **Sleep.** (You may not be able to sleep or you may oversleep, using sleep as an escape from life which has lost its interest. Again, this kind of sleep is unfulfilling, and even though you sleep for long periods, you awaken tired and listless.)

The list goes on. We each have our own personal symptoms:

- feeling grouchy;
- feeling irritable;
- being unwilling and unable to be pleased;
- wanting something but not being sure what it is;
- dwelling on the negatives in life and within ourselves;
- feeling that life is unsolvable and unfair;
- feeling that it will be too much trouble and take too much energy to play golf or enjoy other pastimes that used to be fun;
- feeling hopelessly on a treadmill;
- becoming a cross-bearer;
- being endlessly tired and grumpy;
- feeling that there are too many things to do and too little time to do them.

Or you can be in the "I don't wanna" syndrome:

"I don't wanna go to work."

"I can't think of anything that sounds like fun."

"I don't wanna do my chores or see friends."

A vital key is to realize that burnout is not something that happens only once in a lifetime. It can creep into our lives again and again. If we learn to recognize our symptoms, we can catch it before great damage has been done. Then we can regain our balance quickly instead of needing a longer recovery period.

These symptoms all have in common the dimension of being out of balance. In fact, *burnout is the result of living out of balance.* So often, there is a short-term reward for doing so. For example, there is some big project at work or you are starting your own business or you are going back to graduate school while raising a family or holding down a job—all of which can demand a superhuman effort. In the short term you are willing to pay the price. Then one day you find yourself in burnout without the energy to cope. When in this condition, you often don't have the energy to see solutions. You are apt to be closed-minded to help, so you can become your own worst enemy.

A vital key is to realize that burnout is not something that happens only once in a life-time. It can creep into our lives again and again.

The point is that in the short term the solution may seem to be to live out of balance and push for the immediate goal. However, in the long term, the price may be higher than you expected. You may reach your immediate goal only to lose something of greater worth, such as your physical or mental health, a marriage, or significant and unreclaimable time with your children.

Ellen Terry, mother of two children and president and owner of Ellen Terry Realtors, shares her experience:

> *"Real estate is a unique profession where many of your clients will expect you to be on call even more than a doctor—twenty-four hours a day, seven days a week. Thus work can be all-consuming. When I started in real estate, I realized I was becoming a workaholic and that I would burn out soon if I kept up at the pace I was going. It's easy to become addicted to the excitement and high pressure that comes from working at that pace. But once I stepped back from my frenzied schedule for a moment, I saw that I needed to have more time for myself, and that I could have rewarding, fun times away from work. In the past I defined myself only as a business woman and a mother. I spent too much time focusing on being a 'human-doing,' not a 'human-being.' If I wasn't climbing a mountain businesswise, I wasn't a worthwhile person. But now I am trying to live more in the present moment."*

In the next chapters, we will look at three profiles that lead us into burnout—perfectionism, "fast-lane" living, and the super-human syndrome. Each may sound somewhat familiar to you. Each is linked to high performance in some way and is easy to slip into because most corporations reward and encourage these behaviors through highly visible role models. In the short term each can bring high performance, but in the long term each is a burnout trap. You can easily spot the enormous energy drain of the duality attitudes and behaviors in these profiles. See what you can learn about yourself as we examine them.

Summary

1.   Burnout is the result of living out of balance, typically in an all-work/no-play spiral.

2.   Most symptoms of burnout are "lack of" symptoms, such as lack of motivation, enthusiasm, energy, concentration, and fun.

3.   Learning to recognize your personal symptoms of burnout early can help you turn it around before the situation becomes critical.

4.   Burnout can occur over and over again, so learning to catch it early or, better yet, prevent it can save you enormous energy loss.

5.   When burnout is severe, your perspective becomes distorted and you believe you cannot stop for fun and relaxation. Even fun seems like too much work.

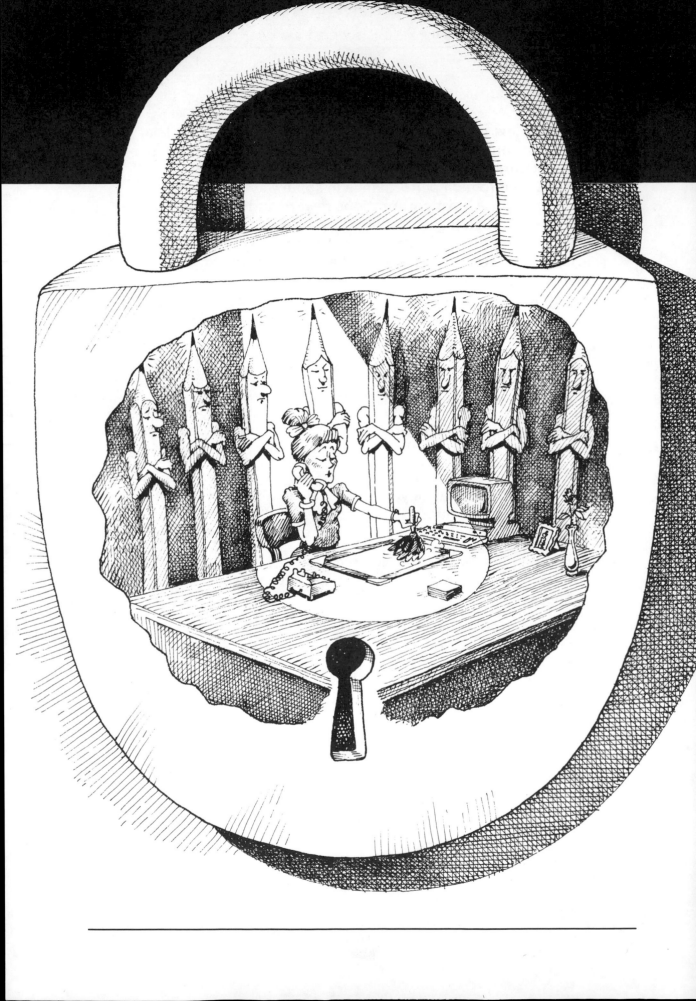

10

THE PERILS OF PERFECTIONISM:

When the Juice Ain't Worth the Squeeze

❝ *[Young people] look at a successful businessman and they don't stop to think about all the mistakes he might have made when he was younger. Mistakes are a part of life; you can't avoid them. All you can hope is that they won't be too expensive and that you don't make the same mistake twice.* **❞**

—Lee Iacocca

❝ *Only the mediocre are at their best all the time.* **❞**

—Gerry Roche,
Chairman, Heidrick & Struggles

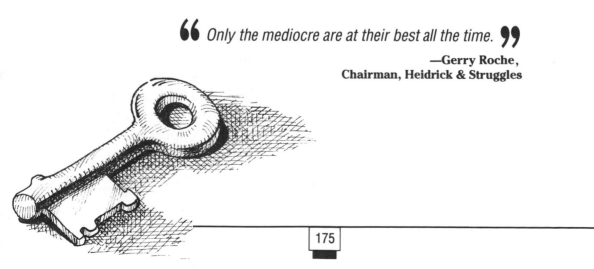

ranted, much satisfaction can be gained by doing a job exceptionally well and by meeting your personal expectations, be it completing a project under budget or giving a flawless speech. But do you devote the same painstaking time and effort to nearly everything you do? And do you perform each task as meticulously as the next? For instance, are your hedges always neatly trimmed, your furniture polished, your inter-office memos formally composed and typed, all pieces of correspondence promptly answered, and so on? In other words, do you place the same expectation of perfection on every project that comes your way?

People who do have taken the dictate "Anything worth doing is worth doing well" far too seriously, for they are unwilling or unable to discriminate between important and unimportant tasks and areas in their lives. Yet many of us believe in this ideal because we had it pounded into our heads by some very influential people, such as our parents, teachers, coaches, or dancing and music instructors. However, this maxim becomes impractical and even unproductive when we grow up and lead extremely busy, complex lives.

ACTION ITEM

▼

Put a check mark next to the statements that describe you.

☐ I expect myself to do well at nearly everything I do.

☐ I get upset with myself whenever I don't do something well, even if I'm a novice at it, such as learning to play a new card game or use a new software program at work.

☐ I suffer through a game of golf or tennis (intended as fun and relief from work) when I'm not playing at my best.

☐ I shy away from trying new things.

☐ I often lose patience with my colleagues or my children if they don't catch on to something quickly.

☐ I rarely think of shortcuts for doing everyday projects, such as home maintenance, chores, meal preparation, correspondence, temporary repairs, and running errands.

☐ I have a reputation at work of being someone who is hard to please.

☐ I usually refuse to start a project unless I have all the optimum equipment or ingredients for it (for example, I refuse to prepare a certain meal because I am out of one of the spices called for in the recipe or I refuse to let my secretary send out a routine letter because one small but not critical piece of information is still missing).

Yet perfectionism is a fairly common personality profile in the business world. The Action Item can help you decide whether this personality profile fits you and, if so, to what extent.

If you answered yes to most of the Action Item questions on the previous page, it is safe to conclude that you have bought into this energy-wasting pattern of behavior. Sometimes it is difficult to recognize these tendencies in ourselves, so you should consider getting your spouse's or friends' judgments about any perfectionist tendencies you might have.

Of course, it is admirable and important to perform well in the significant areas of your life. And most successful people hope to perform exceptionally well—in fact, best—at some of their endeavors. The problem, and energy waste, arises when they can't prioritize the relative value of each task (because all tasks must be done equally meticulously), can't accept a less-than-perfect performance on some tasks (because they can't ever see themselves as doing something with less than their best effort); can't accept imperfection in others (because they can't perceive of value systems other than their own); and are unwilling to attempt something new that they might not excel at (because they can't tolerate the idea of being mediocre at something).

Perfectionism

The *Lure*   is getting to feel perfect, having a reputation of always being right and reliable and exceptional.

The *Payoff*   is getting to feel completely in control, earning people's attention and awe, and feeling that you always meet your highest expectations of yourself.

The *Trap*   is that sooner or later you will find yourself being under a great deal of internal and external pressure to continue doing every single thing perfectly the first time! You will also feel pressured to give everything your utmost effort because you can't risk imperfection. That means you can't risk change, experimentation, and adventure, all of which are key sources of energy. And, finally, perfectionism results in being unable to expand and grow.

Recall a day when you did everything perfectly. Perhaps you gave a tried-and-true speech of yours to a community group, then repeated a reliable sales-pitch formula to a new client, took another potential client out to lunch at your favorite restaurant, and even recommended that she order something that you know the chef does especially well. Later you stayed two hours overtime at the office to triple-check a report of yours, even though both your secretary and public relations director had already proofed it. Mentally recall the specifics of your own perfect day.

Whatever it was like, we can assure you that if you did everything perfectly, you were not growing but were merely standing still, repeating what you had already perfected. On the other hand, on the days when you allow yourself to attempt new skills and to grow, you are bound to make some mistakes. You are also bound to feel unsure and inexperienced at first and to do some things clumsily. But this is a necessary stage to work through if you wish to learn something new and grow as a person.

Unfortunately, many perfection-minded adults rarely risk learning a new sport or game because they become so depen-

> **We can assure you that if you did everything perfectly, you were not growing but were merely standing still, repeating what you had already perfected.**

dent upon the image of themselves as being right and capable that they feel tremendously uncomfortable whenever they return to the role of a rank beginner. Thus they are destined to stay in one place for the rest of their lives, only polishing (perfecting) what they already know. Usually these folks live at less than peak energy. First, they deny themselves the energy-producing experiences of facing totally new situations, processing fresh information, feeling satisfaction at learning a new skill, and even experiencing some apprehension. These experiences, by the way, are key stimulants in the child's world of play. In comparison, repeating routine tasks produces little energy. Second, they expend too much energy worrying about doing everything meticulously, never letting down their perfectionist facade. And by trying to do everything equally perfectly rather than doing some things very well and less important things only satisfactorily, they often squander their time and energy rather than preserving it for their most important responsibilities and goals in their lives. Finally, even when they do participate in activities that should be relaxing and fun, such as playing bridge and tennis with friends and jogging by themselves, they place such high standards on themselves to perform admirably (and keep up that image of being perfect) that these activities become competitive trials filled with pressure. That can take all the fun out of them and turn a potential energy gain into an energy drain. Thus most perfectionists end up expending more energy than they regain. An energy loss cycle such as this will ultimately lead to burnout.

If you fall into this category, here's another way to view your perfectionist expectations. How many people do you know who are truly perfect? And what does it take to be perfect? In fact, perfectionism requires so much time that you may be much less productive and ingenious than those who are less perfect. Perfectionists are forever seeing a tiny flaw to correct. Of course, this consuming attention to every detail, which they feel no one else can handle, takes lots of time. In addition, perfectionists tend to produce less, take fewer chances, stick to procedure rather than create new solutions, and be overprotective about their own territory. And rather than being well-rounded, they tend to be narrow and short-sighted. In contrast, our research into the lives of people considered to be geniuses clearly finds them leading very diverse lives filled with many interests, some they are masters at and some they just find fascinating or enjoyable. But this diversity is one of the primary sources for their discoveries. Their multitude of interests gives them a large basis of knowledge to work from and a constant source of stimulation for new creative links and insights.

If you need another argument against compulsive, perfectionist behavior, consider how much extra time it takes to do everything equally well rather than doing low-priority items just adequately. Take, for example, the task of altering a skirt. A quick tuck in the waistband is a five-minute job, a makeshift alteration that will never show because a jacket always covers the waist. The "proper" way to alter the skirt would be to remove the waistband, shorten it, reset the button or hooks, and then restitch the band in place. This could easily take an hour, but why do it except to be perfect? Only you and the drycleaner's know which you do! (An even faster solution can be achieved with a big safety pin!)

When you catch yourself behaving like a perfectionist, realize that you are experiencing one of the early symptoms of burnout and that there are ways to stop this negative energy spiral. Here are some of our techniques for minimizing this behavior pattern.

Cures for Perfectionism

Cure 1: Harvest the good, or apply the 96% versus 4% assessment rule. When you were a kid in the second grade and you got a 96 on a spelling or math exam, how did you feel? Were you satisfied with the A, or did you browbeat yourself about the four points you missed?

But as an adult, how often do you commute home at the end of a hard day, focusing only on the 4% of your efforts that you didn't do well? Do you often berate yourself for making

a mistake, then fabricate worst-case scenarios for all the horrible consequences that might befall you? And the more you dwell on those few errors, the more magnified they become. By the time you reach home, that 4% feels more like 40%, so you feel frustrated, pressured, and even embarrassed by your "poor performance" or "wasted" day.

You can prevent this negative attitude spiral by guiding your thoughts as you return home each day. Invite yourself to review your day by first congratulating yourself for all the good activities you did. Realize that 90% to 95% of what you did was commendable. While assessing your accomplishments, include the more commonplace or minor things, such as being encouraging to a co-worker who needed your support, controlling your temper during a tense staff meeting, finishing a report faster than you anticipated, giving clear directions to your secretary, eating a healthy meal at lunchtime, and so on. Also, give yourself "points" for the less tangible aspects of your job, such as having good foresight, being creative and innovative, suggesting the most humane way of dealing with a problem, and sticking to your personal ethics. Notice that if you allow yourself some genuine self-appreciation, you will arrive home with more energy and can give yourself permission to play and enjoy the evening. Wait until you are refreshed and more objective (perhaps the next morning) to contemplate what you could have done better that day.

And unless any of these points pose a major problem, limit yourself to a brief evaluation of

- what went wrong,
- what you can learn from your mistake, and
- what you need to do, if anything, to correct it.

Ask, "If I had it to do over, what would I do differently?" or "What can I learn from my mistakes?"

How many people do you know who are truly perfect? And what does it take to be perfect? In fact, perfectionism requires so much time that you may be much less productive and ingenious than those who are less perfect. Perfectionists are forever seeing a tiny flaw to correct.

Two well-known researchers of human behavior and longevity have also reported on the importance of highlighting one's daily successes rather than one's mistakes. Jean Houston and Robert Masters interviewed a large population of highly active men and women in their seventies, eighties, and nineties, such as Pablo Casals, Margaret Mead, Fred Astaire, and Bob Hope. When asked how they had the energy and drive to keep working at their advanced ages, many of them described a phenomenon that Houston and Masters termed "harvesting." For example, a typical response would be: "In my seventies I went through something like a second adolescence. I discovered that I was worrying about all the wrong things. Then I learned how to let go of worry, for it merely saps your energy and enthusiasm. Instead I taught myself how to harvest. At the end of the day I would ask myself what I had learned. And if I had made some mistakes, I asked myself what information I could harvest from them. Thus I put all my energy into learning and none into blaming myself or others, none into feeling badly about myself."

Another practical tip comes from Dave Cole, vice president of HydroCarbon, Fluor Daniel, Inc.:

> *"Let me tell you something that has made a tremendous difference for me. The nature of my job is to spend a great deal of my time solving problems and anticipating problems—it is very easy to get into a less than positive frame of mind when this is your primary daily focus. One simple but extremely effective whole-brained suggestion is, on the way home each evening . . . think only of the good things that happened that day. I've been doing this for a number of months now. It amazes me how many really great things happen during the course of a day. And . . . the benefit is that my wife Donna quite clearly notices the difference when I walk in the door . . . the result is more evening quality time!"*

Cure 2: Put a high value on "failing forward." Failure is a loss only if you fail to learn from the experience. Again, by studying the lives of successful leaders, we have discovered that they commonly see failure not as something to be avoided at all costs but rather as an opportunity to learn and grow.

Thomas Edison, for example, was asked midway in his life how he came to hold more patents than any other person. He answered that he dared to make more mistakes than ten other people put together and had learned from each of them. Then he remarked, "And sooner or later I find a way to patent most of them." Edison knew full well that the creative process involves the technique of turning problems into opportunities and unpolished ideas into gems. So if you are one who dares to venture into problem areas, you will in fact have more opportunities and innovative successes than most others. And people will stand in awe of you, appreciating your pioneering spirit and ingenuity.

Which leads us to another strategy for breaking out of the perfectionist mold: making a list of areas, both job-related and otherwise, that you would like to explore but haven't for fear of not doing well at them. Maybe you have a hunch about an unusual way to solve some problem at work. Maybe you have a daring concept for publicizing a new product your company is developing. Maybe there's a hobby or sport you'd like to take up or a different way to spend your summer vacation this year. You might take time to write down your thoughts. Then we highly recommend taking a chance on these ideas. Though all of them may not pan out to your expectations, surely some will. And the others will bring fresh insights into your life and your work. The main skill to learn from this exercise, however, is how to cope with risk-taking and how to practice stretching into new areas of your life.

Cure 3: Do one thing imperfectly each day.
We are indebted to Dru Scott and her book *How to Put More Time in Your Life* for this marvelous idea. Hard-core perfectionists will find this difficult to do, yet it is an effective first step for breaking out of their mold. We suggest starting off with small things: cooking a new style of food; striking up a conversation with someone whom you don't

know (therefore you can't anticipate their reaction to you); playing a game you are not familiar with; asking your secretary to teach you about an unfamiliar machine or process; reading a book that you think might be "over your head" or contrary to your set beliefs; learning a new hobby or exercise routine. By doing this you will learn to accept your initial feelings of awkwardness and insecurity. You will actually come to enjoy the feelings of challenge and satisfaction that you can derive from trying something new, no matter how unpolished your first attempts are. And you will learn to accept the "imperfect learner" side of you, which we hope will make you feel more willing to attempt worthwhile but uncertain opportunities that come your way.

> **Being willing to do some things imperfectly will save you time and wasted energy. I've applied my "do one thing imperfectly each day" rule to my work routine and discovered some valuable shortcuts.**

On a more practical note, being willing to do some things imperfectly will save you time and wasted energy. I've applied my "do one thing imperfectly each day" rule to my work routine and discovered some valuable shortcuts. For example, the large majority of my mail can be handled quickly by simply writing a note on the bottom of the letter or by dictating an outline of my thoughts that my secretary can later "perfect" into a full response. Then I save my full energy for the 10% of the mail that requires my personal attention.

In addition, I have learned to cut my morning routine in half by wearing my hair in a style that takes much less time, energy, and frustration to "perfect" than my previous style, which required several painstaking steps and numerous touchups during the day. I have simplified my makeup routine as well by using makeup that is easier and quicker to apply and that requires less attention during the day.

I have also learned to have a much less fastidious attitude toward my house. My new policy is to recruit everyone in my family to be his and her own maid. On the whole, each person is responsible for cleaning up his or her dirty dishes, dirty clothes, and clutter. And since no two persons' expectations are identical, this attitude has required my accepting the less-than-perfect standards that my children apply to their own living areas and clothes. While my house is rarely letter-perfect, it is usually presentable and I no longer waste my energy trying to sell other people on my arbitrary ideas about housekeeping.

Jonnie Haug, one of our team partners, explains the enormous gains of climbing out of this energy trap:

"When you are hosting Robert McNamara, Henry Kissinger, and Lord Carington at 44,000 feet, any small error in planning can be embarrassing at the least, especially if you are on a nineteen-hour flight to China as flight attendant for a major international oil company. I learned the hard way how very important it was to rethink and double-check every move and need before we ever took off. Even before that, my parents had stressed such rules as 'Anything worth doing is worth doing well' and 'If you don't have time to do it right the first time, you surely don't have time to redo it!' As a result, I became extremely good at details, prided myself in excellence, and was often referred to by others as a perfectionist. I didn't realize then what a trap this would become. The more I played the role as 'the perfectionist,' the more others would rely on me to remember and tend to details for them. And the more they delegated to me, the less time I had to hang loose and relax. I began to work faster, stay later, get up earlier, and concentrate more intently. Then, in addition to being referred to as a perfectionist and taking myself too seriously, I was seen more and more as 'a hard driver.' More than once I would sizzle silently as the very people who depended on me to be perfect . . . would talk about how hard I worked. I would have loved to have played more if I just hadn't had to carry such a tremendous responsibility. Little did I know then how much this trap was of my own making.

In order to have the energy to deal with the many details of hosting international travel, I would play on days off in foreign countries. I would shop, tour the beautiful cities, and make sure

> **If you wish to be a leader rather than a follower, you must have the courage to be seen as less than perfect. Followers safely learn from the mistakes of the leaders, then smugly hold on to their image of being perfect. But rarely, if ever, do followers know the thrill of blazing trails and discovering new vistas.**

I tasted the food from the finest restaurants available. The adrenaline was flowing! When it was time to get back on the plane for the long trip home, I felt wonderful. I'd had a marvelous time and was ready to attend to details. Unfortunately, fatigue set in before we landed back in the United States because I had exhausted myself on my days off.

I learned the hard way to select one fun thing to do each day that was really important to me—one tourist attraction or one shopping spree. I could always enjoy dinner at a restaurant that was on my 'must visit' list. I learned lunch didn't have to be as important. I learned to save something for the next time. This left me rested but with the feeling I had really enjoyed my stay, seeing one or two important things. I had planned my joy! Looking back, I now see the importance of letting others be responsible for their own details and saving my best effort for the most demanding tasks."

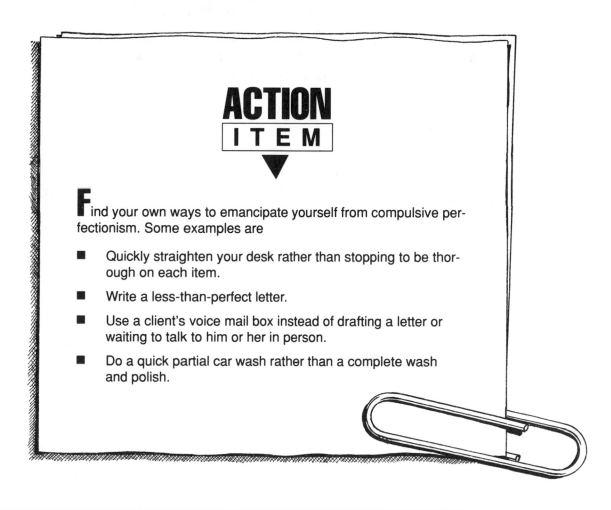

ACTION ITEM

Find your own ways to emancipate yourself from compulsive perfectionism. Some examples are

- Quickly straighten your desk rather than stopping to be thorough on each item.

- Write a less-than-perfect letter.

- Use a client's voice mail box instead of drafting a letter or waiting to talk to him or her in person.

- Do a quick partial car wash rather than a complete wash and polish.

As you decide to let go of your compulsive need to be seen as a perfectionist, you will gain much more energy, time, and enthusiasm. You will also have the energy and desire to strike out in new directions, to discover some untapped talents, and to find new solutions to old problems.

Summary

1. Perfectionists feel the compulsive need to make everything they do look perfect, regardless of how significant or ordinary the task.

2. Perfectionism wastes time and energy on trivia, and it limits a person's willingness to try something new.

3. Balancing perfectionism involves the wisdom to know when a quick but imperfect effort may serve the purpose better.

4. Three techniques for breaking out of perfectionism are "failing forward," doing one imperfect thing each day, and practicing the "96% versus 4% assessment rule."

11

LIFE IN THE EXPRESS LANE:

The Addictive Roar of the Crowd

> 66 *A young bull and an old bull were walking through a pasture one day. As they crested a hill, they saw a herd of cows in the meadow below them. 'Wow!' said the young bull. 'Look at all those cows. Let's run down there and service one of them.' 'Let's walk down there,' said the old bull, 'and service all of them.'* 99
>
> **—Author unknown**

We hear a lot these days about being on the corporate "fast track." Many companies have special programs that identify and train their potential superstars. There are also programs for learning a language in six weeks, a musical instrument in six months, and an advanced degree in a year. Yes, our society worships the concept of speed, often for its own sake. Many of the Olympic competitions are centered on breaking a speed record. Being the youngest person ever to accomplish something is another much-applauded feat. And the *Guinness Book of World Records* is filled with people who went the farthest distance at the fastest speed.

Characteristics of "Fast-Lane" Behavior

With such widespread emphasis on speed, is it any wonder that so many of us live life in the fast lane? For devotees of this lifestyle, every hour is scheduled, from "power breakfasts" to negotiations over the lunch table to client-wooing dinners to late-night work sessions to work-filled weekends. This group also tends to trade in their vacation time for industry conventions and conferences. In fact, fast-lane competitors go about their entire day in high gear, making quick decisions, abrupt changes, and fast moves, always in an effort to reach their destination as quickly and efficiently as possible. In many ways this personality type is the opposite of the infinitely more controlled and careful perfectionists. Although most fast-lane types wish to perform well and make sound judgments, they tend to focus on their broad accomplishments rather than each step they take along the way. And they are willing to take risks and make mistakes in order to beat the other guy to the prize.

Does this description bring certain work partners and friends to mind? Perhaps it describes you as well. Take a moment to recall people you know who are caught in the fast lane. Can you guess what motivates them to live at such an exhilarating yet stressful and exhausting pace?

Fast-Lane Behavior

The *Lure*   is to be out in front and to beat everyone else to the prize.

The *Payoff*   is high visibility, productivity, excitement, admiration, and frequent promotions.

The *Trap*   is that the fast lane is the road to physical and psychological overload.

Let's look at an interesting analogy to help us examine this personality type. Consider the Indianapolis 500, the major race car competition in the United States. Some of the most expensive cars in the world compete, most costing in the range of $600,000. Yet sometimes fewer than half of them are able to finish the race. That's a mere 500 miles, a distance most cars in good repair could handle with no problem. Would you be willing to pay $600,000 for a vehicle that only had a fifty-fifty chance of traveling 500 miles before breaking down?

So why are the performance records of these race cars so horrible? As compared with ordinary cars, these are built to run exclusively at top speeds. And for the vast majority of the 500-mile race they run at only one speed—full throttle. All the other gears are used momentarily. It is rarely the super powerful engine that breaks down, but instead a minor part, such as a ten-dollar water hose or gasket.

If you too have many "fast-track" behaviors, you will have lots of company among the other readers of this book. In fact, we, the authors, occasionally succumb to this behavior pattern as well. For example, we catch ourselves eating lunch as though we're vying for a prize based on how fast we can make the food disappear! We also find ourselves talking too rapidly, giving quick and insufficient directions. Or standing at a desk making decisions and working on the phone, poised for the next leap. Sometimes we second-guess and interrupt other team members, too impatient to wait for them to finish a sentence.

Before we know it, we are so used to doing things at this accelerated pace that high gear is the only speed we feel comfortable in. And like the Indy cars, after a few months of operating at this speed, we experience small "mechanical failures." We begin to get headaches or sore throats, make careless errors, and have interrupted sleep. We also find ourselves stalled along the roadside by relatively insignificant obstacles, such as simple problems that we're too tired to solve. Or we create people problems that take more time and patience than we feel we have. Furthermore, we overlook resources, such as other team members

Apply the race car analogy to yourself. What percentage of your day do you run in your highest gear? How often do you

- ☐ charge through breakfast and your morning routine?
- ☐ race to work, cursing every red light?
- ☐ gobble down lunch at your desk?
- ☐ hurry from assignment to assignment, overbooking yourself in an attempt to force swifter performances from yourself and your staff?
- ☐ miss office birthday celebrations and other small social functions to avoid getting behind?
- ☐ use caffeine and other stimulants to keep you alert and alcohol and sleeping pills to help you unwind?
- ☐ monitor the speed with which others accomplish their assignments and always try to finish before them?
- ☐ frequently ask your printers, programmers, and secretarial help to finish your project faster than they normally work?
- ☐ drive more than five miles over the speed limit?
- ☐ jump at every opportunity to come your way, no matter how overextended you feel?

These are typical behavior traits of fast-laners. If you said yes to more than half of these questions and if you approach most aspects of your life with a "fast is best" mentality, then you have fallen victim to this energy-draining profile.

who could assist us, because we're too busy to delegate or too rushed to realize they are ready, willing, and able to help.

Breakdown, or energy overload, is the hidden danger for everyone who persists in living every waking hour at full throttle. Using the Indy 500 analogy again, remember that everyone needs to schedule regular pit stops—to refuel, to have a minor tune-up, and to repair worn-out parts. Yet fast-lane types are the least likely to slow down when their bodies and minds tell them to because they think that they can't spare the time. They are so consumed with getting ahead that they stop listening to their body's messages; even when their body is screaming for rest or proper nutrition or for some light-hearted fun, they keep pushing on. They frequently experience a major health crisis as a result of heroically tuning out the body's messages.

What keeps fast-lane folks initially revved up is their keen sense of competition, the pressure to stay ahead, and the excitement and intensity generated by their supercharged life-styles. But this kind of nervous energy will eventually wane as physical exhaustion and health problems take their toll. Unfortunately, divorces, poor relationships with children, career burnout, and faulty judgment come from too frenetic a pace that excludes everything and everybody that cannot keep up with the race. In each case, these situations could have been avoided had these people taken the time to slow down, to reassess their long-range values, and to restore their energy resources.

Before discussing some ways to switch out of high gear, we want to point out some key differences between this behavior and the high-energy patterns of children. For at first glance, a child seems to be constantly in motion like our fast-lane adults. However, if you observe children more closely, you will find that they always prefer (perhaps "insist" would be a better word) to do things at their own pace, which will vary from activity to activity. Just try to hurry children through meal time or their morning routine and see how difficult it is for them to speed up and how their nature intuitively tells them to behave. In addition, children frequently switch from intense physical activity to more restful play. And young children are also much less competitive than adults. They don't usually push themselves to hurry through activities, either. In fact, they usually don't feel a compulsion to finish everything they begin.

But for adults, fast-lane living can be addictive as well as consuming. If you fall into this profile, the remedy is not to curb your ambitions. Rather, it is to learn to balance a little patience, plus the art of switching gears, in order to refuel your energy resources.

The Cure for "Fast-Lane" Behavior

The cure is *to use all your gears and to pace yourself throughout the day and week.* By knowing how to balance your high and low gears, you can restore your energy rather than deplete it each day. This skill requires an understanding of what activities genuinely call for high-gear efforts and which activities can be done in neutral or while idling. It also requires a sensible scheduling of projects throughout the day and week which allows for changes of pace.

Imagine, for example, that you are planning a scenic 3,000-mile, cross-country trip with your spouse. Also presume you have planned a two-week vacation and hence do not need to rush to your main vacation site that is 1,500 miles away. Given these circumstances, would you choose to travel like an Indy 500 driver, as fast and aggressively as possible, driving for twenty-five hours straight, stopping only momentarily for gasoline, food, and bathroom breaks? You would reach your destination as quickly as possible, but you would probably need a full two days of rest

to recuperate from the strain of your effort. Even taking two days to arrive, driving twelve hours a day, checking into a motel for eight hours, then hitting the road for a second long day's drive could leave you quite exhausted.

On the other hand, would you consider spreading your driving time out to three or four days in order to drive at a relaxing pace and to enjoy many of the picturesque sights along your route? For example, you might balance one long day of driving with a following day that doesn't begin at the crack of dawn and that includes several hours of sightseeing. Or if you were driving across the desert regions of the Southwest, you might prefer to leave early in the morning, then rest indoors during the most intense hours of the heat before beginning another four-hour stretch of driving in the evening. Or you might find out which stretches of highway would be the most taxing, such as a 100- mile stretch of steep grades and winding roads through the Rocky Mountains. Then you could plan times to rest before and after driving those taxing stretches of your drive.

> **By knowing how to balance your high and low gears, you can restore your energy rather than deplete it each day.**

In addition, you might decide to balance your driving sessions with frequent stops to visit historical sites, regional antique shops, and beautiful parks along your route. You might take an hour out for lunch to sample the local cooking. And you might decide to stop traveling by late afternoon one day in order to tour one of the more picturesque towns that you plan to pass through. By making your trip enjoyable and comfortable, not only would you arrive at your final destination with plenty of energy to spare, but you would also value the time spent getting there.

You can extend this analogy to your work week. Do you spend every day locked in your highest gear, racing from project to project? Or do you attempt to balance the most demanding tasks with less demanding ones throughout the day? In addition, are you aware of your natural biorhythms and the times during the day when you are most alert versus most fatigued? Do you plan your work day according to those normal highs and lows? Like the vacationers plotting out their 1,500-mile trip, you too can plan your work week so that you are not filled with stress and fatigue at the end of each day and work week.

Before your week begins, for example, you could consider the "route" your work will take you and the difficulty of each leg of your trip. Then with those factors in mind, you could create a work and break schedule that allows for lots of challenge and productivity but that isn't thoroughly grueling. In addition, you could go a step further by scheduling your most difficult and stressful tasks during your most energetic times of the day, then following them with easier, more relaxing tasks. You could also follow a very stressful day with an easier one, and grant yourself a relaxing night at home after a previous night burning the midnight oil. By creating a balance between high-energy exertion (loss) with times of energy restoration (gain), you can minimize your energy drains and can maintain high energy levels overall.

We'd like you to begin to recognize which projects at work demand the most of your energy. Start noticing which leave you feeling the most pressured and fatigued and which make you feel the most enthusiastic and stimulated. Also notice which tasks are the most relaxing.

By realizing which tasks drain and build energy, you won't have to wait for the weekends to try to recharge your energy. You will be better able to fine-tune your performance each day and avoid huge energy drains. You will begin to feel the benefit of switching gears throughout the day and will learn how to save your top gears for the times when you need to accelerate the most. All these tactics will help you avoid the fate of the Indy 500 race cars, with their 50% chance of breakdown before they reach their final destination or, worse yet, a crash or total wipeout.

Think not only of using three speeds but also reverse and neutral. In a meeting or sales call or when delegating work to a team member, if you begin with a relaxed, friendly few minutes just to enjoy

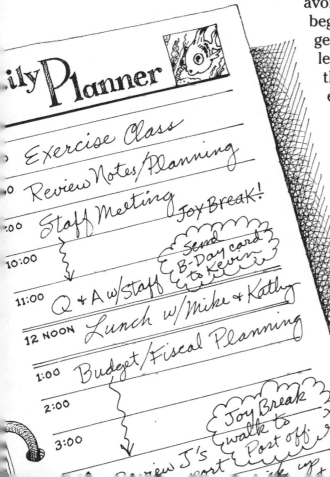

that person, much more can be accomplished when you get rolling with the work. Think of using neutral when you seem to be going nowhere on a project. Shift into neutral and just coast for a few minutes. Give yourself a joy break or a brief rest to refresh your mind. Think of using reverse when you realize you are off on the wrong foot or direction. Saying "I'm sorry" or "I was sure wrong about this. What other options might work better?" can indicate a healthy attitude for a balanced team player.

Summary

1. People caught in the fast lane spend their entire day in high gear, filling every minute with meetings, work, and socializing. They tend to be highly competitive and goal-oriented, and rarely slow down and spend time alone.

2. The cure for fast-lane living is learning to use all your gears and pace yourself throughout the day. Frequently using neutral, reverse, and low gear can bring you far greater energy, productivity, and innovative behavior over the long term. Discovering how to truly relax is another antidote.

12

THE SUPERHUMAN SYNDROME:

Retiring Your Cape

❝ *About the time we think we can make ends meet, someone moves the ends.*

—**Herbert Hoover**

❝ *Good judgment comes from experience which comes from bad judgment.* ❞

—**Source unknown**

❝ *Much has been given us, and much will rightfully be expected from us. We have duties to others and duties to ourselves; and we can shirk neither.* ❞

—**Theodore Roosevelt**

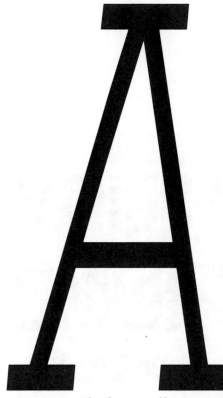third profile that leads to exhaustion is the superhuman syndrome. It has received a good deal of attention by the media, particularly as it relates to women geared toward careers, but it is equally applicable to men. As one who played superwoman for many years before suffering a serious case of burnout, let me describe some common patterns for this personality type.

Characteristics of the Superhuman Syndrome

The most basic underlying compulsion for superhumans is to be all things to all people. A typical male superhuman will strive to achieve maximum success at his job while maintaining a high profile in his community. He might also attempt to have quality time with his spouse and children each day. We might find him serving as an officer in the Chamber of Commerce, leading his son's boy scout troop, volunteering to work for every United Way fund-raising campaign, supervising a monthly neighborhood cleanup, and scheduling a major home fix-up project every summer, doing the work himself. He may also feel somewhat responsible for the well-being of his friends and staff. Thus he frequently invites his divorced brother over to dinner, his widowed secretary out to lunch, and his neighbor's "problem child" over to the house for motivational talks. He

The most basic underlying compulsion for superhumans is to be all things to all people.

rarely has a relaxing lunch by himself or a jog alone around the park because he reasons that he can use that time to meet a potential client or teach his son another football maneuver.

Similarly, the superwoman usually holds a full-time job while going to night school three evenings a week to advance her career opportunities. Of course she still expects her house to look as spic and span as during the five years she stayed at home to raise the children, so she spends at least ten hours each week cleaning house. She continues to teach the Sunday school class she has led for eight years; she still manages to make homemade Christmas presents and goodies for most of her relatives; she still serves on the executive committees of Planned Parenthood and a local art museum. She also takes an active part in her children's school activities, plants an extensive flower garden each spring, plays Sunday-night bridge with her husband and friends, and relishes her role as an always-available friend to a growing number of women. Her daily shower is about the only time she has just to herself because every other spare minute is spent ministering to her children's, husband's, relatives', employees', and friends' many needs.

Superhumans are extremely outer-directed, sensitive, and responsive to the needs and requests of others but have long since lost touch with their own inner needs and messages. Instead of prioritizing their concerns and interests and limiting their involvements, they rarely say no to any request made of them—which means they rarely have a moment to spare on their individual needs and interests. Everyone admires their zeal and often asks them where they get the energy to do so many things.

On the outside, Schweitzer, Mead, and Edison appear to exhibit the superhuman syndrome as well. They involved themselves in a number of diverse activities and led very busy lives. But they learned how to *balance* their energy by scheduling time each day to rest and enjoy time alone, absorbed in an activity of their own choosing rather than constantly pouring their energy out to one recipient after another. This outlet provided them with a vital source of private, personal satisfaction and creativity, both of which are sources of mental and emotional energy. Moreover, they knew how to balance a set number of tasks and activities rather than spreading themselves too thin by constantly piling one new endeavor on top of another. But superhumans get *out of balance,* doing everything possible for others while leaving almost no time to tend to their personal needs.

Finally, Schweitzer, Mead, and Edison had a gift of inspiring and encouraging others to be a vital part of their team. They served as mentors and coaches to an energetic team of young proteges. Each benefited from the energy and accomplishments of a committed and inspired team.

The Superhuman Syndrome

The *Lure*   is be everyone's hero!

The *Payoff*   is to feel needed, vital, well liked, and admired.

The *Trap*   is having all your energy lapped up by an endless procession of causes and people, which will ultimately result in, you guessed it, *burnout.*

It might help to examine the reasons underlying the superhuman syndrome. I confess that I foolishly struggled "heroically" to play this role for many years. I'm sure my first mentor was the comic-book hero for whom this syndrome is named. Try to remember the type of life-style Superman led. His entire existence revolved around rescuing people and doing good deeds. He never seemed to have a hobby or enjoy a summer nap in a hammock. Did he ever stroll hand in hand with his sweetie enjoying the fun of courtship? He couldn't afford the time to get married either, to take a vacation, or to have Thanksgiving dinner with his adoptive parents. Nor was he ever seen with a gravy stain on the front of his suit or baggy knees in his blue tights. Even with all his breath-taking heroics, he never seemed to have those awful rings of perspiration you know where. He seemed to exist only to perform heroic deeds and rescue others.

Another indicator of the superhuman syndrome is the number of roles you perform, especially if your goal is to give a hero-

sized effort to each. For example, the two and one-half years I commuted to Columbia University while teaching full time and raising my son in Dallas was one of the most "heroic"—and hectic and exhausting—times of my life. My list of roles included

■ much-admired single mother who was actively involved in my son's life;

■ full-time associate professor who was always available to my university students (I carried a double teaching load of graduate students and directed a major research project involving 5,500 children, teachers, and parents);

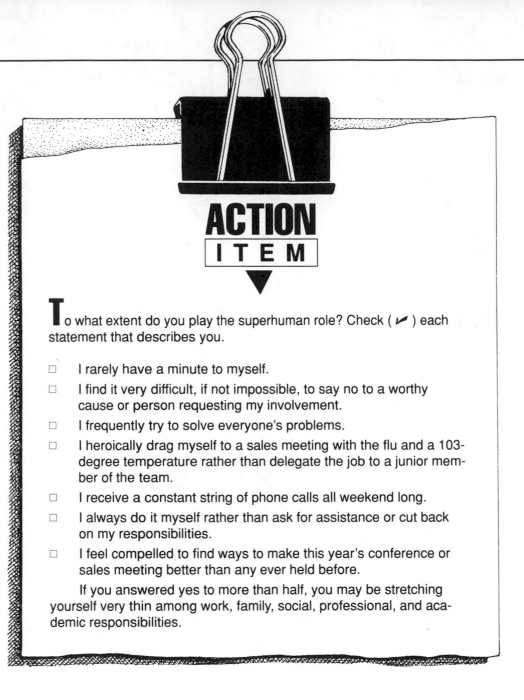

ACTION
I T E M
▼

To what extent do you play the superhuman role? Check (✔) each statement that describes you.

- ☐   I rarely have a minute to myself.
- ☐   I find it very difficult, if not impossible, to say no to a worthy cause or person requesting my involvement.
- ☐   I frequently try to solve everyone's problems.
- ☐   I heroically drag myself to a sales meeting with the flu and a 103-degree temperature rather than delegate the job to a junior member of the team.
- ☐   I receive a constant string of phone calls all weekend long.
- ☐   I always do it myself rather than ask for assistance or cut back on my responsibilities.
- ☐   I feel compelled to find ways to make this year's conference or sales meeting better than any ever held before.

If you answered yes to more than half, you may be stretching yourself very thin among work, family, social, professional, and academic responsibilities.

- ■ doctoral student aiming to make excellent grades and to complete my program in record time;

- ■ community worker involved in women's groups, religious education, the Children's Medical Center Psychiatric Program, the Texas Scottish Rite's research on dyslexic children, and eleven other community research projects;

- ■ gardener with a thriving flower garden;

- ■ single homemaker who frequently hosted get-togethers for friends and graduate students;

- problem solver to an average of eight to ten needy students;

- attentive daughter to my parents; and

- recipient of an award as an outstanding professor at Southern Methodist University the same year I completed my doctorate with high honors.

"How can you manage to do it all so well?" was the comment I often got from my neighbors, friends, and work associates. Since I was held in such high esteem, I totally believed in the superhuman role I was playing. At the time, I wouldn't dare let anyone down by (shudder!) passing up a challenge or simply referring someone's request for help to another resource. Like Superman, I was so used to giving to others that I rarely gave myself permission to receive from others without wanting to outdo their favor in return! For instance, if a neighbor brought me a covered dish when I was sick, I felt compelled to return the dish with a fresh-baked casserole in it. A gracious "thank-you" was insufficient for the likes of me. Translating this situation to the work force, superhumans might attempt to cut their operation budget by 4% even though they have been asked to cut it only 2%, or they might write a fifty-page report when a ten-page report with supporting visuals or case studies would have sufficed.

Those of us with the superhuman syndrome think we are invincible. We also may think our primary motivation is to share our warmth, spirit, and talents with everyone who appears to need it. But *underneath that powerful exterior is an insecure person begging to be needed.* We don't feel valuable unless we are helping someone.

With the exceedingly full and diversified lives that most of us lead, the large number of roles we try to fill is not highly unusual. People who are adept at establishing a healthy give-and-take between these roles and their personal energy needs can manage to maintain most of them. But I, like other superhuman hopefuls, tried to perform each role to the best of my ability, which led to my ultimate undoing. If I had been energy conscious, I would have cut back on the number of social and household duties I fulfilled during my very demanding two and one-half years of commuting to Columbia. I could have decided to clean house only every other week. I could have taught my son how to make ten-minute dinners and relied on the most nutritious of the frozen dinners available for half our meals. And I could have let the flower garden go one year, or cut back to planting only a tiny garden. I could have delayed the home renovation projects. I could have shifted my entertaining to be more casual—a covered dish rather than me preparing a five-course meal for twelve people, for example. And I could have encouraged my long list of people coming to me for lengthy listening and support sessions to seek qualified counseling, freeing me to enjoy time with friends instead of always performing a service. Or I could have invited a friend to combine our socializing with our weekly shopping or cleaning duties.

Kay Russell, one of our team members, formed a creative group with three friends when they all were homemakers with small children. To make their hectic lives more fun, they planned frequent lunches and all pitched in for an hour and cleaned house or accomplished a similar "un-fun" chore for the hostess before lunch (a shared covered-dish affair). Meanwhile their eight children enjoyed playing, with one mom supervising. They also traded out child care for each other, using playful "coupons" for number of children, hours kept, and so forth. The toddlers are now in college, and all four families still thrive on eighteen-plus years of creative friendship.

Instead of choosing any of these possible alternatives, super-humans often try to maintain their normal roles and commitments while expanding their schedule into eighty and ninety hours per week of work and traveling combined with their already busy schedule. By sleeping less, relaxing less, eating on the run, and skipping meals, they push and push themselves. They become mentally, emotionally and physically exhausted. They also tend to look for new causes to pursue rather than taking care of their own personal needs and areas of growth.

Surprisingly, a person with low self-esteem often lies behind this profile. The superhuman typically does not call on others for help because of the need to be needed. Perhaps this life-style leads to the most out-of-balance scenario of them all. As superhumans pile more and more activities and rescue missions onto their agenda, they have less time to do each activity well. They end up rushing through everything so hurriedly that they actually get less pleasure from each task they accomplish and each person they spend time with. And ironically, the more they do, the more they feel pressured to do.

Once you have established this pattern of behavior and these dependencies in your life, it is very difficult to change (and to disappoint all those people counting on you, you might be thinking). But in the long run, you will be doing everyone a favor.

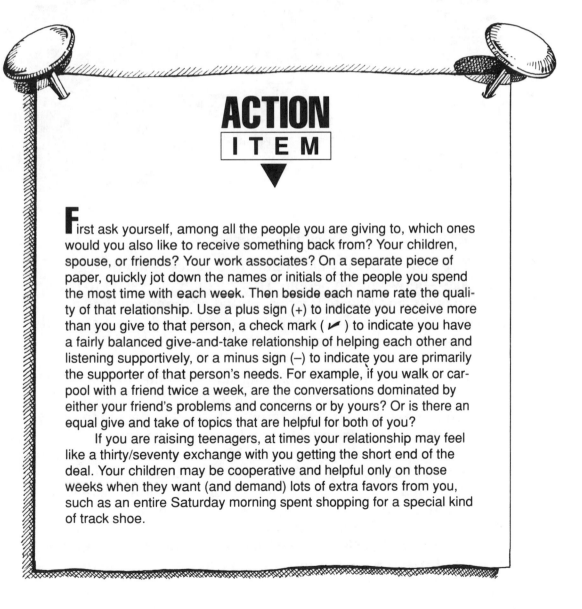

ACTION ITEM

First ask yourself, among all the people you are giving to, which ones would you also like to receive something back from? Your children, spouse, or friends? Your work associates? On a separate piece of paper, quickly jot down the names or initials of the people you spend the most time with each week. Then beside each name rate the quality of that relationship. Use a plus sign (+) to indicate you receive more than you give to that person, a check mark (✔) to indicate you have a fairly balanced give-and-take relationship of helping each other and listening supportively, or a minus sign (–) to indicate you are primarily the supporter of that person's needs. For example, if you walk or carpool with a friend twice a week, are the conversations dominated by either your friend's problems and concerns or by yours? Or is there an equal give and take of topics that are helpful for both of you?

If you are raising teenagers, at times your relationship may feel like a thirty/seventy exchange with you getting the short end of the deal. Your children may be cooperative and helpful only on those weeks when they want (and demand) lots of extra favors from you, such as an entire Saturday morning spent shopping for a special kind of track shoe.

The Cure for the Superhuman Syndrome

The cure is *reciprocity*, which refers to balance—an equal give and take—between two people. That's a difficult lesson to learn, knowing why and how to invite a mutual exchange of time and services from others and promoting interdependence instead of dependence. It involves taking off the hero's cape and becoming a balanced person again.

When my mentor, Jerry Spalding, a management consultant in Dallas, first asked me to do the kind of objective assessment found in the Action Item, I felt rather offended at having to rate the qualities of each friendship as if I were comparing the rates and policies of a lending institution! After all, I wasn't being kind and helpful to all these people with the expectation of their re-paying me in a like manner. Yet Jerry taught me how to create a much more mature and fulfilling type of relationship with others. He showed me that when I was not requesting an equal amount of assistance and strength back from others, I was allowing them to neglect their own inner resources. I was also denying them the satisfaction of giving something of equal value back to me. This is called "learned dependence," and I was teaching this quality left and right without realizing it.

I now realize how damaging it can be to encourage others to become dependent on me rather than to develop their own sense of confidence and self-reliance. What I had created with many people was a guardianship relationship, with me as the center of power and wisdom. It led them to rely on someone else to "leap tall buildings" rather than to learn how to scale their own obstacles, no matter how long it took. In contrast, Jerry taught me to develop win/win relationships. I became their coach rather than their guardian angel by encouraging them to begin solving their own problems. Ultimately, this type of "empowering," or "enabling," relationship results in many mini-heros learning to be team players rather than one superhero flying above all the rest. Jerry also taught me the importance of developing a few friendships with people to whom I could look for help and support. He became one of those significant friends and mentors.

Here is how I taught reciprocity to my graduate students. While an associate professor at Southern Methodist University, I often stayed two hours late listening to my students' personal as well as academic problems. The same students tended to come back week after week for more advice and insight. Even when I had stacks of papers to grade and materials to read, I felt obligated to listen and help. Then Jerry advised me to make a reciprocity list for my office door. Entitled "Tasks Ann Would Be Grateful for Help On," it was a collection of responsibilities I needed to do that someone else could accomplish. My list included picking up my son from school or taking him to the library to do homework; taking the dog to the vet; getting stamps at the post office; returning or checking out books from the library; picking up clothes at the cleaners; and taking film to be developed.

It's easy to say NO when you have a burning YES within you.

Then whenever a grateful student would chime in, "Your listening has helped me so much. How can I ever repay you?" I would mention the list outside and sincerely thank them for the offer. Perhaps you are wondering if any of them felt insulted by the list or by my other suggestions for repaying one good deed with another. In the case of my students, only one of them took offence during the three years I used this tactic. And as I reflect on it, the one who got in the huff was the most abusive of my time; she easily found another willing ear to listen and shoulder to lean on.

Another true example of reciprocity in the work force comes from one of our Energy Engineering seminars. An executive secretary explained that her desk was located close to the copier machine. Employees expected her to help them with every problem that arose with the equipment, which on some days left little time for her own work. She admitted that she enjoyed feeling needed and being praised as "the only one who could work miracles with the copier." But this role became too time-consuming. And since she had allowed everyone to become dependent upon her, she knew it was her responsibility to teach others to share the burden with her.

Her solution was to make a chart of all the types of problems she was called upon to correct. As each problem arose, she invited the person she was helping to learn the procedure, then to sign his or her name next to the problem that he or she now knew how to correct. And the next time that same problem arose, the woman told the person needing help to turn to any name listed beside that problem. Her biggest challenge was to resist the plea for immediate help but rather to politely yet firmly refer to the list. Within a few weeks she had trained a large staff to be both self-reliant and team-motivated when it came to dealing with the copier. And she stopped letting others constantly sap her flow of energy and concentration. She had taught the valuable lesson of *reciprocity.*

In other chapters we will share many more examples of creating reciprocal, energy-sharing relationships with co-workers, friends, and family members. But for now, look at your list of relationships in the Action Item. Put a star by those that are sapping more energy than they are giving back. Then rest assured that within one to three months of patient but firm coaching, you will be able to teach these people how to have energy-sharing relationships with you rather than energy-draining ones. When doing this, consider author Wayne Dyer's statement: "People treat us the way we teach them to treat us."

Now that I am learning to limit my roles and balance my commitment to each activity, I am delighted to find that my accomplishments and friendships are more special than they were before. And I realize that I don't have the uncontrollable urge or even the burning desire to involve myself with everything that crosses my path. But by wisely managing my energy resources, I do have the time and motivation to participate in many select areas of life. And now that I have stopped teaching "learned helplessness" in favor of self-reliance, my relationships are much more rewarding and energizing.

**"People treat us the way we
teach them to treat us."**
—Wayne Dyer

Summary

1. Superhuman personalities overload themselves with a staggering number of tasks and roles to perform. They want to be all things to all people, finding it hard to refuse any requests for help.

2. As superhumans pile up more and more activities in their lives, they have less time to do things to their satisfaction and have almost no time for themselves.

3. Surprisingly, low self-esteem underlies this overwhelming need to be needed.

4. Typically there are several impossible, superhuman roles going on simultaneously, not just one (super parent, super engineer, super community leader, super friend, etc.).

5. The cure for the superhuman syndrome is reciprocity. Invite some balance back into your life by allowing others to take care of themselves and to contribute to your life, enhancing their value and your resources.

THE CURE FOR BURNOUT:

Learning to Refuel Your Tank

66 *The greatest despair is to not become the person you were meant to be.* 99

—**Kierkegaard**

66 *You don't grow old. You get old by not growing.* 99

—**E. Stanley Jones**

66 *Making a living is necessary and often satisfying; eventually, making a difference becomes more important.* 99

—**David Campbell, author and vice president, Center for Creative Leadership, Greensboro, N.C.**

ortunately, it usually takes a lot longer to get yourself into burnout than it takes to get yourself back into balance. The key is to know your own symptoms. And the earlier you recognize the symptoms, the less time you will spend in a drained, burned-out position.

In our research, which has come not only from personal testing but also by tracking many programs and research models focusing on burnout, there seem to be at least twelve key lifestyle factors affecting energy. There may be other factors that affect you. Be open to your own sense of what is best for you.

Descriptions of twelve energy factors and their significance follow. At the end of the chapter is a self-test for rating yourself on each of these factors. After you have rated yourself, pick the one factor that is most important for improving your energy and gently increase the amount of attention you give to this factor. For each of the following ask yourself, "What percentage of the time do I get an adequate amount of this?"

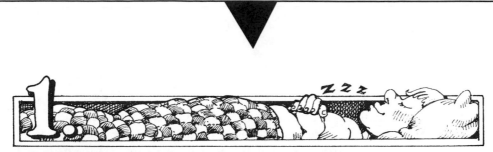

Proper Rest

We encourage you to base your assessment of this feature on a subjective response of what you feel you need. Some people seem to need much more sleep than others. It can have to do with how soundly you sleep, how hard you are working, and what other ways you find to rest between sleep periods. Some people need eight to ten hours while others seem to do fine on four or five hours of sleep. Without worrying about whether the amount you sleep is "right," what percentage of the time do you feel adequately rested?

Good Nutrition

We know generally that too much salt, sugar, fat, cholesterol, and caffeine will lower performance levels. They interfere with the chemistry of your brain and impede optimum performance, and they can plug up your cardiovascular system, causing your heart to pump harder, your body to get less oxygen, and toxins in your blood to be less effectively filtered out.

We also know now that salt, sugar, fat, and caffeine are addictive. The more you eat, the more you want. And the more salt you add to your food, the less you taste it, so the more salt you want. These are called soft addictions but work much the same as the hard addictions of nicotine, alcohol, and narcotics. They have the most control in your life when you are out of balance. So getting your life back into balance can be an important first step toward getting these soft addictions eliminated from your eating habits.

Caffeine stimulates the central nervous system and can produce a variety of effects elsewhere in the body. Depending upon how much you consume, it can increase your heartbeat, speed up your metabolism, and promote secretion of stomach acid. Psychologically, the effect of caffeine has been described as a "lift." However, you won't feel more pep when you drink your coffee, but instead will feel worse without it. There is a substantial body of solid scientific evidence supporting the view that moderate amounts of caffeine (about 500 mg per day) are not a threat to the health of the average adult. According to the March 1988 issue of *Consumer Research*, six ounces of coffee contain 180 milligrams of caffeine, six ounces of tea contain 70 milligrams, and twelve ounces of cola soft drink contain 45 milligrams of caffeine. So to get the benefit from your daily cup of coffee, you need to keep your daily limit to two cups or less.

Other studies indicate that coffee and tea, even if decaffeinated, act as a diuretic. As such, they flush out significant chemicals from your system which are necessary for your brain to function most effectively. So drinking lots of water daily (which increases significant chemicals to the brain) can be as positive for your energy and productive thinking as a heavy coffee habit can be draining and debilitating.

Keeping this in mind, what percentage of the time do you enjoy eating for energy or good nutrition? (You may notice that we purposely avoid the term "diet" because to us it has a negative connotation of being deprived or eating other than what you might prefer. We think it is essential that you link positive words to your food and drink choices. So you pick the terms—eating for energy, eating clean, eating for high performance—whatever motivates you to make healthy choices for yourself.)

Think of the changes in your eating habits as permanent rather than as a temporary diet. When you decide to gently improve your eating habits for life, that is when you begin to make real progress. At age forty-four, after going back and forth from a size 14 dress to a size 10, gaining and losing the same twenty pounds over and over for about twenty years, I got down to a size 6 dress and have stayed there for the past seven years. The secret is to have many other ways to have fun rather than eating junk food. Walk or enjoy some form of aerobic exercise daily. (This changes your metabolism so that you think better and process your food in more productive ways, as you enjoy eating for energy.)

Another secret is to buy and bring into the house only energy food. For example, make sure that there are always plenty of fresh, appetizing fruits and vegetables in the house. Instead of an alcoholic or soft drink beverage, try a cool glass of sparkling water with a twist of lime in the evening. Whole grain breads with high fiber round out meals with occasional portions of fish and white chicken meat. Steamed vegetables can be an alternative to meat, and fruit for dessert is a nice change. Be sure your meals are balanced, and slowly try some changes to see what fits you best. We encourage you to get your mate in on this. It makes all the difference when you team together to surround yourself with only healthy food choices.

We also use this idea in our office. We take turns bringing fresh fruit for snacks. We limit the coffee and enjoy mint tea most mornings. Also, six to eight glasses of water a day can really help your energy by keeping your system flushed out and clean. We find that keeping a glass of water in front of us encourages us to drink more water and less caffeine. These are all habits we have developed over time. There can be a big payoff in new-found energy if you choose to change some of your energy-draining habits. We find that if we keep focusing on the energy benefits and reward ourselves for positive choices (and waste no energy feeling guilty when we backslide into poor choices), we keep moving forward. The more we mentally link energy with eating choices, the easier it becomes to make good choices.

Daily "Nonstressed" Aerobic Exercise

Probably a minimum of twenty to forty minutes a day of non-stressed aerobic exercise is needed to bring your mind and body back to optimum. To be aerobic, you need to get your heart rate up to 120 beats per minute and keep it there for a minimum of twenty minutes. Another easy gauge is to exercise hard enough to sweat. The American Heart Association suggests the following target heart rate formula: subtract your age from 220. This is your average maximum heart rate. Your target zone is 60% to 75% of your average maximum heart rate. (Multiply your average maximum heart rate by .60 to .75.) Sustain your target zone rate for fifteen to thirty minutes three times a week.

In the past eleven years, a new medical field has emerged which links our moods, attitudes, thoughts, and body chemistry. Called psychoneuroimmunology, this field provides a scientific explanation for the positive effects produced by the "power of positive thinking." As Janet Hopson points out in the July 1988 issue of *Psychology Today*, thoughts actually alter body chemistry by changing the levels of hormones, endorphins, and other key chemicals which affect the brain, the immune system, and subsequently our perception of energy. We therefore believe it is important to choose to *enjoy* exercise. If you get up early to run but are reminding yourself all the while how you don't like it, you are blocking the beneficial effects of endorphins with your attitude.

If you think you don't have a choice in this, try changing your attitude. Spend a week seeking out all the reasons to see your exercise as a positive. For this period of time don't allow the negatives to creep in. We think you will find it is just a matter of what you choose to focus on. It can be as simple as choosing to change your focus. However, the bonus is that you can perhaps double the benefits of your aerobic exercise by replacing the negatives in your self-talk with positives.

Time Alone

Know that each of us is different in this personal need. It may vary from time to time. In thinking back over your normal current pattern, how would you rate your need for time alone at this period in your life? Both highly creative people and people who are unusually productive in unique ways seem to require some significant time to be alone with their own thoughts. This may be an important part of their morning jogging routine. Or it may be quiet time alone when they get up very early or arrive at their work place before others are there or the phone begins to interrupt their private thoughts.

Teaching children to treasure and use time alone not only helps the child develop a valuable lifelong habit that can lead to balance and high performance but also helps the child understand a parent's need for precious alone time on a daily basis.

Time to Read and Learn

It is easy to get so busy that you feel as though you have no time to read and learn. Yet these are times when we may be spinning our wheels and not even be aware of it. Taking the time on a daily basis to glean new ideas—new food for thought and inspiration— is just as important as enjoying regular, nutritious meals. Henry Ford once said, "A man who doesn't read is no better off than a man who can't read."

As you consider the various ways to make this happen for yourself within a busy schedule, think of the variety of reading spots available. You might try keeping magazines by your bed or in the den (to read during TV commercials), your car, or the bathroom. A smaller collection could go in your briefcase.

Spiritual Growth

Do you have daily habits to fill this need for spiritual growth? Are you aware that there are stages of development in your spiritual life just as there are in your physical development? You may fill this need by daily devotional or inspirational reading or by meditating and prayer. You may focus on a collection of inspirational poems or take walks in nature.

Robert Greenleaf's essay "The Servant as Leader" describes the paradox of being able to serve those you lead as an essential quality of leadership. This can be seen in the role model of Jesus, Buddha, Gandhi, and other great leaders. Do you regularly take care of this aspect of your life so that you can be a steady and trustworthy role model? What percentage of the time do you find daily time to focus on your own spiritual growth?

Intimacy and Love

It is easy to get so caught up in the busy-ness of our lives that we go through the motions of loving our mate and our children without taking the time or devoting the attention to creating and experiencing new feelings and new gifts of love to be given and received. This may or may not be linked to sexuality. It has more to do with depth of feeling and the sense that we are valued and genuinely cared about than how it is expressed.

If you are not one to say "I love you" to your spouse or children, perhaps because they are teenage or grown, you might want to rethink this. By choosing to break this habit you may find not only new joy in the relationship but a wellspring of new energy related to the newly freed feelings. Many male executives in our executive development programs found the courage to break out of this cultural norm and discovered their renewed relationships with spouse and grown children to be a major turning point in their lives and a source of great personal energy. It takes real strength and courage to make this choice. And the paradox is that these behaviors are usually avoided because they have been thought to represent a lack of strength. What percentage of time do you get and give an adequate amount of intimacy and love?

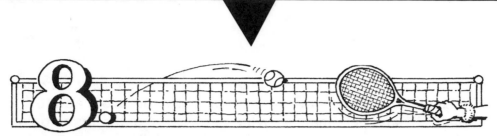

Fun, Joy, and Play

If these only happen "when you have time," which hasn't been very often these days, then let us recommend a great book to you. Written by a young, creative father and minister, Tim Hansel, *When I Relax I Feel Guilty* can be an enormously freeing resource for you.

Are you waiting until you "finish all your work before you go out to play"? That was good advice for you as a child, when your work could be finished in a reasonable period of time—say forty-five minutes or an hour. Yet now, if you were to finish everything there is for you to do—at work, at home, in the community, in your extended family—how long would it take? Several lifetimes for many of us. As a responsible, creative adult, the more you accomplish, the more you discover that needs to be done. Play, fun, and joy can provide the energy needed for work. So we need to rephrase the above rule to read something like "Plan your joy as thoughtfully and as frequently as you plan your work." Or "Be sure to balance your work with refreshing, invigorating play." Many of us haven't played for so long, really letting go and freely playing, that it is truly difficult to think of doing so, much less knowing how. What percentage of the time do you get an adequate amount of fun, joy, and play to keep you refreshed, joyful, and energized?

Quality Time with Family and Friends

It is so easy to catch ourselves just going through the motions, especially with family and friends. So often we give our quality selves to our professions and work. And then when we arrive home, our families get what is left of us, which is often a tired, grumpy, lifeless, unimaginative person. If we have just described you more accurately than you might wish, *be gentle with yourself!* You can learn to bring your best self both to your work and to your family and personal life. What percentage of the time do you claim quality time with your family and friends?

New Interests or Hobbies

Many busy people have long since given up hobbies and time-consuming outside interests as something that doesn't fit their life-style. Yet in our research, we noted that most high-energy people typically have many hobbies and outside interests in their life, each feeding new energy and insights into the other.

We encourage each participant in our Energy Engineering seminars to explore some new interests or even some old hobbies once enjoyed but given up as too time-consuming. We encourage people to give themselves permission to start but not finish a hobby. Often something that seems like it would be fun and enjoyable turns out not to be. Give yourself permission to try out many possibilities so that you can discover the few that do fit you.

Perhaps you have a kit or hobby in your closet that you once started but then lost interest in, and now you refuse to let yourself get into another hobby till that one gets finished. May we recommend that you promptly give it away on the next birthday or anniversary that comes up: "Here's a great model or quilt, and it's already started for you. Such a deal!!!!" Or give it to charity or a home for the elderly. Someone would love to pick up where you lost interest. And you need to emancipate yourself from this guilt trap and move on to new possibilities. This is where we get confused and apply our work habits ("Finish what you start. Be persistent and disciplined. Follow the rules.") to our play. If instead you will let the little kid in you do it his or her own way according to interest and inclination, we think you will find a whole new level of energy and creativity unleashed.

One power plant superintendent who now spends lots of happy evenings designing stained glass mandalas and building unique kaleidoscopes told us how he discovered the importance of daily time for joy breaks and play: "It has saved my life . . . if not physically, then mentally."

If you are not sure where to begin on this but know that you probably could really benefit by discovering some new, exciting outside interests, you might start with a trip to the library. Or try some hobby shops, craft shops, or sporting goods/outdoor recreation stores. Don't stick to the norms here. Some men have discovered that they were unusually good at needlepoint or stitchery. Women may equally enjoy hobbies typically seen as male-oriented.

What percentage of the time do you allow yourself to enjoy an adequate amount of refreshing, renewing time immersed in outside interests or hobbies? (It is interesting to note that throughout history so many of the major contributions and breakthroughs came from amateurs, from people's hobbies rather than from their vocations. The Wright brothers ran a bicycle shop but on the side had a passion for flying. The root of the word "amateur" means to love. Here again is the link of passion and play to significant mental contributions. Copernicus was an amateur astronomer. Ben Franklin, Thomas Jefferson, and many others made major contributions from the love of their hobbies while making their living at other more conventional areas.)

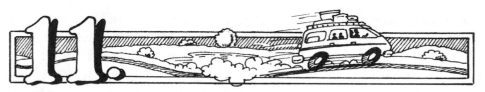

Regular and Frequent Vacations

Have you ever known yourself or others to finally take a vacation and then have trouble letting go and truly relaxing? Perhaps it takes the form of needing to stay on schedule instead of doing what you feel like doing when you feel like it.

Being on vacation calls for a different type of thinking and response. Often it is more important to switch into these responses than to geographically be in a certain spot. Leaving the location of our typical life can be helpful to this process. By practicing, even if for only twenty minutes or two hours a weekend of "being on vacation," we can keep this part of our playfulness active and intact.

The idea of regular vacations led us to find a way to make a part of every business trip, even if it were only a part of an hour, a vacation of sorts. We find that even calling it a mini-vacation helps to remind us and others of its purpose. We might take a twenty-minute sidetrip through a craft boutique or request a sidetrip through a historic area. Or plan an extra day to hike through a wilderness area. It takes pre-planning and this, we find, is a big part of the secret. If we creatively keep work integrated with refreshing joy breaks, we work with more energy, productivity, and creative problem solving. Indeed we find that we get more done of higher quality in less time with more time and energy left to enjoy other dimensions of our life! This, after all, is one of the primary goals of Energy Engineering. What percentage of the time do you get an adequate amount of regular and frequent vacation time to keep you refreshed and at your best?

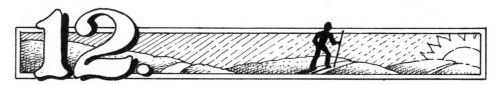

Sense of Purpose

The health care profession is learning that a sense of purpose in one's life is not only key to having vital energy and motivation but perhaps to continuing to live. Statistics indicate that within two years of retirement if one hasn't replaced career purpose with some new purpose or commitment, frequently health fails and in some cases life ends. Pleasure alone seems not enough to energize life. Purpose and a sense of making a difference is essential.

Abraham Maslow in *The Farther Reaches of Human Nature* regards purpose as the key to life and explains how a sense of purpose differentiates what he calls "self-actualizing people": "self-actualizing individuals (more matured, more fully human), by definition, already suitably gratified in their basic needs, are now motivated in other higher ways, to be called metamotivations . . . in all cases . . . they are dedicated people, devoted to some task 'outside themselves,' some vocation, or duty, or beloved job. . . . something for which the person is a 'natural,' something that he is suited for . . . even something that he was born for . . . The dichotomizing of work and play is transcended." In another section Maslow describes the "I want to" coinciding with "I must." Maslow thought purpose was so essential to the quality of life that differentiated his self-actualized person that he developed his Theory of Metamotivation.

Noted psychiatrist Viktor Frankl thought that one's sense of purpose was so essential to quality of life that he created a whole new approach to psychology called Logotherapy, which assists the patient in finding meaning in life. As one defines a clear sense of purpose in life, one experiences a commitment, drive, urgency, even enthusiasm to get up in the morning and contribute to the goal.

Mid-life crisis is a classic example of what happens to our energy when focus and purpose are lost. When we begin to realize that we won't live forever and maybe won't ever reach our goal of being CEO of the company (or whatever our life-dream has been), we may go into a depression. The "empty nest" syndrome is another form of losing touch with one's identity or purpose in life and feeling without direction. Depression is often linked to lack of exciting dreams or goals for life. When we feel limited and boxed in, a victim of our current circumstances, we can suffer from an overwhelming loss of energy and loss of general enthusiasm for life.

Getting back in touch with dreams or coming up with new purpose can renew energy and zest for life. Going back to school, starting your own business, writing a book, taking up a new hobby, getting started on a fitness program, learning a foreign language and planning a trip to use it, taking a leadership role in a community project, renewing your spiritual growth, getting out of your rut and investing in a new vision of possibility—all this has to do with the importance of purpose in boosting personal energy.

> **"We fear our highest possibilities . . . We are generally afraid to become that which we can glimpse in our most perfect moments, under the most perfect conditions, under conditions of great courage."**

In reflecting on these twelve factors, you may be painfully aware that what you know to do for yourself is far away from the

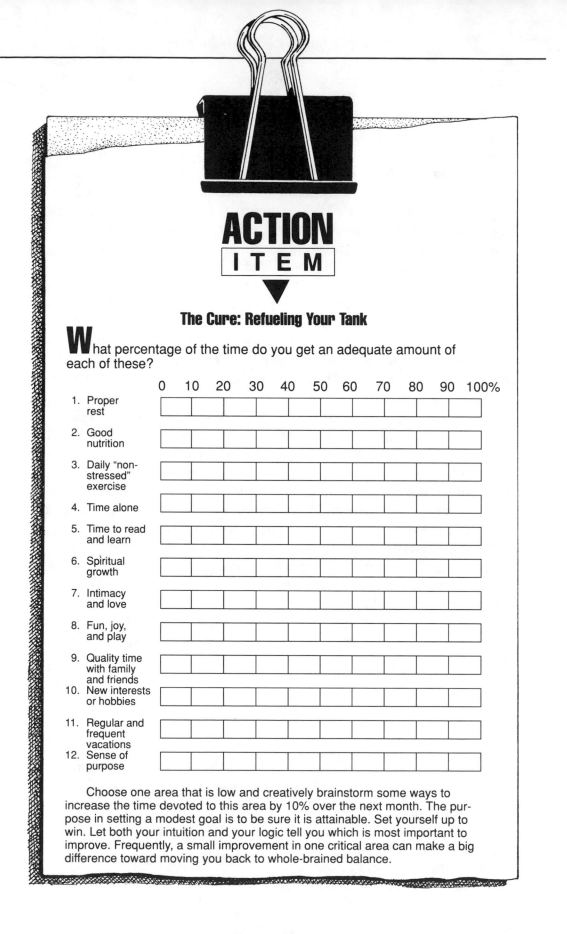

ACTION
ITEM
▼

The Cure: Refueling Your Tank

What percentage of the time do you get an adequate amount of each of these?

0   10   20   30   40   50   60   70   80   90   100%

1. Proper rest

2. Good nutrition

3. Daily "non-stressed" exercise

4. Time alone

5. Time to read and learn

6. Spiritual growth

7. Intimacy and love

8. Fun, joy, and play

9. Quality time with family and friends

10. New interests or hobbies

11. Regular and frequent vacations

12. Sense of purpose

Choose one area that is low and creatively brainstorm some ways to increase the time devoted to this area by 10% over the next month. The purpose in setting a modest goal is to be sure it is attainable. Set yourself up to win. Let both your intuition and your logic tell you which is most important to improve. Frequently, a small improvement in one critical area can make a big difference toward moving you back to whole-brained balance.

daily choices you make. So why don't we do the best that we know? Why don't we exercise daily, make healthy food choices, quit smoking, and devote quality time to family? You may think lack of time is the reason, but it's often just an excuse.

Abraham Maslow, in his work on the self-actualized person, helps us understand this clinging to our weaknesses as the Jonah Complex, as we noted earlier. This has to do with the tendency to run away from the opportunities to rise to our highest potential. As Maslow explains in *The Farther Reaches of Human Nature*, "We fear our highest possibilities . . . We are generally afraid to become that which we can glimpse in our most perfect moments, under the most perfect conditions, under conditions of great courage. We enjoy and even thrill to the godlike possibilities we see in ourselves in such peak moments. And yet we simultaneously shiver with weakness, awe, and fear before these very same possibilities."

Enormous energy can be consumed in avoiding these opportunities as well as grieving many roads not taken. The self-assessment in the Action Item can help you reflect on where you are holding yourself back and where you can make significant gains through moving toward balance.

Summary

1.   The twelve factors of life in which you can improve overall quality while regaining energy and restoring balance are

      ■ rest
      ■ eating habits
      ■ daily aerobic exercise
      ■ private time
      ■ reading and learning
      ■ spiritual growth
      ■ intimate relationships
      ■ experiencing joy and fun
      ■ relationships with friends and family
      ■ interests and hobbies
      ■ vacations
      ■ a sense of purpose

2.   Trust your intuition and begin to find creative ways to bring your lowest-rated factors into play to replenish your energy.

Energy Engineering Strategies:
Tools to Synthesize Energy

AUCTION TODAY

14

FOUR STEPS TO NEW ENERGY:

The "Big E"

66 *I want to be completely used up when I die, for the harder I work, the more I live. I celebrate life for its own sake. Life is no 'brief candle' to me, but rather like a splendid torch which I hold in my hand at this moment in time, and I want it to burn as brightly as possible before passing it on to future generations.* 99

—**George Bernard Shaw,** *Man and Superman*

66 *The way I see it, if you want the rainbow, you gotta put up with the rain.* 99

—**Dolly Parton**

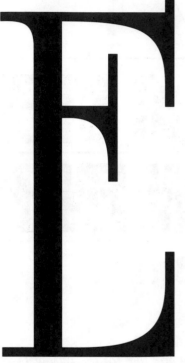arly into our work on energy, we stumbled onto a rather basic approach to what we now call Energy Engineering. It began simply by observing what gave us energy and what drained our energy. We each made our own list and each was different. One of our lists looked something like the one shown in the diagram.

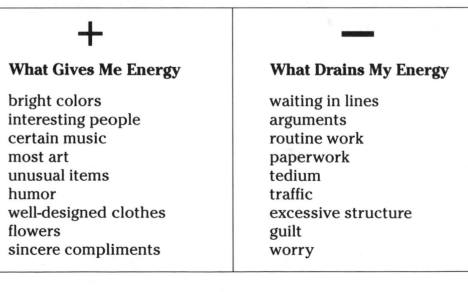

+	−
What Gives Me Energy	**What Drains My Energy**
bright colors	waiting in lines
interesting people	arguments
certain music	routine work
most art	paperwork
unusual items	tedium
humor	traffic
well-designed clothes	excessive structure
flowers	guilt
sincere compliments	worry

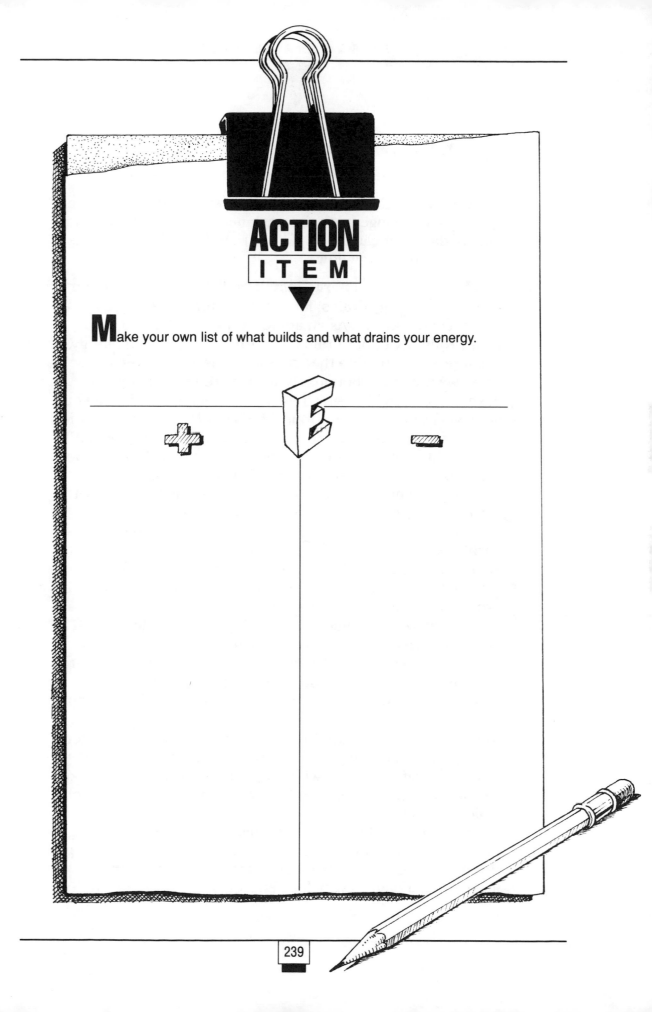

ACTION ITEM

Make your own list of what builds and what drains your energy.

Four Energy-Building Steps

Now we can apply the following four steps to gain new energy:

1. **Observe what gives you energy and what drains your energy.** This can change from circumstance to circumstance and time of day, so it can be helpful to train yourself to become aware of your energy flow.

2. **Block unnecessary energy loss.** If "guilt" or "worry" are on your list of energy drains, let's start by simply letting go of these two behaviors. As an adult, they do nothing to help your productivity but drain an enormous amount of energy. It is interesting to note that guilt helps us as children know when we are out of bounds. When we are very young, we have a strong right brain (the basis for feelings and guilt) but not a well-developed left brain (the basis for ethics and rational, abstract judgment). So guilt protects and warns us until we are older and able to use judgment and logic to guide our behavior. Notice how often our guilt is not logical, such as feeling guilty because there are dirty dishes in the sink or the gutter needs repair after working long hours at the office.

    It took years of practice to get good at guilt, so it will take a while to unlearn it. But it can make a big difference in your energy once you block or stop this energy-draining habit.

    Avoid any other energy-draining habits that are nonproductive and unnecessary (such as worry or nagging). Sometimes we lose energy by creating problems for ourselves. Georgia Ulrich, a creative octogenarian and researcher who practices Energy Engineering strategies, shares this wisdom: "I find that many problems solve themselves while I work at other tasks. When I hit a snag (such as getting things scrambled as they come from the Xerox machine— front and back pages are the worst), usually late in the afternoon, I leave it overnight. The next morning, when I am fresh, it works itself out easily, without pressure. This saying makes the pressure more fun: 'Miracles we do instantly. The impossible takes a little longer.'"

    Another good example of blocking unnecessary energy loss would be to find ways of coping with inevitable energy drains such as traffic. Most of us are usually in traffic at least twice a day. So why lose energy over it? An alternative would be to accept it as part of your choice to live and work in a big city. Then find ways to make your time in traffic a plus rather than a minus. You might do this by leaving early to allow yourself extra time during periods of peak traffic. Try traveling with tapes you enjoy, either of relaxing music or of seminars or reviews of research, so that you can make use of and benefit from any traffic delays. By planning ahead and rethinking your attitude choices, you may discover that it is easy to relax in traffic and feel no energy drain.

3. **Balance by linking.** Add an energy gain to an energy drain, or wear something you particularly like on a day when you face tasks which drain your energy. Here are other examples.

    Get help from a person you enjoy on a task that drains your energy. Plan trade-outs with people of opposite hemisphere dominance. You can learn from their opposite work style, and they may also find times when you can be an asset to them.

    Add color and unusual tools to routine paper tasks that are usually dull and uninteresting. In our office we use colored file folders; large, unusual paper clips; and an oversized, well-designed solar calculator to help us to enjoy the routine paperwork that is an essential part of our work. The colorful and unusual items not only make the work more fun for us but help us retrieve things by appealing to the right hemisphere (which is more visual than the left).

    A real problem for right-hemisphere-dominant people can be keeping up with many projects in motion. When we take files out to work on them, we put them inside a certain colored file folder for the time being. This makes it easier for all of us to locate the yellow or orange file, rather than trying to locate the "Time Management" file from several hundred manila files also being processed around the office.

    If a project is urgent (meaning that it must go out today), we put it in a red file folder. Everyone in the office knows not to put anything on top of red folders so they won't get buried and forgotten. Our team is conditioned to check around for any red folders to be sure that essential work is done and mailed before quitting time.

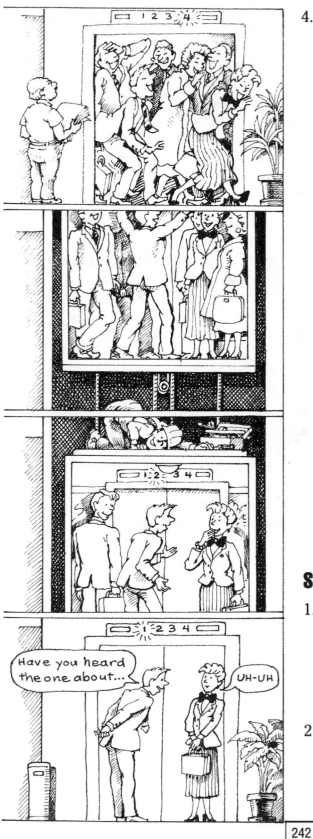

4. **Build energy by looking for new opportunities to tuck energy pluses into your day.** The secret here is not to wait until your energy is completely exhausted to do something about it. If you frequently renew and build your energy in small doses, it's like topping off your gas tank. This can be a quick phone call to a friend or mate to plan a place to meet for a romantic dinner. It might be a quick thank-you note to someone who has given you special help. It might be trading out a neck rub with a work partner, taking a brisk walk, or taking the stairs two at a time to get the toxins out of your system. Or it could be totally relaxing for five minutes with your eyes closed, taking yourself via fantasy to a refreshing place you would love to be.

Summary

1. Become your own research lab and observe what drains your energy—whether it is long lines, heavy traffic, or excessive noise.

2. Learn to block unnecessary energy loss by not dwelling on worry and guilt. Also

ACTION
ITEM

Now you might teach the four steps to new energy to someone you care about. Then each of you might plan your own way to put them to work for yourself. You might use "choice accountability," which means that you each choose to make yourself accountable to the other in a week (you set the deadline) to tell the other what you tried and how it is working. One important tip here: no nagging. Let the process be one of inspiring and encouraging each other through your positive role model. But put no energy into reminding the other of what he or she was supposed to do. Let this be a free choice. If you are gaining more positive, productive, enjoyable energy on a daily basis, this will be obvious and motivating to most others around you.

You might want to challenge yourself with the following.

Can you live _____ % (fill in the blank) of the time at 90% energy or above?

We would encourage you to set your goal just above where you are now and continue to increase it as you learn new ways to make progress. Slow, steady progress is usually much longer-lasting than abrupt, giant steps.

block energy drainers by eliminating them when possible. If traffic is a drain, try commuting before or after peak hours, exercising after driving home, and driving a less-used route.

3. Compensate for an energy drain by adding an energy gain to it. For example, if you hate to garden but love jazz music, put on a portable cassette player and listen to your favorite tapes while pulling weeds.

4. Don't wait until your energy is completely exhausted to do something about it. Look for any opportunities to tuck five-minute energy breaks into your day.

CHAPTER 15

CHAINDUMPING VERSUS POSITIVE VENTILATION:

How Teams Play "Ain't It Awful?"

❝ *People spend most of their lives worrying about things that never happen.* ❞

—**Molière**

❝ *The problem isn't the problem—the problem is the attitude about the problem.* ❞

— **Kelly Young, age 19**

Just as certain individuals can exude a positive attitude and high energy, other individuals can drain your energy. Have you noticed yourself suddenly feeling pessimistic, depressed, or fatigued after talking with a particular person? Sometimes you might feel this way in the midst of the conversation and wish to cut the talk short.

Chaindumping—A Contagious Energy Drain

A few years ago we were called in to help a company in trouble. The energy, morale, and motivation of the group was really at the bottom, and their financial picture was moving that way fast! We were hired to teach them how to increase their energy. But first we wanted to see if we could get a clearer picture of the problem.

We spent a few days just observing, and one behavior looked all too familiar. One fellow we will call Greg (not the real name) came to work with a heaviness to his walk. He stopped at the receptionist and grumbled about the traffic delay that morning, the high pollen count, his kids who had "made him late," and his car that was requiring repeated service. As he slowly moved on down the hall, we noted the reception- ist looked a bit more tired and her voice sounded heavy as she answered the next call.

It's easy to see that chain- dumping is unhealthy both for the dumper and for the listener. So why do we do it?

Greg next stopped in to re- tell his tale of woe to an associ- ate, only this time the traffic de- lay was five minutes longer and in his story about his car, it had required four rather than three return trips to get the transmission fixed! At mid-morning Greg was in the coffee room retelling his same litany of woe. His voice was heavy and his posture slumped. Soon others were playing "Can You Top This?" with horror stories on trying to get cars repaired, what a pain kids are, and so forth.

By day's end, we had overheard Greg dumping his problems on six occasions. Each time, his stories became worse as he would feel more and more the victim of these unlucky circum- stances. We began to notice not only the familiar pattern of Greg's behavior and its effect on him and those around him, but the contagious nature of the process as well. Others became echoes of him, each dumping their own tale of woe on first one person, then another.

In an effort to help this group gain insights into some of their energy drains and begin to discover new options for taking charge of their situation in positive ways, we named this behav- ior pattern *chaindumping,* which means to dump your problems on first one person and then the next. These are the symptoms of chaindumping:

1. **The same complaints get unloaded again and again.**
2. **The person telling the story is always the victim.** This is called victim mentality—a person becomes the victim of everything: job, spouse, the weather, age, car, the traffic, etc.
3. **Exaggeration is used.** Details grow and get worse with each retelling.
4. **The problems get dumped on anyone who will listen.** One airing of the bad feelings is never enough. The teller seems to pick up steam as he or she repeats the tale.
5. **There is low or no awareness of other choices.** This would include ways the person could become proactive, plan ahead, turn negatives into positives, etc.

6. **There is low or no energy.** You can frequently hear a whine in the voice or a lot of heavy sighs and groans along with the story.

We can all probably think of times when we were champion chain-dumpers. At least I can. When I went through a divorce, I must have worn out all my friends retelling my sad story, laying all the blame elsewhere and putting lots of energy into feeling sorry for myself. It was not until much later that I was able to let go of all the anger and blaming. Only then could I begin to learn how I had contributed to the many problems. Only then did I begin to discover many positive options for opening my relationships to healthier and happier outcomes.

Through counseling I learned the damage I was causing to myself by retelling my problems over and over so many times. Think of a very long gash on your arm that must be sewn up with thirty-eight stitches. What if you went around reopening the wound to show each friend how bad the gash was? Each time, the scar tissue would build and the wound would take longer to heal. Nothing would be gained and your chances of a healthy healing would grow less and less through this process.

This is a good metaphor for our emotional life as well. Our subconscious doesn't know the difference between a real event and the emotional reliving of an event through remembering or retelling the details. Each time you emotionally go back through all the incidents, it is like having the event happen one more time. Through this process you can experience a bad argument or painful loss many times just by retelling it again and again. And if you position yourself as a helpless victim with no power to change the outcome, you convince your subconscious again and again that it has no other choices.

On the other hand, this is why positive reframing of a negative experience is so effective. If we rethink the experience as we would like for it to have been, we are then rehearsing and practicing other options for the future. The next time we find ourselves in a similar situation, we will have these positive, proactive behaviors rehearsed and ready like familiar friends.

It's easy to see that chaindumping is unhealthy both for the dumper and for the listener. So why do we do it?

Victim Mentality

If you listen carefully, you will often hear evidence of low self-esteem sprinkled throughout the stories. I may tell you of getting caught in endless traffic or complain about the heavy workload of my job. Victim behavior and a feeling of being overwhelmed are two other patterns often present. One way to better understand these negative behavior patterns is through Karpman's triangle. This concept explains the dynamics of the roles of Persecutor, Rescuer, and Victim.

When you establish a relationship, you can assume any of these three roles, but regardless of which role you take initially, you will eventually take on all three. Let me explain through my own out-of-balance habits.

I am most likely to be a rescuer initially. Here's a typical scenario from my past. If Sue is piled high with work and moaning that she will never get caught up and has to get a proposal out before going home, I might volunteer to stay late to help her (rescuer role). This becomes a rescue when I take on her problems as my own (as a victim), not seeing other alternatives for her or for myself. Perhaps in my eagerness to help her, I for-

get that I have promised my son that I will attend his soccer game and my husband that I will meet him there as well. When I finally leave work and remember my forgotten promises, I rush to the soccer game already late and very likely begin to blame Sue on the way. I might whine: "If Sue had only planned ahead, she wouldn't get herself in such binds and need to be bailed out. I can remember when she wasted time on the phone to friends or came back late from lunch. Her poor planning has sure made a wreck of my evening." Then as I arrive at the game I might be filled with blame (persecutor role) toward her. It is now all her fault that I had to stay late (victim role). I couldn't just leave and risk losing the client. (Can you see how I have mentally found other ways to blame her and feel victimized, never seeing or admitting that it was I who originally volunteered to stay late and help?)

You can see this pattern in parents racing around on Sunday night to help their kids find supplies for science projects that they must hand in on Monday but that kids remembered only late on Sunday evening (victim). Or maybe a father volunteers to coach a daughter's basketball team and then feels like a victim of the endless hours and many additional duties, blaming the other parents for not helping.

On the other hand, if you prefer the victim role, it is safer and easier to let others rescue you than to figure out problems on your own. Then if something doesn't work out, it is all their fault. And you can not only feel sorry for yourself for having the problem but also for having to deal with someone who louses up the solution.

If we rescue our children, spouses, friends, and colleagues rather than teaching them to take responsibility for themselves, then we become their victims, being called upon again and again to bail them out. On the other hand, if we begin to learn to ask for what we want in advance and to firmly but politely insist that people treat us fairly, it's amazing what good things can follow.

> **Rescuing is doing for others something that they need to do for themselves. If you rescue others from the results of their behavior, they will repeat their mistakes, only to need rescuing again and again.**

Life became far more pleasurable and successful when I began to put as much energy and imagination into exploring positive ways to invite others to meet me halfway in solving problems as I had into blaming others and creating sympathy for myself through dramatic "poor me" routines. This process helps us understand that we are conditioning or teaching the people around us how we want to be treated by our actions and reactions. We can choose to take charge of our lives proactively and give up our victim mentality.

Chaindumping—An Expensive Addiction

We're not sure it is scientifically accurate to label chaindumping as an addiction, but as we observe it in ourselves and others, it seems to fit the definition: to give oneself habitually or compulsively to something. Chaindumping is not only contagious, but once it gets going, it seems to grow. You can notice it in families or in work groups. If the parents come home chaindumping, the kids will quickly learn to blame their problems on teachers, friends, their poor eyesight, their siblings—it's easy to find someone or something else to blame—thus avoiding looking to themselves for the causes and solutions to their problems.

If the boss blames upper management, other departments, slow mail, or difficult clients, soon those working with the boss learn that the game is to blame others before they blame you. In fact, people waste lots of energy documenting with paper trails so they can't be blamed.

Victims seek out other victims to help them feel justified in their points of view. Victims avoid dumping on those who might hold them accountable for their roles or opportunities to effect change.

By now you see how we can get on a roll, going through our day dumping negative feelings and stories on innocent friends, family, and fellow workers as we contaminate our day and drain energy needlessly. But don't we all have times when we need to dump and grumble?

There are two points to notice in discovering new perspectives for solving this problem. First, you always have the choice as to whether you will give away your power and become a victim of circumstance or others. Or you can proactively seek ways to affect your situation. There is no freedom without responsibility. When you begin to look for ways you can take responsibility, you not only will begin to discover more and more positive options but very likely you will experience new energy. Viktor Frankl, who was a prisoner of the Nazis for four years, teaches us that even in the most severe circumstances, the final freedom is the freedom to choose our attitude. "No one can harm me with-out my permission. They can harm my body but they cannot harm me. I have control of that," Frankl declared. His insights teach us the enormous potential of becoming proactive and self-directed, not even blaming ourselves, but instead seeking positive options and ways we can bring them into being.

Second, when you need to let off steam about a situation, you can ventilate (express negative feelings) positively —in ways that are responsible and not harmful to others. Here are some tips on that process.

Tips for Positive Ventilation

1. **Know when you need to ventilate** (let out negative feelings).

2. **Choose your listener wisely.** This is a time when you will be most tempted to complain to a listener who will side with you and against the other party. Be fair about this. For example, don't ventilate to your child about your spouse. Your children can't be objec-tive, and putting them in a position of taking sides is unfair.

Neither is it fair to ventilate about the company or your boss to new employees. They don't have the history with the company to know whether you are speaking from facts or feelings, and typically when we ventilate, it is our feelings speaking.

3. **Warn your listener that you wish to ventilate and ask permission before doing so.** This person may not be able to listen to your problems just now. He or she may be in emotional overload with the situation as it is. Typically we might say, "Got a minute?" This can be a trap because we usually just get started in the first minute. The whole story may take far longer. So here is the next step.

4. **Set a time limit in advance.** "I need five minutes to ventilate. Are you at a place where you can listen?" This request is far more fair to the potential listener.

5. **Have the listener keep time while you pour out your feelings.** Since your purpose is to ventilate negative or pent-up feelings, really get them out. Exaggerate, moan, groan, be dramatic and outrageous, adding generous self-pity and self-defense. You might even have so much fun with this that you will break into laughter. But at least all the garbage gets expressed and the vulnerable little kid of your right brain gets affirmed and heard in the process.

6. **Ask for more time if you run out of time but still have more feelings to pour out.** But here is where the balance of accountability comes in. You know in advance that you choose to take responsibility for balancing the energy drain of pouring out negative feelings by contributing something positive for an equal amount of time. This might include blissful silence, taking a walk, enjoying a cup of tea, or making positive comments about the same situation. Making this contract with yourself will probably cause you to ventilate in a hurry.

7. **Now shift and balance the energy drain with some kind of energy gain.** Sometimes I shift and tell the positives of the occasion I have just groaned about. Other times I recall why I am very lucky to be who I am where I am. This not only brings energy back to my patient listener, it also brings me back into balance. Always I find I am amazed at how my feelings shift when I do this last step. Let's say I am overwhelmed with the demands on my time by clients. When I shift, I recall a time when we had no clients and were looking for business. Suddenly the problems look like good fortune and I have to grin in embarrassment that I would view my success as a burden.

I learned this lesson from my husband, Larry. Early in our marriage when he would come home from work, I would be filled with complaints about contractors remodeling the house and problems with the kids. He would invite me to get my running shoes. To get him to listen I would have to keep up with him. The more I complained, the brisker his pace became. I learned to grumble quickly because I didn't have his stamina, and I sure wanted him to hear me.

One evening when I was particularly filled with woe, I stopped my sad saga just long enough to ask when we were going to turn around and start home. "As soon as you have finished airing problems," he said with all the patience that let me know he could walk on for hours. It was getting dark and I was ready to turn around right then, so I announced that I was through complaining. We turned toward home and after walking a few blocks, I remembered just a few more complaints. Without saying a word, he turned the other way. I got the message quickly.

I don't want to paint the picture of Larry as being an unsympathetic listener, for that would be unfair. What I learned is that it is far more constructive to sort through problems when you are both walking briskly. The aerobic exercise seems to also help me process more objectively and creatively so that my thoughts are less likely to get blocked by emotional dead ends. By balancing the time spent on problems with an equal amount of renewing, trouble-free silence or cheerful conversation on the walk home, we experienced a healing bond. I would encourage you to find your own equivalent.

Protecting Yourself from Chaindumping and Other Negative Behavior

"If you want to change others, change yourself first." We don't know whom to credit for this quote, but it is one that continues to inspire and help us as well as protect others from our overzealous

In chaindumping, the right brain is in control in a destructive, half-brained process. In positive ventilation, both the left brain and the right brain become partners in finding ways to get your needs met while not harming either the listener or the party you may be struggling with.

attempts to change them. We are amazed at how effective it is just to work on changing ourselves. As we enjoy working on a team where we all strive to practice these ideas, we are aware daily of how others' good habits help us change for the better. Far more effective than criticism is the role model of positive options. Here are some other tips we find helpful in protecting ourselves from negativity:

1. **Raise awareness.** Invite your closest associates and

ACTION
ITEM
▼

Spend several days noting which people you regularly talk with. Also analyze how you feel after each conversation. Ask yourself which persons

1. make you laugh or smile?
2. express the attitude that life is rewarding and fun?
3. are willing to try new things and inspire you to do the same?
4. are self-sufficient and capable of solving their own problems?
5. exude good health, enthusiasm, and vitality?
6. spend most of their time complaining about their problems?
7. think that life is unfair and that all their efforts will be thwarted?
8. always remind you of what could go wrong whenever you want to try something new?
9. frequently ask you for help and say they don't know what they would do without you?
10. are basically uninspired people who seem to get little enjoyment out of life?

The first five traits are the marks of an energy builder, someone who offers you an energy boost. The last five traits signal an energy drainer, someone who drains your storehouse of positive thoughts and energy within minutes.

family to learn about chaindumping and the positive alternatives. We find others most open to the concept when we simply ask for help as we seek to change. You might describe the behavior you want to change and the ways you plan to work on it. Then ask your listener to help by encouraging any positive changes and gently reminding you if he or she sees you falling back into old comfortable, negative habits. When I expose my own less-than-admirable behavior, this confession seems to free others to admit that they too might benefit from similar changes. The process seems to be as contagious as is negative behavior. Only the energy reverses as positive change brings positive energy increases.

2. **Have fun.** Use humor, but be gentle. Unfortunately, most American humor is built on put-downs and negatives. Sometimes it is hard for us to see ways to be funny without discounting ourselves or others. But this is worth some effort because put-downs to self or others cause the vulnerable right hemisphere of our creative little-kid self to wither or withdraw. On the other hand, positive, wonderful fun invites the little kid in us to venture out and be at our best. Be sure to laugh with others and yourself, not at them. And if you catch yourself being negative and sarcastic with your humor, a sincere and genuine apology can make all the difference. This may take some practice, but it's worth it. Humor is a great way to build energy and relieve stress. It also stimulates creativity and innovation, which is a key to finding better ways to get things done.

   During our workshops, audiences laugh the most when we reveal mistakes that we have made which remind them painfully of themselves. If it is safe to laugh with us, then it is safe to laugh with themselves. And out of this healthy laughter we can then search for healthier ways to turn our problems into opportunities.

3. **Give your negative habits names.** Pretend they are invisible people, then have fun laughing at their ridiculous (but familiar) solutions to problems. We picked up this great idea from a woman who kept us regaled with tales of the Travel Agent (the part of her that is going to leave home and make them all sorry if they don't agree with all of her ideas!), Priscilla Pig (who solves any difficulty by searching for something fattening to eat), Dudley DooRite (who insists that everything be done perfectly,) Aunt Maude (who criticizes her behavior and dress if it isn't strictly Victorian), and the Committee (which refers to all the critical voices in her head). She might say, "The report looks great as is. Dudley DooRite would have us both redo it till the last T is crossed perfectly, but for this client and our current deadline, let's go with it."

4. **Celebrate at the first sign of positive change.** Don't wait until you or others are perfect to acknowledge and celebrate growth. We find that the more we generously recognize and reward change and growth, the more we keep them going for ourselves and each other.

5. **Keep your "emotional raincoat" handy for those times when emotionally draining people are around.** We find that just getting a mental picture of protecting ourselves with imaginary foul-weather gear helps us remember to make the mental shift and not lose energy unnecessarily.

6. **Collect positive people.** Plan ways to spend more time with them. Their energy, enthusiasm, and behaviors are contagious.

7. **Look for mentors.** These people can coach you on ways to stay proactive and positive. Ask for and practice their tips and insights.

Bob Gary, an executive at TU Electric, tells how he surrounds himself with positive people:

"I 'date' high-energy people. I put them on my calendar and make a point of spending time with them. Sometimes it's simply taking a walk down the hall with them. At other times, I try to 'hook onto their energy' when I know they are celebrating some kind of success. For instance, I will call to congratulate a guy who is having his twenty-fifth anniversary with the company, because being with high-energy people gives me an energy break in and of itself. I have to deal with low-energy people, too, in my job. I have found the best thing is to challenge those who have a basket full of woes to take time off in order to feel better about themselves. Sometimes I team them up with high-energy people to give them an energy boost and make them feel a part of our team."

Summary

1. A chaindumper focuses on a veritable avalanche of problems in his or her life and drains everyone's energy by spreading contagious pessimism, gloom, and dissatisfaction throughout the office.

2. Chaindumping, classic half-brained duality, creates a victim/persecutor/rescuer triangle in which all are losers.

3. Learn and become a role model for positive ventilation, a whole-brained way to express and work through frustration and anger balanced by a healthy consideration for others.

DESIGNING AN ENERGY ENVIRONMENT:

A Nest for Innovation

66 *Creative clutter is better than tidy idleness.* **99**
— **Author unknown**

66 *I used to have a naive theory . . . that no one willingly lives in a state of disorder; therefore what causes it is lack of time and lack of money. [But I have learned that] a tendency to order or disorder in life comes very early; more money . . . simply leads to more mess.* **99**

— **John Fowles**

66 *Imagination is more important than knowledge, for knowledge is limited while imagination embraces the entire world.* **99**

— **Albert Einstein**

In Chapter 7 you learned the many benefits of adopting a work style that supports your brain dominance. The same factors hold true for your work environment. Think of that space as the physical domain in which your mind must operate and your psyche must dwell. And like your work style, your office's structure, decor, ambiance, and organizational setup can either enhance your personal energy or detract from it.

Brain Dominance and the Work Environment

In a set of interviews that Marilyn Zdenek conducted for her book *The Right-Brain Experience*, a variety of creative people were asked, "What do you find stimulates your creativity?" "My nest" was one of the responses. Our studies also validate the power of having comfortable and dynamic surroundings. But again, what feels right to one person won't necessarily accommodate the next. To test this premise, just walk past a row of private offices in a large office complex such as a university or a public relations firm and witness the huge diversity of office decors and styles.

Some desks will be almost bare with just one neat stack of papers centered in the middle and an appointment calendar off to the side. All pens, paper clips, tape, scissors, and other assorted supplies will be arranged neatly in drawers. The walls will have few decorations—possibly a framed degree and professional certificates, a photo of the employee shaking the hand of some government official, and a small picture. But in the office right next door, the desk might be covered with a collage of papers, supplies, coffee cups, pen holders, paper weights, books, and framed photos of the family. The walls will display an assortment of items, too — a crowded bulletin board, a large calendar, prints, plants, an arrangement of photos, and overflowing book shelves. Chances are, if the occupants of the "neat" and the "cluttered" offices were forced to switch desks and work styles for a week, both would be pulling out their hair in two days.

We moved into a time of sterile, basic work spaces void of anything reflecting the person employed there.

By now you know enough about hemisphericity and its influence on personal work styles to identify which brain dominance belongs to each office. In addition, you can probably cite many reasons why a right-brained employee might feel restricted and uninspired by the first office, and why a left-brained employee might feel disorganized and "crazy" working amid the chaos in the second office. The third important point to understand, both as a manager of other employees and as a manager of your own work style, is that this dichotomy does exist, to the benefit of both types of workers. Of course there are many other variations of preferred office environments as well.

Managers and office policies that encourage individual expression in each employee's work site enhance employee morale and energy levels. Unfortunately, the Industrial Revolution fostered an "egg carton" mentality that carefully divided life into separated times for work and play. Standardized methods of production and a heavy emphasis on conforming to the standard were also introduced. This emphasis on standardization affected our business environments, too. We moved into a time of sterile, basic work spaces void of anything reflecting the person employed there.

Among the business trends that we have witnessed in the past twenty years is the less-is-more, all-business style of designing the office where family photos (and any other personal aspect of one's life) and informal decorative items such as colorful pencil holders, favorite plaques and posters, and so on were all typecast as unprofessional. These items were also thought to be distractions from the work at hand. Another idea promoted by many time management courses was to keep the desk perfectly clear of everything but the one folder of information needed at the moment. A disorganized-looking work space was considered an indication of a disorganized mind (right-brained folks know otherwise!). It was also assumed to be distracting to the worker.

The latest office decorating trends have let up on this idea, allowing much more freedom for each employee to decorate and organize his or her own space. Without even counting the energy factor here, the fact that most people spend more continuous time in their work space than in any other room in their houses (except perhaps their bedrooms, and much of that time is spent asleep) underlies the importance of the work setting.

Making Your Office a "Nest"

Another way to look at it is that your office is your home away from home. And the more personalized and comfortable it can be, the more you will enjoy living in it. It is truly your "nest."

Science fiction author Ray Bradbury is reported to sit amid a collection of memorabilia much like the inner sanctum of the Smithsonian. In an interview he noted that he prefers for his phone messages to be left in the pattern in which they fall, much like "fallen leaves." He added that it distresses him to have some well-meaning person come by and "straighten them up into a singular, uninteresting pile."

We are stressing the much-maligned messy desk first because it is this style that often needs defending. Have you ever worked with a group that made fun of someone because of the disheveled state of his or her office? If people understand that there is true "method in the madness"—a hidden order within the clutter— then their jokes are not hurtful. But we have witnessed cases in which the state of a person's office made him or her truly suspect by the more conventional people among the group. We've heard comments ranging from "It's a wonder she can find anything in all that mess" to "I'm afraid to give him the file for fear he'll misplace it" to "If this is what her office looks like, can her home be any better?" to "I wonder if his brain is as fuzzy as his office." As you learned when reading about duality, this response is a typical "if-it's-different-from-me-it-must-be-wrong" attitude.

The truth is that many of our most famous geniuses, including Edison, Mead, Darwin, Einstein, and Picasso, have surrounded themselves with work clutter. One of our favorite sayings is "Clutter is the sawdust of a busy mind." A cluttered desk usually indicates that the person thrives on jumping back and forth from project to project and enjoys the stimulus of seeing his or her work in progress. Furthermore, in most cases the person is aware of the exact location of each item amid the clutter. If you have a right-brain dominance, have you ever filed materials away (in an effort to make your desk look presentable) and then later searched under every heading you can think of in an effort to relocate them? And all the while you're muttering obscenities because you can vividly remember where they were lying for six weeks before you filed them. Again, this happens because right-brained folks respond much better to visual stimuli

> **Clutter is the sawdust
> of a busy mind.**

(leaving something out in sight) than to abstract stimuli (filing or putting something out of sight in a logical, left-brained category). Plus they are such inventive thinkers that they can come up with fifteen possible topics under which to file an item, not just one "right" topic.

As for my own office, I seem to crave and create clutter as a predecessor as well as a product of my creative work. And I seem to need the stimulation of lots of materials and textures around me in order to get the creative juices flowing. I collect old photographs; toys; colorful, oversized, and whimsical objects that interest and amaze me; cards and letters that convey warmth and strength; and all kinds of office equipment and supplies that give me an energy lift when I use them.

This premise that certain environments can actually be a catalyst for creative thinking is shared by many artists. In an *Architectural Digest* article, here's what novelist John Fowles says about the relationship between his work space and his own creative dynamics: "Good novels are like good wild plants; they grow out of dirt, the mess of the earth as it is, not as it should be. Almost anything preplanned or decided before a novel is written is potential death to it. The enterprise depends to an enormous degree on sheer luck, and such luck simply does not flourish in the closed universes of immaculate order."

On the other hand, Duane needs a minimalist design work space in order to be creative. He relates:

> *"I can't think clearly when my in-basket is overflowing, books and reports are stacked high, and too many supplies are cluttering my desk. If I don't have time to deal with the mess, I will go to an empty conference table to work or simply clear the top of my desk by putting everything in a stack or in a box. But the most important thing is to have a large, clean surface with one ruled pad and a black pen if you are asking me to create something new."*

Barbara's office is a blend of right- and left-brained preferences:

"I need both neatness and clutter (visual contact with my work in progress) at different times and stages of my work. Since most of my writing projects involve lots of references and materials, my large desk is scattered with papers and books by mid-morning. In addition, I work on five or more different projects in an average week, plus five other projects that are on the "back burner" constantly, waiting for me to make time for them. I need for all of them to literally be in view and within arm's reach of me, or else I feel a kind of nervousness, as if I have abandoned them or might forget them. I could not understand this reaction until I took Ann's seminar and discovered my right-brained need for visual references. And now that I know the reason, I don't fight this reaction; instead I acknowledge this need by keeping my work nearby in plain sight.

But if things get too messy, that frustrates me as well. So on the other side of the coin, I have some strong left-brained needs, such as wanting my environment to look soothing and neat. And when office clutter builds up, I begin to feel irritated. In fact, at times I feel that I can't settle down to work until I have restored beauty to my office and have cleaned up the dishes, newspapers, etc. left in the kitchen and dining area from breakfast.

My solution has been to strike a balance between both needs. In the morning I allow fifteen minutes or so to reorganize and clean up. This routine gives me satisfaction and energy and helps my brain get prepared for the work I'm about to dive into.

Another way I balance my right- and left-brain needs is to keep my different projects in a neat stack of colorful folders placed on the far side of my desk. Thus, all my tasks are in view, but my desk top doesn't look messy. I also have a white wire mesh cart with three trays. The cart itself looks attractive, plus there is ample room for my various-sized tablets, my appointment calendar, my dictionaries, and other materials I'll be using that day. I place it right by my chair for easy access. And by the close of the day, my supplies are arranged in the cart rather than scattered all over the floor and desk.

Ann helped me realize the importance of having an aesthetically pleasing space to work in, especially since I do most of my work at home. Having my house look fresh and inviting has always been important to me, but I tended to neglect my office. Often it was the last room to get repainted and decorated. In

*addition, it ended up being the catch-all room for boxes, my
exercise bike, and various nonessentials. After meeting Ann,
I took a critical look at my office and decided it was by far the
ugliest room in my entire house. No wonder I wasn't eager to
lock myself away in there each day. No wonder I kept making
excuses to carry my work into other parts of the house. I took
a day off and set about improving it. I bought colorful rice-paper
blinds, installed and painted extra shelves, covered the ugly
computer table with some material, hung some handmade glass
wind chimes, and moved in a few plants."*

Personalized Work Spaces Boost Business

Here's another environment story about an entire company that
opted to personalize its setting rather than stick with a bland,
conventional office decor. Some years ago our team was hired by
a financial institution that was having a problem with employees'
low morale. It was during a time when the savings and loan companies in the country were first experiencing a sagging economy.
We were asked to try to boost morale and increase motivation
within the work group. Upon visiting the newly built corporate
office, we first discovered that all of the staff were required to
wear matching uniforms of sorts. Each office looked a lot like the
next. Only one piece of art hung in each office, and that had been
chosen by the architect. The environment reflected the corporate taste of the architect but not the people who spent nine
hours there each day.

Our first suggestion was that everybody take themselves
shopping for a "toy"—something they wanted but didn't need.
There was a limit of ten dollars on it so that each person would
feel comfortable with the assignment. They were to bring their
item into their work space and note whether the toy made any
difference in the way they were feeling. Among the toys selected
were a yo-yo, a crystal prism, a bag of marbles, a windup jumping
frog, a kite, a tiny teddy bear, a book of poems, and a game of fid-
dlesticks. Before long, people were getting acquainted with a new
side of each other by viewing and playing with the toys. Initially
there was some nervous laughter, but soon it became genuine joy
as people began to discover the power of play in their work
place. There was a noticeable new energy within the group. The

fun of sharing childhood memories of toys, favorite games, and other kinds of play stimulated new topics of conversation and new feelings of warmth. Much of the gloom-and-doom atmosphere lifted. And instead of worrying about slowdowns and other obstacles, the groups began to engage in creative problem solving. They were challenging themselves with more positive questions, such as "What do we have to offer the changing needs of our society?" and "If the trend is away from savings institutions, how can we change with the times?" In addition, a broader group of employees were invited to join the brainstorming groups.

Next each person was encouraged either to rediscover a hobby or find a new one to enjoy. They were to risk attempting new interests. After exploring their ideas for one month, they were asked to bring some aspect of their interest to work with them. One trust officer began to bring wood carvings he had been collecting. A woman brought her needlepoint. Watercolors of favorite fishing spots in Colorado filled one office. Desert plants were added to another. Soon each corner of this formerly cold and ultrasophisticated building began to warm up with the personality of the people who worked there.

Within six months of the beginning of this project there were some noticeable changes, changes which encouraged the leadership to celebrate the courage it took for them to risk supporting these seemingly irrelevant ideas. Absenteeism and days out had dropped significantly. Much higher energy and enthusiasm were present in all departments. And the "bottom line" had even improved significantly.

When we began to search for possible explanations, we found several. First, customers waiting to see trust officers commented that they would wait longer to talk with the officer whose office felt most comfortable to them. The offices had one glass wall so customers could see the interior from the waiting area. One man had model airplanes very neatly arranged in wall cases. He was a precise person with a great need for order and conformity. He attracted the confidence of those customers who also had a need for precision and order.

Another officer next door had a collection of antique farm implements on his wall. He even had an old pickle barrel for a stool like the old country store where he grew up. Several weathered signs from a grocery store were placed here and

there. His office was the essence of clutter and memorabilia. And he attracted folks who felt a trust and security from this part of history. He recounted that one fellow who had done business with them for years stopped by to ask about some of his collection. It turned out that they had grown up not far from each other. In the course of their visit, the fellow came to decide to shift some of his major investments into their trust department. The officer felt sure that without his collection of memories, the link to their past would never have happened and the idle chatter would never have taken place. Yet these were the seeds for the new relationship.

Second, without realizing it, we had encouraged each employee to fill his or her work space with items that expressed each individual's brain dominance. Being surrounded by these items felt harmonious to their self-image and work style, thus reducing stressors and stimulating extra energy.

Remember that change is another stimulant of energy for whole-brained and right-brained folks. After you look at the same picture and chair in the same spot week after week, you fail to notice it very much. It becomes part of the expected pattern of things. At a time when life seems to be changing faster than you might wish, familiar surroundings can give you security and energy. But at other times, lack of change can breed monotony. Thus some people rearrange their furniture from time to time and bring in new pictures, books, and decorative items to stimulate a sense of renewal.

One particularly creative president, Peter Van Nort, did a rather revolutionary about-face with a traditional office:

"My present office setup evolved over a period of twelve years. My first step in moving away from the standard office came when I recognized that I did not like to have discussions with people across a desk. So the initial thing I did was to turn my desk to face a wall to make such conversations impossible. Then I created a general seating area in my office, with chairs surrounding a coffee table. I also added a tree to the office and gradually began to bring in personal mementos, things that triggered a reaction or questions from visitors to my office. These included framed finger paintings from a child, a patterned wall hanging, a model outhouse. Later I brought in one of my favorite books and laid it on the coffee table. The book has lots of photos with interesting phrases beneath them.

Furthermore, I have never liked sitting down at a desk to do my reading and paperwork; sitting all day long makes people groggy. So I replaced my desk with a drafting table where I can stand up and work. In the early 1980s, I also was concerned with stimulating ideas and motivation sharing among my staff and visitors to my office. I added items that would stimulate a conversation, and turned all my walls into whiteboard areas for brainstorming. These help me illustrate my ideas as I talk, and I welcome others to use the boards as well. Anyone who walks into my office can immediately tell that it is different and that I am open to fresh ideas. I guess the office has a startling effect on newcomers, such that it stimulates more informal and less conventional thinking.

The most recent items I have added are photos of my family and my collection of toys. The toys evolved with the concept of joy breaks. I have a model of a 1946 American Flyer train, a gyroscope, jacks, Silly Putty, finger puppets, and anything else that catches my fancy. Often I notice people fooling with the toys during a meeting, and I think that's good—it's a tension breaker."

As you can conclude from the examples above, it all comes down to knowing what kinds of offices and work styles will boost your energy and what saps it. You may already be aware of energy factors, both pro and con, in your current office. Looking back at the list of stimulants for your brain dominance can give you clues about your energy gains and drains.

If you are a top corporate leader, you may feel very nurtured and energized by your traditional corporate office and easily overlook the message. But look again and rethink with us. When you are at the top, you finally have permission to work in an office rich with leather furniture, beautiful woods, and tasteful art. The view is usually

inspiring. You are surrounded by awards, pictures, and mementos of your achievements and high points in your career. But go five levels down in the corporation and you may find sterile, look-alike cubicles with metal furniture and few or no pictures. Standard phones and calculators are visual reminders that the worker is not special, but one of many. Can you see why you might enjoy coming in early and staying late whereas the average worker might feel more like she or he is coming to a cell? If by starving the senses we starve the imagination and deplete the renewal of energy for ourselves and others, doesn't it make sense to empower and encourage our team to create a nurturing environment for themselves?

Designing a Whole-Brained Office Environment

Brain integration is another angle from which to approach the redesign of your office. Rather than create an area that reflects a heavy right- or left-brained proclivity, why not design elements of your office that will promote whole-brained thinking and behavior? A left-brained person can greatly benefit from having items that will stimulate his or her right brain as well, such as brightly colored folders, paper clips, tabs, and so forth. Anything that appeals to a sense of beauty or sense of humor will also engage the right brain, as will memorabilia from childhood. In addition, family photos, handmade objects from children, and anything else that evokes emotion will stimulate the right brain.

On the other hand, a right-brained person can redesign certain aspects of his or her office to increase the ability to stay organized. Some left-brain-oriented items that we use include colored files and folders, clipboards with "to-do" lists and "action items," calendars and schedules, boxes, shelves, containers, and briefcases. Visual people find it helps to use large clear-plastic boxes for all the files and research of a project while it is current. With a large label, it can't get misplaced and it's easily portable during the working life of the project. We use several brightly colored clipboards to keep up with pack lists, curriculum orders, and other working papers that are used by several people and, therefore, easily misplaced. We also keep different briefcases for different clients so they can be packed and ready prior to a trip without confusion.

The best way to get an accurate assessment of your individual energy gains and drains is to observe your response to all aspects of your work space. By simply becoming aware of these reactions, you can discover which aspects of your current environment are working for you and which are working against you. The second step is to bring extra high-energy items into your office. You may also choose to redecorate and rearrange your space as well.

The list of possible high-energy factors is almost limitless, but the following is a grouping of the major categories for you to consider:

■ personal items included in your work area (photos, art work, inspirational sayings, humorous and playful items, reminders of past achievements, favorite vacations, indicators of your outside interests, etc.);

■ overall visual aesthetics (color of walls, carpet, and decorations; style and condition of the furniture; existence of windows and quality of the scenery outside);

■ noise level (quiet office versus noise from the rest of the building; music you can or cannot control; noise from equipment);

■ furniture (Is it comfortable and effective? Does your chair give you a backache? Does your computer give you eyestrain? Is your typewriter efficient, or would the flexibility of a word processor be more than worth the cost difference?);

■ health factors (air quality, lighting, and temperature control);

■ atmosphere (What other settings does your office currently remind you of? What setting is one you would find appealing to work in—a secluded library nook? a clean, streamlined, high-tech research area? a plant-filled sunroom? a creative workroom?).

Office Environment Research Studies

Duane recently visited a landmark research facility studying a number of these office environment variables. The Environmental Simulation Laboratory (ESL) at the University of California at Irvine is the first full-scale university laboratory for the study of office space. It tests workers' reactions to a multitude of environmental factors. For example, the ESL has blood pressure and pulse-testing equipment so that physiological effects can be measured. Soon it will measure adrenaline levels as well. Researchers have also come up with several different yardsticks of productivity, including performance speed

Not only is it true that worker performance on the job is enhanced by attention to the environment, but the converse is also true: nonattention to the environment can lower performance.

and accuracy. Worker morale and mood are also being examined. Explains director Daniel Stokols, "We want to see how these stress levels correlate with changes in the work environment, such as whether people are put near plants, away from plants, whether they're crowded together in a bull pen or more separated with some privacy. We think that those kinds of alterations of the space of an office can have important effects on physiological arousal and stress."

Some of the elements that will be considered at ESL are how close workers can be to one another and still be comfortable; whether they need to see other workers; the ideal degree of enclosure around a work station; whether the space as a whole would benefit from natural lighting; and whether music should be playing in the whole office or only in certain areas.

In the March 1986 issue of *New Age Journal*, Sandy McDonald reported a six-year study done by the Buffalo Organization for Social and Technological Innovation (BOSTI). BOSTI's research indicated that a better-designed environment can increase employee performance to the financial equivalent of 15% of each person's yearly salary. MacDonald writes, "After studying six thousand workers in more than one hundred offices nationwide, BOSTI's researchers determined that, with depreciation, employers could invest about $8,000 per professional in work-environment improvements (above and beyond normal operating costs) and still come out ahead."

Not only is it true that worker performance on the job is enhanced by attention to the environment, but the converse is also true: nonattention to the environment can lower performance. Jean Stellman, co-author of *Work Is Dangerous to Your Health*, writes,

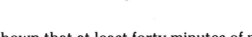

"Research has shown that at least forty minutes of productive time are lost each day because of poor workplace design."

Another fact that comes up repeatedly in research is that the more people are separated behind closed doors, walls, and other barriers, the poorer communication is. After studying this research, Duane decided to move his work space from a partner's desk we shared on the second floor to an open-area work space shared by four production staff. After trying this arrangement for several months, we decided to make it a permanent change because of the increase in communication. Working side by side with production staff, Duane was able to catch misunderstandings due to unclear instructions and misinterpretation.

Permission to "Break the Rules" Energizes Your Environment

As a part of our research, my husband and I have been experimenting with our living spaces at home. We had one of those traditional living rooms with a small grand piano in a lovely bay window surrounded by a blue silk sofa, two formal French Provincial chairs, and a heavy gold coffee table. It was elegant and lovely—and rarely used. Our daughter, Cathy, would go there to play the piano and her dad would come to sit and listen. But other than that, it only got used for parties too large for other rooms to hold all the guests and for Christmas.

We began to wonder how we could use this space so that it would be more inviting, more energizing. My husband loves music and had played the saxophone and clarinet as a boy. At age fourteen he played professionally in a jazz group, but had since given it up. He decided to buy a used clarinet and enjoy playing again. I bought a used set of drums. We added a large bass fiddle and a synthesizer. An antique armoire now holds the various music cases, a library of music, my tap shoes, top hat, and silver wig. In the corner is an old wooden pony cart filled with stuffed animals and dolls. There are several tall captain's chairs upholstered in antique silk tapestry to invite guests to join in the fun of singing along or just becoming a lively audience. As a spoof, there is even a tin cup to invite tips for the musicians.

Now about once a week we enjoy an evening of music following an informal dinner. And often at mid-day someone wanders in to enjoy a few idle moments of making music on one instrument or another. Guests at first are amazed, amused, and generally puzzled by this unusual arrangement of musical instruments, toys, and furniture. But soon, they are infected by fun and permission to become a kid again and enjoy the playful part of themselves.

Now this won't be the perfect environment for your home or office. But discovering what will invite joy and generate a new enthusiasm and commitment for your work can be a delightful adventure worth taking. If you fear that others will discount you for breaking the norms of conventional office arrangements, share these energy strategies with them and perhaps they will soon realize that you are on the cutting edge of change, setting the pace for increased energy and innovation in the work place.

> 66 *Here's a whole-brained practical joke on the world's left-brainers. Keep one drawer of your desk empty and each night stuff (and I do mean* stuff *) everything from your desk in it—pencils, papers, files, paper clips, coffee mugs, the works. Your desk is immaculate and only you know the truth. The risk: if you are going to be away for a few days, be sure to rinse your coffee cup—a giant spore may take over your office if you're gone long enough.* 99
>
> —**David A. Wilson**
> **National Director, Professional Development**
> **Ernst & Young**

Summary

1. Scientific research validates the impact of environment on energy, productivity, and stress.

2. Typically, top corporate leaders have permission to enrich and personalize their office environments. They consistently seem to have more energy and motivation, too. On the contrary, lower-level employee work spaces are usually much less imaginative and personalized; energy and motivation often suffer from this.

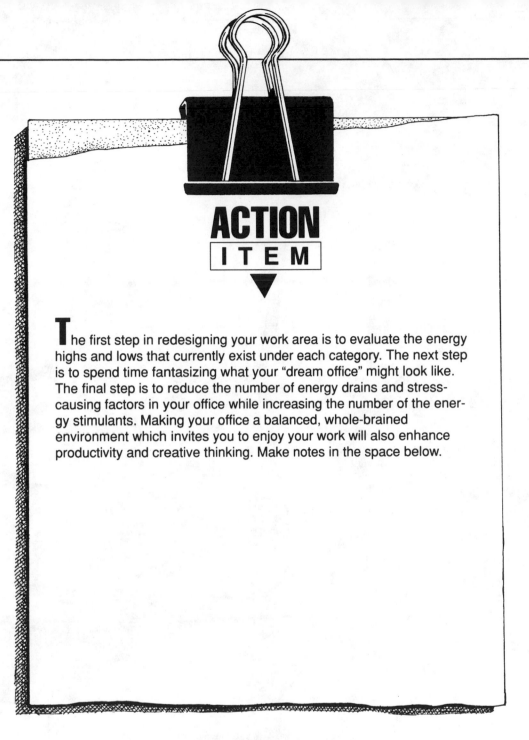

ACTION
I T E M

The first step in redesigning your work area is to evaluate the energy highs and lows that currently exist under each category. The next step is to spend time fantasizing what your "dream office" might look like. The final step is to reduce the number of energy drains and stress-causing factors in your office while increasing the number of the energy stimulants. Making your office a balanced, whole-brained environment which invites you to enjoy your work will also enhance productivity and creative thinking. Make notes in the space below.

3. You have more control over your environment than you think. Adding colorful folders and accessories, artwork, playful items, family photos, and anything that evokes positive emotion will stimulate fresh energy. Getting out of mental ruts can increase your energy, too.

4. Most people have more control over their home environment than their offices, so you may want to evaluate your home to discover its high-energy possibilities.

17

IMAGING:

Daydreaming as a Source of Energy

> ❝ It's a matter of attitude, thinking like a winner. The most significant techniques we teach are inner talk and visualization. Get those butterflies in your stomach flying in formation. ❞
>
> —Judy Foster, *The Mental Athlete*

> ❝ Imaging gives me a formal start to the day. If you don't set out a plan for your day, the day tends to control you more than you control it. ❞
>
> —Ed Platt, Manager of Generations
> Eastern Gas Plants, TU Electric

> ❝ I have often been afraid, but I would not give in to it. I simply acted as though I was not afraid, and presently the fear disappeared. ❞
>
> —Theodore Roosevelt

> ❝ What you can do is limited only by what you can dream. ❞
>
> —Dick Rutan, *Voyager* pilot

One of the most powerful, energizing techniques you can apply to your work day is *imaging,* or visualizing. This mental exercise is a well-established practice among Olympic and professional athletes, and it is quickly gaining popularity in the business world as well. Author Tom Peters (*In Search of Excellence*, *A Passion for Excellence*, *Thriving on Chaos*) has mentioned forms of imaging in his books, as have Michael Ray and Rochelle Myers, the authors of *Creativity in Business*, and many other business and creativity professionals. Here's how it works.

Suppose you are waking up on a beautiful, sunny Saturday morning. You think about all the fun you will enjoy that day, alone and with your friends, playing golf, planting flowers in the garden, hiking in a state park, or lying in a hammock reading a good novel. You are filled with anticipation and energy as you throw back the covers to start the day.

Now presume that you are waking up on an icy, gray Wednesday. The news on the radio tells of dozens of accidents piling up on the freeways. You visualize a long, tedious drive to work with many traffic delays. You feel tired before you even get out of bed, and you slump to the shower in a bellicose mood. Once at work, you review your schedule, grumbling about your back-to-back meetings and the unfinished report decaying on your desk. Your energy sags even more.

But what if you were to receive a surprise call from your honey inviting you to spend an all-expense-paid weekend at a nearby ski resort? Might your mood and energy level instantly shift, allowing you to enthusiastically attack all your projects with the knowledge that a wonderful reward was waiting for you in a few days?

For most people, the answer is yes. What you anticipate, or vividly imagine, will directly affect not only your energy but your performance as well. Research in psychoneuroimmunology indicates that our brain actually produces chemicals that can either add to or block and drain our energy and our performance. Just as adrenaline gives us an instant boost of energy, so can endorphins and a multitude of other self-induced neuro chemicals affect our physical and mental states. In addition, under negative stress and pressure the brain signals the release of chemicals which block the immune system, making us more vulnerable to disease and cloudy thinking. You can take control of this process, however, by becoming aware of and guiding the images you create.

Roger Peterson in *USA Today* has reported that "Skaters, skiers, triathletes, and a host of Olympians tell us each night on television how they visualize their winning performances. It may sound like a snow job, but the sports psychology techniques could make us all winners, if we applied them." During the 1988 summer Olympics, many athletes discussed their use of imaging to mentally rehearse (and, in essence, experience) a perfect dive, a flawless skating routine, a winning race, and so forth. This technique works because *the brain does not distinguish between a "real" physical experience and an imagined one.*

What you anticipate, or vividly imagine, will directly affect not only your energy but your performance as well.

Thus if an athlete fears giving a bad performance and visualizes what it would be like, he or she is actually programming the brain to repeat that bad performance.

Gold-medal diver Greg Louganis is an avid believer in the power of imaging. He adds relaxing music to his practice of visualizing perfect dives. In fact, he mentally rehearses each dive approximately forty times prior to the actual performance. Then, when he prepares for the real dive, he simply replays the music in his mind and dives to the sound of it. In this way he avoids losing his pacing under the pressure of competition.

Louganis's use of music is important because calming music is an effective tool to help induce a state of alpha. Alpha is a slowed-down level of brain waves, approximately eight to thirteen waves per second, that relaxes people and "awakens" the subconscious. For best results, imaging should be done in this relaxed alpha state when the human mind is most open to suggestion and most capable of dissolving fatigue.

Imprinting Failure or Success

Actually, you already know how to do imaging and probably do it regularly. You practice it whenever you worry and dwell on problems. Unfortunately, this is imaging backwards, preparing yourself for failure.

Anytime you worry about a future event, you are imaging. Remember that imaging is simply reviewing or rehearsing mentally a past or future occurrence or action. Some people do this with words such as "My boss will never approve this" or "I don't know how I'm going to make it through the meeting without losing my temper." Other people focus on mental pictures, such as the image of themselves stuttering and losing their place while giving a speech. Feelings, sounds, tastes, and smells add even more impact to the images. When people dwell on their worries and fears, another negative reaction occurs. Visualizing a negative event invites the brain to imprint the expectation and sight of this event. What results is a method of subconscious programming that may affect its true outcome. Can you recall when you last voiced or visualized a fear? Do you practice this kind of backward imaging on a daily basis?

Our point here is to establish the fact that you already are quite skilled at the art of imaging, even if you use it in a disabling rather than an empowering way. But if you become aware of when you are imaging your worries and fears and choose to either replace those negative thoughts with positive ones or with possible solutions to the problem, you can create an energy gain out of an energy loss. Thus, learning to replace these negative

mental habits with positive counterparts is an important aspect of high-energy maintenance.

But before you learn the process of imaging, let us warn you to be patient with yourself and not to worry if you can't block all your imaging of fears and guilt right away. It takes lots of practice to become good at it, and imaging fear seems to come easier to people than visualizing success. The first step is simply paying more attention to your random thoughts and becoming aware when you are worrying, then choosing to replace these thoughts with an equally vivid positive expectation. You might ask yourself, "What would it be like if the best possible things happened?"

The Process of Imaging

We recommend a several-step method of imaging, with energy benefits linked to each step. In order to place you in control of the process, we'll explain the how and why behind each of the steps.

1. **Prepare your body through relaxation.** First, get into a comfortable position. Also, if you want to listen to slow, calming music (such as classical baroque pieces like "Largo," the Pachebel canon, or the contemporary selection "Zamfir"), turn it on. Then follow this procedure:

   - Stretch, yawn, or shake out any stiffness in your body.

   - Close your eyes, if possible, to give you privacy and block visual interference.

   - Focus on taking long, slow, deep breaths.

   - Allow your body to utterly relax, and put any worries out of your mind. As you breathe slowly and drift into a state of relaxation, your brain waves will move into the alpha field, allowing an integration of your logical self (left brain hemisphere) and your imaginative, emotional self (right hemisphere). Listening to the music will also help you synchronize your brain waves, heartbeat, and breathing into a relaxed, rhythmic flow.

   - Focus on the process of deep breathing for a few minutes. Enjoy the volume of pure, fresh air coming into your lungs. Visualize your blood becoming oxygen-rich, your brain receiving increased oxygen. And as you exhale, visualize the toxins of stress and pressure leaving your body along with any fatigue, discomfort, or pain you may be experiencing. If you want to create a visual metaphor for this, such as dark smog or dirt being blown out of a vacuum cleaner, you can increase your brain's response to the process. As you inhale, visualize pure, fresh air coming in and revitalizing your body.

By learning to take slow, deep, controlled breaths, your brain waves will become synchronized to your heartbeat and blood pressure, letting the brain and body become aligned. And by getting yourself in sync mentally and physically, you will have more power over the experience.

2. **Prepare your mind by releasing anxieties.** The next step is to take a mental trip to a favorite place. Visualize the environment in detail—its colors, textures, emotions, tastes, smells, sounds, and so forth. Think of the good feelings you had there, the moments of success, love, fun, or spiritual renewal. Really free yourself to be there again. However, if you wish, you can change any details, such as your age, who you are with, and what happens. What is important is to make your fantasies as rich, pleasant, and supportive as possible.

   When creating vivid images of positive events, you will cause your brain to release a cocktail of natural chemicals such as endorphins, which were released during the initial experience. The body enjoys the results of reliving the experience. And with these brain chemicals come not only new energy but a boost to your immune system as well.

3. **Imprint scenes of success in your mind.** Now you are ready to plant, or imprint, images of daily habits of successful performances that will lead to optimum energy. If you are trying to change your life-style into a healthier mode of living, you might start by seeing yourself waking early and enjoying a brisk walk. Then see yourself eating a nutritious breakfast and having a relaxing commute to the office. Then go through your day, visualizing habits that will enhance your energy, such as taking frequent joy breaks, appreciating yourself and others for what goes right, using humor to defuse stress, and drinking six to eight glasses of water.

   Or you might want to visualize your success at something. If you are studying a new computer program or a foreign language, see yourself enthusiastically learning and utilizing your new skill. Or if you are preparing a presentation at work, visualize yourself successfully giving the talk. Feel yourself being confident and calm, see your listeners giving you nods of approval, and hear your voice speaking clearly and smoothly. Focus on all the clues and signals which would indicate that you have been highly successful and received with enthusiasm.

4. **Reward yourself with a mental vacation.** We also recommend putting a good balance of play, celebration, and simple enjoyment into your imaging sessions. If you use imaging only to visualize yourself accomplishing a goal, you give

yourself no permission to play and relax. But by including images of yourself relaxing and playing, you will automatically look for ways to bring a healthy balance into your life.

When to Use Imaging

Imaging can be very helpful in changing your mental set. The term "mental set" refers to the attitude you choose to take regarding a certain task or that you experience both immediately before and after the task. Your mental set is another, more subtle form of imaging that most people overlook. But like imaging, your mental set can have an enormous impact on both your energy and your performance.

If the ideas in the Action Item on the following page sound familiar, that's because we also discussed attitude shifts in relation to *dualistic thinking*. There we discussed how forcing yourself to do something you've decided you won't like drains energy and throws your right and left brain hemispheres into opposition. Practicing visualizing exercises is, therefore, another way of achieving synergy between your right and left brain hemispheres. Visualizing is just another way of addressing the same problem, another solution to attitude-linked energy losses.

Here's how Loren V. Sprouse, district manager of AT&T's Southern Region, changed a negative mental set using positive visualization:

> *"I needed to write a lengthy report during a time when I was already experiencing a work overload. I estimated that it would take several days to complete. I even considered asking someone else on my staff to do it for me, but I couldn't figure out how to get the information from my head to another's without writing down nearly all the details myself. Rather than begin with the project in this dualistic mind set, I decided to attempt writing the project in a different way.*
>
> *First I tried visualizing what the finished report would look like and how it should be organized. I imagined writing down my ideas as if I were being interviewed by someone. I had an 'a-ha' kind of insight about formatting the report in a question-and-answer style, with myself considering what kinds of questions my readers most wanted to know about the issue, and in what order those questions would logically flow. Another important insight*

ACTION
I T E M

Run a test on the mental sets operating in your own life. Simply select a task that you usually do not enjoy. Check your mood and attitude just prior to the task. How long does it take to talk yourself into starting the project? How quickly and efficiently do you perform it? Do you find yourself making more mistakes on it compared with other projects? Could attitude possibly be the reason for more mistakes? Do you find yourself fighting to keep your concentration glued to the task at hand? How do you feel when you've finally finished?

Now compare this mental set with one you have about something you relish doing. Ask yourself the same questions and contrast your two sets of responses. Also compare the different energy output that you experience.

The next time you plan to start an initially undesirable task, try reframing your mental set. Spend a few minutes just before you begin it to consider all the positive reasons for doing a quality job. Even if the task is not particularly enjoyable for you, you can maintain an energy-building attitude toward it if you remind yourself of the overall importance of your task to the rest of your team. Or consider what it might indicate if you did not have this task to do. For instance, you may not enjoy creating a prospective budget for a new client. But if you didn't have that new client, you might not have such a respectable sales quota for the month.

I had was to try dictating my thoughts rather than putting them on paper because dictation comes easier for me than writing.

I had never imagined being able to dictate a first draft of a policy paper that was this complex. Yet to my amazement I had a respectable first draft after about forty-five minutes. Another helpful technique I used was mind-mapping to bring forth and tie together my thoughts. Later, as I read through the typed copy of the report that my secretary produced, I was surprised to find that very few revisions were needed. I wondered how many other jobs I might have accomplished in one-half or one-quarter of the usual time using this new method. Since then, I have used this method with equal success for several different writing projects."

After trying the imaging technique described in the next Action Item for a few days, notice how you feel when you arrive home. You will probably feel more deserving of and ready for a restful, pleasant evening, because you will gain inner permission to relax by realizing how much effort has gone toward your work day. You will also pick up energy by re-experiencing your wins for that day.

On the other hand, if you focus on what you didn't get accomplished or what you did poorly that day, you will probably arrive home feeling anxious and undeserving of relaxation. You might push yourself to try and get caught up by working several hours that evening. But too often when we try this, fatigue and/or resentment impairs our work. In addition, without a chance to unwind and restore our energy reserves, we arrive at work the next day feeling burned out. So if your evenings are lacking in fun and relaxation, this imaging exercise is a key step toward granting yourself permission to change your evenings by changing your mental set.

Other Times to Practice Imaging

People go through two alpha windows, or natural periods of experiencing alpha brain waves, at least twice each day: once when they awaken and again as they drift off into sleep. Thus, what you choose to dwell on during these alpha periods becomes powerfully imprinted in your memory because your mind is far more open to suggestion, or imprinting, in alpha than in the normal beta state. For instance, can you recall waking to a particular song on the radio? Then off and on for the rest of the day, did you continue to hear that song in your mind? Or you may have awakened from a troubling dream and felt the haunting mood of the dream linger for many hours.

In addition to the morning and evening exercises suggested in the Action Items, there are other great opportunities for imaging. One is when you wake up at night and are trying to get back to sleep. When that happens, you may be experiencing some

Spend a few minutes at the end of the project to imprint again all the positives of the project. Think of these as two positive mental "bookends" that come immediately before and after your task performance. Mental set can make an enormous difference by creating whole-brained synergy as a foundation for your work.

painful memory that keeps you awake. But whatever the reason, if you can gently guide your mind toward a positive image, you can create a good experience out of these wakeful minutes. Positive visualizing will help you fall back to sleep with a beneficial mind set. But if you stay awake for a long period of time, comfort yourself with the knowledge that research has proven that your body can get the same benefits from positive imaging and relaxing as from sleep.

Another way to take advantage of those wide-awake times at night is to get out of bed and harvest your thoughts. Suppose you wake with your mind racing, focusing on all the things you want to accomplish during the next day or week. If you quietly retire to your study or kitchen table and write down your thoughts as they pour out, you may be able to get two hours worth of work done in much less time. Simply stay with your thoughts until your mind empties or until you feel ready for sleep again. Usually the process of recording these thoughts will reassure your mind that you will act upon them, and then you will be at peace to sleep again.

Visualizing can also be done in connection with energy breaks at the office. For some other examples of when, how, and why to incorporate imaging into your new, high-energy life-style, here are several personal stories attesting to its effectiveness. Ed Platt, manager of generations for Eastern Gas Plants, TU Electric, had these comments:

> *"Imaging is a very powerful tool, and I use it in several key ways. First, I usually start my morning off with an imaging exercise. I lie in bed for a few minutes, reflecting on my plans for the day. I imagine the things I want to accomplish and I review the projects I have scheduled.*
>
> *I also use imaging as a rehearsal for all important meetings and presentations that I make. I'll do up to half a dozen imaging*

ACTION ITEM

Imaging on Your Way Home from Work

As you travel home from work (or if your office is at home, choose a time toward the end of your work day), spend a few minutes recalling only the positives of your day. Think of the goals you accomplished as well as the healthy habits you practiced, the nice conversation you had with a friend, the compliments you received on a recent project, the new idea you came up with, and so forth.

At first it may be difficult for you to congratulate yourself on the good aspects of the day rather than worrying about problems or disappointments that surfaced. If so, this will show you how unaccustomed you are to revisiting your wins. Yet imaging the positives is a highly effective habit of peak performers. Think of it as a mental dress rehearsal for future performances. Also, remember that your subconscious mind cannot tell the difference between a real experience and a remembered one. So to recall a win is like reliving it again. And if your mind insists on thinking about what you did wrong or badly, replay that experience, doing it correctly this time.

sessions where I visualize the results that I hope to get and the impression I hope to make. For example, I will see myself remaining calm and positive during a potentially difficult or emotional encounter, like a difficult employee evaluation. I'll hear the conversation, see the other person's reactions and the way I look, the body language I use. I'll image the decisions that are made. Then I let my subconscious mind work on this image as I go through the rest of the day. And by the time the real meeting takes place, my body and mind feel prepared.

The few times I haven't gotten the results I wanted, I have followed up by replaying the scene in my head, but visualizing the results I wanted to have. That way I'll be better prepared next time."

Bob Gary, a Texas Utilities executive, describes how he uses imaging:

"The big thing I learned about imaging is that the eyes are virtually an extension of the brain. But your eyes don't have to be open for your brain to receive powerful messages from it. It's like breathing in the sense that you can do it unconsciously, or if you think about it and control it to give you a higher level of oxygen . . . and energy, then it will be that much more refreshing an experience.

On the average, I practice imaging at least two to three times a day. Often I do it in the morning or later at home in the privacy of my study. But I do it whenever I feel the need to. I have learned to capture beautiful sights, like when I'm on vacation or during the holidays when my family is gathered together. I say to myself, 'This would be a great imaging sight to save,' and I [imprint] the sight in my mind, because it really sticks.

One of the most effective times I used imaging to change my mental set and give me positive energy was when I was scheduled to give a sworn deposition for a major lawsuit. I knew it was going to be a potentially intimidating experience because we expected TV cameras, lots of attorneys and reporters, and days of questioning. Plus I was going to be the first person from my company to testify. I wanted to set a good example, to turn it from a negative to a positive experience for myself and those who would come after me. So I decided to spend a lot of time imaging how I would like to appear and how I wanted the proceedings to go for me.

I visualized playing every question put to me as if it were a major poker hand with high stakes on it. I would either win or lose the biggest poker game of my life based on that hand. I also decided to dress up for the occasion, to look my best, to project lots of energy, and to turn the cameras into a plus. My opponents expected me to be wary of the cameras, but I insisted that we not start until the cameras were in place. That kind of unnerved the other side.

The questioning went on for two weeks. Instead of feeling drained and stressed out, by the end of the third day my opponents and the attorneys were asking me where I got all my energy and confidence. I was a good fifteen years older than them, but they were bushed at the end of each day. But I had more fun testifying because I went in there with a positive attitude, and I applied what I know about maintaining energy and a sense of humor. The whole experience was actually an energy gain for me."

In the following case study you will hear how a creative servant/leader used imaging over and over again to help his team create a vision and overcome impossible odds in achieving an impressive success. Notice the many ways in which the problem (recovering from a major industrial fire in record time) became an opportunity and positive imaging changed the beliefs which significantly increased the energy of the participants. Notice too that the imaging he created with his team all was brought about through typical business practices done in atypical, creative ways. T. L. Thompson, manager of support services at TU Electric, tells this story:

"In February, 1987, we experienced a major fire in one of our power plants. It destroyed all the major electrical components in the unit, which are used to furnish us with supplemental electricity during the peak summer months.

The recovery period for this type of destruction is typically very long. Even if the crews worked overtime and on weekends, at least nine to twelve months would be the anticipated time needed for repairs. The problem of rebuilding our plant was compounded by its age, which meant that all the replacement equipment had to be re-engineered. Also, half a million wires and cables needed to be hooked up to the replacement equipment.

We also knew that if we did not get the plant on line by mid-July we would have to buy the supplemental power from another company. So we set July 1 as our target date to be back in operation. At our first staff meeting, I wrote 'July 1' on the board and asked each manager to write down the single obstacle that would most likely prevent us from reaching that goal. Most wrote 'engineering,' so I took over that assignment to show my commitment and belief that our objectives were possible. And in the face of lots of advice from top experts saying that we could not possibly meet the deadline, we decided to go for it.

We selected the members of our recovery team based on several factors: their knowledge of our operation, their ability to supply goods and services, and, most important, their attitude about our potential to achieve our July 1 goal. We ended up hiring five corporations to supply our major needs. We sat down with the top people and first got their commitment to do everything in their power to meet our objectives. Some said, 'Well, it's never been done before, but we'll do all we can to get there.'

Another critical step we took when choosing our team was to identify the special 'window of opportunity' available to each company. We knew that one of the firms, for example, wanted the opportunity to improve its track record and reputation within our company. By doing an especially high-quality performance on this project, the firm could achieve this objective. I promised to share my evaluation of its performance with others throughout our company.

A second firm had done maintenance work for us but not construction work. Its future objective was to move into that field, so we awarded it the construction contract along with the opportunity to show its ability in that area.

When choosing our internal team for the recovery project, we started off by discussing both the problems and the opportunities. But we focused more on the benefits that this project could bring us, and I asked the team to list our own windows of opportunity. Their answers included developing the expertise of our

ACTION
ITEM

Morning Exercise

Upon waking, gently review your day in sequence, imaging it to be as positive and beneficial as it could possibly be. Include some fun breaks, too, as well as the healthy life-style habits that you would like to acquire. As you visualize your day, see others responding to you in supportive ways. It is fascinating to discover that as we imagine others reacting positively to us, they very often do end up behaving that way. We may not have been aware that our body language and other subconscious forms of communication were contributing to their previously negative reactions to us.

If you have a tendency to fall back to sleep while doing this exercise, try getting out of bed gently. Either sit in a chair or begin your morning routine while you do your imaging. You might even try imaging while you are getting showered and dressed in the morning. Breathe deeply during this time, and do not listen to the news or talk to anyone. A tape of alpha-oriented music is also helpful to maintain a relaxing state of mind. In fact, some people report that a warm morning shower is such an excellent setting for their imaging exercise that they call it "doing their morning mantra."

personnel, building credibility among personnel, and building relationships among staff both internally and externally.

But we still had to design a formal plan for putting our objectives and opportunities into real life. We created different teams to brainstorm on new and faster ways of accomplishing the job, since the normal methods of attacking the problem would not let us meet our deadline. One novel solution was for the construction personnel to create their schedule by planning backwards from the July 1 due date. On the engineering side, we decided that by handpicking the top-qualified professionals in the field, we could control our quality and goods and services enough to eliminate 50% of the normal review process. We also moved everyone in the design stage to the site of the project rather than having them work from their out-of-town offices, which increased efficiency. A third unconventional method was to put the construction management people in charge of the engineering schedule.

In addition, every Friday the head of the engineering company flew to Dallas and reviewed the week's progress. He and I made independent evaluations, then compared our notes over lunch. Sometimes our assessments agreed, sometimes not. We also had a meeting with his engineering staff each Friday to discuss our evaluation and to keep them focused on our goals. This frequent contact gave his personnel a great career-enhancement opportunity as well by giving them a chance to work closely with the president of their company. That provided another energy boost for them.

As far as positive imaging goes, I already had my philosophy on visualization in process before the fire. I believe that no one goes for a day without visualizing—you either image the negatives or the positives. Of course, at first I had to do some of both, because you can't just focus on the roses and not see the weeds threatening to overtake your garden. But you can visualize those weeds being removed in a positive fashion. And I clearly visualized the positive objectives for all of the support staff. And once you have a vision, you can come up with your 'to-do' list to make it happen. I also realized the potential for a mid-project letdown, so I imaged those things that would keep 600 people all working happily at something they believed in. My main energy source during this period was the strengthening of relationships with our people and our support companies.

From a morale-building standpoint, one very positive thing was the creation of a pep-rally atmosphere at the plant. We hung banners saying, 'July or Bust.' And some entrepreneurs

designed and sold items such as 'July 1' tee shirts that many employees wore. The enthusiasm was infectious, from the top to the bottom of the employee ladder. In fact, the degree of commitment and enthusiasm from our people was probably the most important factor in reaching our goal.

Furthermore, there was no such thing as suggesting a solution that would not support our July 1 goal. At our daily management meetings, we strictly considered only those steps that had to be taken to achieve our objective. Still, I'd say that before June 1, about 50% of our people truly believed we would make our goal while 50% hoped we would. But by June 1, when most of our equipment and cables were in place, everyone realized that our goal was very feasible and the excitement level hit a high. We all felt a buildup akin to the William Tell overture.

Then we had a minor setback a few days before July 1. A freak fire occurred in one of the transformers. It could have been a major catastrophe, but we located a transformer that would fit our unit, and it was installed within four days. Although this pushed us five days outside our initial goal, we still had the power plant ready for the July 15 energy peak. We considered our record-breaking efforts as a great success. We *held congratulatory dinners and did many other things to personally thank everyone for their super efforts.*

The final result is that the plant has run as well as any of our other units, plus it had fewer start-up problems than normally occur. Choosing a team of high-quality people was one reason for our success. But having 600 people working on a project means dealing with the average worker, too. I believe that our above-average performance came from the positive attitudes and enthusiasm that spread through the entire work force."

ACTION ITEM

End-of-the-Day Exercise

At the close of the evening, as you are drifting into sleep, guide yourself through a review of the day. Focus on the positive events. If you come to a memory of something you don't feel was your best effort, skip over it. The first step is to reinforce positive experiences. Next, allow your mind to consider any negative events, but this time imagine them as you wish they had been. This step provides a mental rehearsal for the next time the opportunity presents itself, which may be tomorrow or later that week.

As you go through this second step, though, be careful not to be judgmental or to revive whatever harmful emotions you felt that day. Emotions felt while remembering something add power to the imprinting. So if you think about failing to win a new account, for example, and you let yourself feel self-anger or resentment or a drop in confidence, you have just imprinted an expectation of these emotions and the accompanying behavior.

If you still feel sufficiently awake to proceed to a third step, look into the future and imagine what you would most like to happen for you in one, three, or five years. Be inventive, outrageous, and have fun with this. You can get enormous energy and drive by creating vivid pictures of your dreams. In fact, depression, which is a dramatic energy blocker, frequently is linked to a person's inability to imagine good things happening in the future.

Summary

1. Research shows that the mental images you entertain while in a relaxed state will directly influence your performance.

2. You already know how to do imaging, and you do it regularly. Whenever you worry or dwell on problems, you are imaging "backwards"—you are mentally rehearsing for problems and disappointments to occur. However, learning to image positively will make a significant difference in your energy, motivation, and future performance.

3. You can easily learn to image positively by relaxing your body, clearing your mind, and imprinting scenes of success in your mind. A last step in imaging is to reward yourself with a mental vacation. This is important because it balances your expectation for successful work with permission for refreshing play. You can do this mental exercise with or without slow-paced music.

4. Mental set is the attitude you choose for a task just before and just after it. Think of mental set as two bookends surrounding a task. By carefully reframing your mental set with positive expectation, you can significantly improve your performance level.

5. There are two important times in the day—on first waking in the morning and going to sleep in the evening—when it is important to have positive images present in your mind. In these natural times of alpha, your brain is highly susceptible to suggestion, so you will want to specifically guide your thoughts toward positive outcomes.

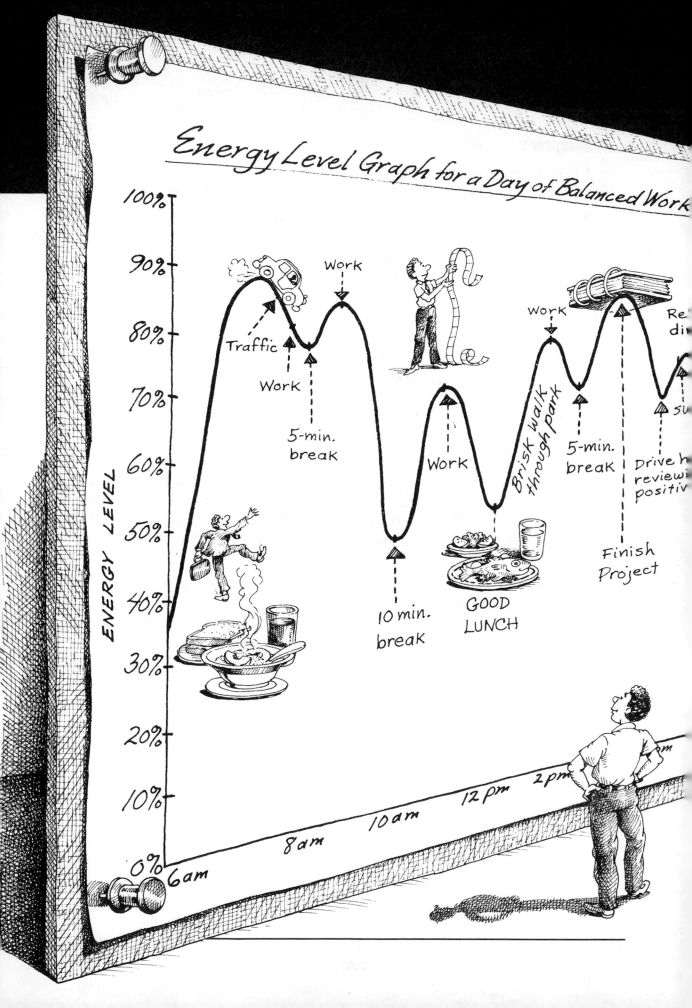

18

CHARTING YOUR ENERGY PLAN

66 *It is important to allow yourself to have some fun. Don't be afraid to have fun with people sometimes. I always try to have something close at hand to anticipate, such as a visit with a friend. Sometimes I will shop for books during a work break—I love to browse through shelves for ten minutes. Or at lunch I might go look at a new tennis racket I'd like to have. Using these short breaks to get away briefly from the office and its problems is especially helpful when you are having a tough day. I also recommend a break for a short walk around the block if you reach a mental roadblock. It is amazing how well a walk will clear your mind and bring back your enthusiasm.* 99

—**Jerry Farrington, Chairman and CEO, Texas Utilities**

66 *Men are made strong not by winning easy battles, but by losing hard-fought ones.* 99

—**Dick Bass, *Seven Summits***

his chapter will show you a way to analyze and discover your energy patterns over a typical day and week. The next step is to create ways to infuse positive energy into down times. In our research we noted that high performers such as Jerry Farrington consistently gave themselves permission to claim new energy before current reserves were depleted.

For example, if you enjoy weekends but not your job, the obvious need is to do something to make your job more satisfying and energizing. Changing your work space, adding more appealing tools to work with, taking energy breaks through the day, or going back to school to add skills so you can qualify for a more challenging, enjoyable job are a few strategies to consider.

If you start high on energy on Monday and steadily go down to a low on Friday, you may need some fun to look forward to and renew you through the week. Enjoying a hobby in the evenings, taking a fun course at a community college, and enjoying aerobic exercise with a friend or mate are a few ways to creatively counter this drain.

The primary goal is to step back and look for the bigger picture in regard to your energy. Over the year there may be high- and low-energy periods. The time of the year when you prepare

ACTION
I T E M

▼

You may want to quickly chart a profile of your energy level during an average day on the graph below.

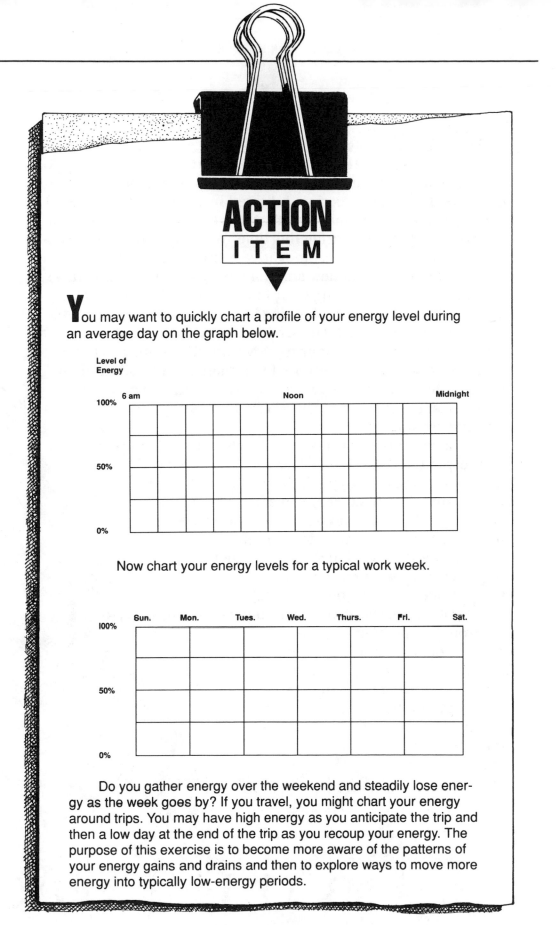

Level of Energy

	6 am					Noon					Midnight

100%

50%

0%

Now chart your energy levels for a typical work week.

	Sun.	Mon.	Tues.	Wed.	Thurs.	Fri.	Sat.

100%

50%

0%

Do you gather energy over the weekend and steadily lose energy as the week goes by? If you travel, you might chart your energy around trips. You may have high energy as you anticipate the trip and then a low day at the end of the trip as you recoup your energy. The purpose of this exercise is to become more aware of the patterns of your energy gains and drains and then to explore ways to move more energy into typically low-energy periods.

budgets may take lots of emotional energy and typically cause you to be tense and testy. If you plan ahead and enter this period in excellent mental and physical shape and then plan some fun or treats through this period, followed by a wonderful weekend vacation reward, you may find that you can totally change your energy to high levels during this time. You will also have the bonus of a creative, flexible, innovative attitude to bring to your team and of wonderful new solutions to typically draining tasks.

A final idea is to bring your family and/or business team into thinking about and planning long term for energy in typically low-energy times. Think of money management as a metaphor. If you just spend your money until it's gone, you have far fewer options than you do if you plan ahead and think of the big picture. And the more you practice these creative strategies, the less time you will find you spend in low-energy slumps.

Remember that it is important to listen to your body and respond to what it is telling you. You may need to take a long weekend to just relax and do nothing to allow yourself to become renewed. Don't feel guilty about this or think that you should always be bouncing with abundant energy. Rather, seek out balancing states that bring your life the richness that feels right for you. A lazy, relaxed weekend may be wonderful and pleasurable. But this can be very different from just landing in a tired, depressed heap after a whirlwind week. It's fun to discover how many positive choices we have with regard to energy and balancing our energy. The choice is there for each of us!

BURNOUT

Study the two charts in this chapter to see how productive a balanced work/break schedule can be compared with an all-work/burnout schedule. Using breaks as periodic energy replenishers and as rewards for completing a segment of work, you can maintain a good level of productivity and motivation throughout the day. And by the close of the work day, you will not only have enough energy left to enjoy your family and other activities (such as hobbies, reading, journal writing, etc.), you will also feel entitled to a break in the evening because you will feel satisfied with the amount of work you have accomplished that day.

Just the reverse is true when you fall into an exhausting and guilt-ridden all-work spiral. This is how the scenario often goes. Instead of taking a restorative break at 10:00 or 11:00 a.m. when your concentration and interest start to decline, you admonish yourself and push on. But the longer you work, the lower the quality and quantity of your output. You drink cup after cup of coffee in an attempt to stay alert, but that makes you feel more jittery than invigorated.

By lunch you aren't as far along on your project as you had hoped, so you refuse the offer to go to lunch with your work partners. Finally, you give in to hunger and fatigue at 1:30, but only take time to get a fatty fast-foods burger at an outlet around the block. In fifteen minutes you are back to work. Your energy hasn't really been restored because you worry about your work the entire time you're away. Nor has your stress diminished because you ate so fast you couldn't relax. You work through the afternoon feeling tired, distracted, and disgruntled. Several times you have to redo your work because of careless errors. You also need to reread many passages since you can't maintain your concentration. And though you are slowly progressing, you feel little satisfaction because you know your work is mediocre at best.

At 4:00 p.m. you call your spouse and say you need to stay late to finish your project. You are reminded of a 7:00 p.m. appointment with your daughter's teacher. Reluctantly you agree to attend, but you insist on staying at work until 6:30. Despite more coffee and a candy bar, your fatigue increases. In the last half hour at work you barely produce anything worth keeping. Furthermore, you are listless and distracted during

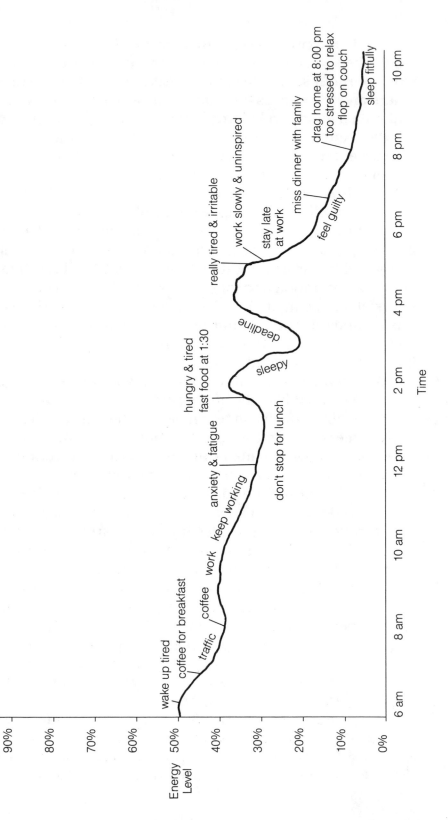

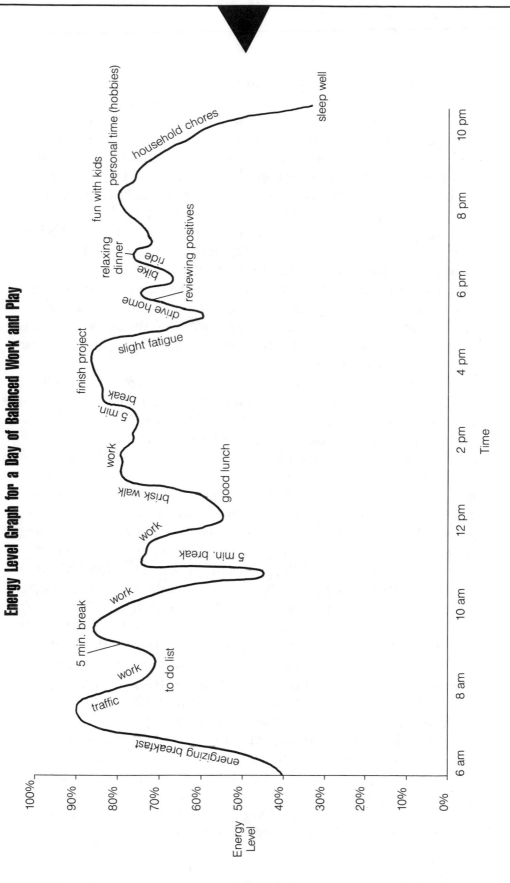

Energy Level Graph for a Day of Balanced Work and Play

energizing breakfast
traffic
work
5 min. break
work
to do list
5 min. break
work
5 min. break
work
brisk walk
work
good lunch
finish project
slight fatigue
drive home
reviewing positives
relaxing dinner
bike ride
fun with kids
personal time (hobbies)
household chores
sleep well

Energy Level: 0%, 10%, 20%, 30%, 40%, 50%, 60%, 70%, 80%, 90%, 100%

Time: 6 am, 8 am, 10 am, 12 pm, 2 pm, 4 pm, 6 pm, 8 pm, 10 pm the meeting with the teacher, and you leave feeling guilty as well.

Once home, you are too tired to do anything other than fall asleep on the couch in front of the TV. You haven't done anything to relieve the built-up pressure, though, so you sleep fitfully at night. You arrive at the office the next morning still feeling tired and pressured and lacking confidence, destined to repeat another day of low productivity and high anxiety. Each day gets worse until you fall prey to an illness or mental burnout.

Many of us have fallen victim to this all-work spiral. We have also heard it referred to as "the harder I work, the farther I fall behind" or "the hurrier I go, the behinder I get" syndrome. As the illustration of the balanced work/joy breaks spiral shows, the ninety minutes of idle time each day (a minimum of four five-minute breaks per day plus at least forty-five minutes for lunch) will be more than compensated for by the added energy and productivity you will gain.

We certainly are not the first people to realize the benefits of taking frequent breaks. If you review the profiles of creative people in Chapter 3, you will find that break-taking was an integral aspect of their work styles, too. Schweitzer had his music and gardening to break up his work day. Playful and mischievous, Thomas Edison had impromptu jam sessions with his staff whenever his work became tiresome. He also took frequent motor trips across the country. O'Keeffe liked to begin her mornings and end her days with either gardening or long walks. And Mead devoted her break times to her child, to cooking, to her parents, and to entertaining conversation with her colleagues. Our study of the lives of other geniuses and highly successful business leaders has turned up a similar break-taking pattern in their lives as well.

From our analysis of their work patterns and life-styles, we believe that most of these people had well-balanced, or integrated, brain hemispheres. They intuitively seemed to understand the need for shifting their concentration during the day and for giving their creative, whimsical right brain a chance to surface after intense spells of left-brained thinking.

This chapter concludes with the field research from insights of several of our clients who have discoverd the benefits of breaks. Perhaps their examples will provide you with the best verification for the many high-energy benefits of taking breaks both at work and in the evening. Some of these quotes also attest to the value of working according to your brain dominance.

Paul Smith, principal training specialist for Texas Utilities, shares these observations:

"There are several things that I do to build energy both in my personal life and professional life. When teaching a class, if I notice that the students seem to be losing energy, I try to stop and take a break, do a magic trick, do an in-class exercise where people have to participate physically, or play a quick game."

Ed Platt, a Texas Utilities engineer, tells this story:

"About two years ago I found myself coming home from work totally drained. I had no energy for any activities except my job and family. I had no interest in hobbies and outside activities. At that time I knew nothing of Energy Engineering.

In November 1985, my wife and I went to a stained-glass shop and commissioned a special piece of glass for an anniversary present. The owner told me I should take a class and learn to do glasswork. It seemed like the right thing to do, so I started a new hobby. As I went through the course, I found that anyone who tried could create attractive stained glass. Over the next two years I made more than seventy-five pieces of stained glass. Over time, the patterns became more complex and larger. The amazing thing was that I had time to do this when I had felt that I was so tired I could do nothing else. I found myself working on projects in small blocks of time and having several projects going at the same time. When I came home from work, the glass projects were a release and an energy builder. The handwork let me forget about other cares. The elements of color, texture, and form were not in anything else I did and thus made the work more enjoyable.

I learned a very important lesson as people became interested in my glasswork. Several times I committed myself to projects and schedules rather than just letting it happen [at my own speed]. It was not nearly as much fun or energizing. Now when I work on a piece for someone, it is without a schedule. For me, committing to a schedule was contamination of my joy time.

My stained glass hobby has also revived some other hobbies such as photography. Again, I discovered that I can find time and have energy to do things that I could not before. It is a thoroughly enjoyable hobby that

Remember that it is important to listen to your body and respond to what it is telling you.

has had benefits far beyond its cost, and in my mind incorporates many of the Energy Engineering concepts."

John H. Carlson, vice president for Gas Plant Operations, TU Electric, confirms the value of energy breaks:

"I learned as an adolescent to play the piano for my mother. (The lessons were a very left-brained, disciplined experience.) In retrospect, the entire effort was an energy drain and a somewhat frustrating experience. I quit studying and didn't play the piano for about ten years. After college and a family of my own, I discovered how energizing music can be to me and what a wonderful tool it is to build relationships with my children. I had been curiously wanting to learn how to play the guitar and at twenty-seven taught myself the basics. At thirty-seven I bought a fiddle and an old pump organ. At forty I purchased a mandolin and dulcimer. At forty-two I was given a mountain banjo. All of these I have learned to play with varying degrees of expertise (I don't play any of the instruments very well).

I use these instruments in 'engineering my energy' by playing one or more almost every evening after dinner. I have used a predominantly right-brained approach to learning, as I favor 'playing by ear' as opposed to reading music. By selecting an instrument and playing for not more than thirty minutes, I can feel more alert and relaxed to spend an evening with my family. Playing music, especially when it is spontaneous and from a right-brained perspective, is very therapeutic and energizing."

Summary

1. By charting your energy for a typical day and week you can become more aware of your patterns of energy highs and lows.

2. You can plan and practice energy strategies to increase energy levels during low periods. You can also plan your most demanding work to take advantage of your natural energy peaks.

3. Get into the habit of taking breaks regularly so that you don't allow your energy reserves to become depleted.

4. If you are proactive with your energy during the day, then you will arrive home with sufficient energy to have fun with your family.

5. Having a variety of hobbies and outside interests gives you something fun to look forward to and enjoy during times when you might otherwise just be tired.

19

GETTING YOUR DAY OFF WITH A BANG!

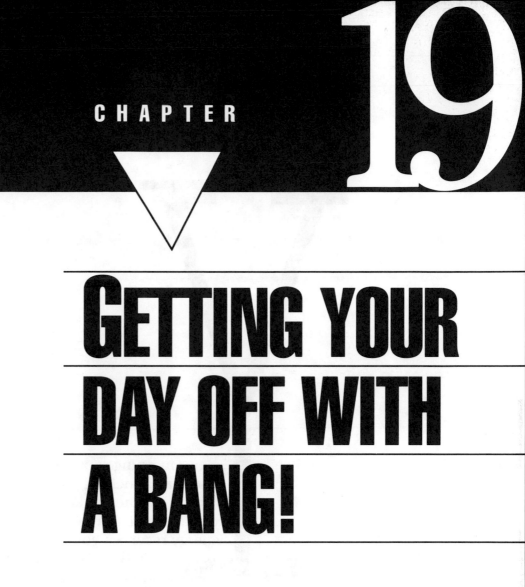

❝ *Life's too short to jump-start a three-watt bulb, because once you get it started, it's only a three-watt bulb anyway.* **❞**

**—Dr. Robert Ballard, Director,
Center of Marine Exploration,
Woods Hole Oceanographic Institute**

❝ *You can count how many seeds are in the apple, but not how many apples are in the seed.* **❞**

—Ken Kesey

❝ *Life is a grindstone. Whether it grinds a man down or polishes him up depends on what he is made of.* **❞**

—Old proverb

Your morning routine is the metaphorical launching pad for your day. It can determine the kind of mental set you arrive at work with, the amount of energy reserves you have on hand, and even the degree of productivity and success you experience throughout the day. Yet many people don't count their day as starting until *after* they arrive at the office. They routinely allow many stressful, low-energy events to trip them up during the "first lap" of their day, although morning is the time they should be locking into a good, steady pace.

This chapter will take several of the concepts and strategies explained previously and put them together so you can get a clear picture of how to begin a high-energy day. These ideas have been used by numerous professionals to build and preserve their morning energy reserves.

Patsy Fulton, president of Brookhaven College, describes how she starts her day:

> *"I keep myself on a morning exercise program that is terrifically important to me. I get up at 5:30 a.m. and am at the gym by 6:00 four to five days a week. I do an hour's worth of aerobic exercise and weight training. While I exercise, I don't bog down my*

mind with problems. Instead, I focus on making my exercise time a refreshing, creative experience.

Back home, I also give myself some vital 'sit and think' time. I have a cup of coffee by the window, watch the bird feeder, look at nature, and let these scenes give me an up feeling. I purposely do not listen to the radio or the news, but make the morning a more quiet, reflective time.

My breakfast consists of a cup of coffee, a bowl of cereal, some juice, and lots of vitamins. After dressing, I'm off to work, but I use my drive there as a time to get centered, too. I go down a country road with lots of trees and fields. This doesn't always come easy, but I try to concentrate on the changing beauty outside my window, not on any work concerns.

Because I know that once I step into my office, I will be in constant demand, going from one meeting to another. So I need to have that time alone in the morning to focus inward."

Morning Menu

- WAKE-UP IMAGING
- MORNING EXERCIZE
- HI-CARBO BREAKFAST
- POSITIVE MENTAL SET
- REWARDING COMMUTE
- EARLY ARRIVAL AT WORK

Wake-up Imaging

Remember, one of the most effective times to image is upon waking, when your mind is still in the "alpha window" and very open to imprinting. This is also an ideal time for establishing your goals for the day, rehearsing upcoming tasks, framing a positive attitude, and visualizing yourself performing at your best.

Here's how Barbara uses her morning visualizing time:

"Because my husband likes to listen to the news upon waking, I usually wrap a blanket around myself and settle on the living room couch. Then for the next ten minutes, I get in touch with my waking thoughts. While deep-breathing, I listen to whatever my subconscious has been dwelling upon. Sometimes it's a wonderful line for a poem, sometimes the solution to a writing problem or personal conflict that I've been pondering over, sometimes it's the need to write down the many things I hope to accomplish that day, and sometimes it's simply the desire to eat a special breakfast or to call a friend for lunch. Next, I 'program' two imaging exercises. The first is to see myself efficiently accomplishing whatever my main goal for that day is. The second is a more general goal—that I sustain my sense of confidence and creativity for a very long piece of fiction I'm working on. At times I fantasize winning a writing prize or receiving an acceptance letter in the mail. After that, I stretch, look out the window, and look forward to all the potential the day has for me."

Morning Exercise

Exercise at any time of the day is great for reducing pent-up stress and increasing your energy levels and overall stamina. Here are a few reasons why exercise gets you going in high gear in the morning.

First, exercise increases the flow of blood through your body and to your brain. This means that much more oxygen is coursing through your brain than usual. Conversely, lack of oxygen is one cause of fatigue, the thing that triggers yawning or a fainting spell. But by giving your brain a rich oxygen boost through exercise, you will not only recover from morning drowsiness; you will also make your mind more alert and ready for intense concentration.

Just ten minutes of mild to vigorous exercise will stimulate this enhanced blood flow. This could include taking the dog for a walk, doing a short stretching and calisthenics routine, and walking or jogging in place as you watch the morning news.

If you want to give your system an even bigger blast of energy, schedule twenty or more minutes of morning aerobics. True aerobic exercise, such as vigorous walking, jogging, swimming, skating, dancing, tennis, and cycling, requires constant movement. It also requires a level of physical intensity that produces heavier breathing, a faster heart rate, and sweating. But most important,

> **Exercise at any time of the day is great for reducing pent-up stress and increasing your energy levels and overall stamina.**

this type of exercise will increase a person's metabolism up to 25% for four to six hours, a significant physical energy boost. Aerobic exercise changes the chemistry in the body, getting rid of toxins and producing endorphins and other hormones which increase creativity, silence negative self-talk, and increase the likelihood of brain integration. You will be more patient and a better team player, more receptive to others, and a better listener after twenty to thirty minutes of aerobic exercise. Aerobics creates energy and makes you feel alert, open, tuned in, ready.

Morning aerobics may be the solution for those who are not naturally energetic upon waking, for those who don't normally feel alert until 10:00 or 11:00 a.m. A natural "aerobics high" is also a good substitute for caffeine in the morning.

There are surprisingly many exercise opportunities for people early in the morning. Several cable television channels, such as "Lifetime," offer instructor-led aerobic exercise programs. They usually air between 6:00 and 7:30 a.m. Most YMCAs, YWCAs, and other fitness centers present a range of before-work exercise programs, some beginning as early as 5:30 a.m. An indoor stationary bike is another wonderful exercise opportunity for a morning workout. We have many clients who read the paper or watch the morning news while getting their twenty-minute cycling workout. And again, with morning aerobics, you get the benefit of a sustained energy boost that will keep you going straight through to the lunch hour.

Betty Hudson, vice president of government relations for Fluor Corporation, makes morning exercise a vital part of her high-energy routine:

"My morning begins at 5:30. First I walk the dog, enjoying the quiet streets at that hour. Then I do an hour of exercise at my home. My workout consists of one-half hour of aerobics followed by one-half hour on a rowing machine. By the time I get to work, I'm in full gear, ready for a fast-paced day. I've also found that morning is the best time to schedule my exercise routine because my job requires so many evening social commitments that they would interfere with noon or nighttime exercise. But the mornings are my own . . . and I like the feeling of [taking care of my personal needs] before devoting myself to the needs of the company. On those days that my travel schedule does not allow me to exercise, I truly miss it."

Healthy Breakfast

Farmers and others engaged in hard physical labor have long known the importance of having an energy-sustaining breakfast. Of course food, particularly calorie-converted blood sugar, or glucose, in your bloodstream, is the body's key source of physical energy. If your last meal was dinner the night before, your blood sugar will be at a low ebb when you wake up ten to twelve hours later. (Imagine how hungry you would feel if you didn't eat for ten hours during the day.) Some people do not feel hunger upon waking because their metabolism has slowed down during sleep or because they grab some juice and coffee upon waking. But neither of these drinks will provide enough calories to sustain the body's energy needs until lunchtime.

Furthermore, upon waking, the body's bloodstream probably contains no more than 80 to 120 milligrams of glucose per each 100 milliliters of blood. This condition will normally set off an energy-depleting chain reaction that causes the cells to draw sugar reserves from the liver. If food is not ingested soon, lower and lower blood sugar levels will still result. Thus, waiting until noon to eat (a full sixteen or more hours since last night's dinner) constitutes the first stage of a genuine fast. Anticipating a real threat of starvation, the body will enter a lowered metabolic/ shutdown phase to conserve your remaining blood sugars, proteins, and fats (your energy reserves).

Many debilitating symptoms come when the body is deprived of ready calories. Fatigue, foggy thinking, fainting sensations, queasiness, and intense hunger are common ones. Imagine trying to perform at your best under those circumstances. In addition, *drinking coffee on an empty stomach to overcome these symptoms only tends to stimulate the symptoms further.*

While skipping breakfast is the worst way to start your day, you should also avoid breakfasts that are high in fats and/or simple sugars. Current dietary research is uncovering the role of fats in making the bloodstream more viscose, thus slowing up the flow of oxygen to the brain and other cells. This explains why many people feel sleepy and sluggish after a heavy meal of fatty foods. Typical breakfast foods that are sky-high in fats include bacon, sausage, and other meats, gravy, cream, greasy fried potatoes, and buttery or cheesy sweet breads.

On the other hand, grabbing breakfast out of a vending machine or the corner doughnut shop will probably result in a nutritionless meal of simple sugars. Whereas skipping breakfast plunges your glucose levels to an unhealthy low, eating sugary foods, especially on an empty stomach, will usually create a blood-sugar imbalance that needlessly wastes energy as well.

The best foods to put in your bloodstream in the morning are complex carbohydrates and high-fiber items. Unlike simple sugars, most complex carbohydrates will not raise the blood sugar too high, and fiber slows down some aspects of digestion, helping you feel fuller longer.

The cereal manufacturers have finally jumped on the health bandwagon, and many brands offer unsugared cereals composed of high-fiber grains and seeds (whole wheat, bran, oats, rye, corn, and flax seeds). Natural-grain hot cereals are excellent sources of high fiber, too. Using a low-fat or skim milk on your cereal will keep your fat intake to a minimum. On the hot cereals, go light on (or better yet skip) the butter and syrup.

Eating fresh fruit with whole grain bread or muffins is another high-energy breakfast option. Low-fat yogurt (some brands offer no-fat varieties, too) is another light item that will give you dairy protein as well. And speaking of protein, there is nothing wrong with having an occasional egg if you do not have a cholesterol problem. In fact, some nutritionists recommend having a sustaining, high-protein/low-fat egg breakfast if you face a particularly demanding morning or if you anticipate having a late lunch.

A final word on caffeine products. In addition to the fact that they can exacerbate many health hazards, such as high blood pressure, caffeine is simply not necessary if you jump-start your morning with exercise and a good breakfast instead. Although one cup of coffee or black tea is rarely harmful, we strongly encourage you to switch to juice, herbal teas, and water as your beverage of choice for the rest of the day after your morning cup of caffeinated or decaffeinated coffee or tea. Be aware that many regular and diet soft drinks contain caffeine as well.

A Stress-Free, Positive Mental Set

Think back to the scenes of the Olympic athletes preparing to appear before the audience and judges for their next event. The television camera showed many of them sitting alone, often with their eyes closed, deep-breathing and mentally rehearsing their performance. Others were huddled in a corner with their coaches, getting a last-minute pep talk. Some of them refused to watch their competitors going before them to avoid losing their concentration and positive mind set. Most actors, musicians, and other artists practice some form of this pre-performance discipline as well.

What this amounts to is maintaining a calm physical and mental posture and a positive mental set. Like these athletes and performers, you too can conserve your morning energy reserves and positive attitude by avoiding stress-causing situations as you get ready for work. Look back at the morning energy profile you completed for Chapter 18 and identify which activities and interactions tend to drain your energy and produce stress. Which of these can be changed or avoided to create a less stressful morning for you?

To begin with, if you wake up just a half hour before you need to leave the house and start to work, you have so little margin for error that virtually anything that goes wrong will throw you off schedule and make you worry about being late. For instance, if you snag a pair of hose or nick your face while shaving or if you receive an unexpected phone call, you may be set back five minutes in your race to get out the door in half an hour. It will be difficult for you to have a peaceful morning within such a high-gear setting.

The same applies to allowing yourself the minimum amount of time to drive or commute to the office. One traffic snag or delayed arrival of your train can instantly put you on edge because you have programmed into your morning absolutely no time to spare.

Other than the time factor, are there other areas where you have left yourself open to needless stress in the morning? Do you neglect filling the gas tank in your car so that you are frequently on empty when starting out, with little time to spare for a gasoline fill-up? Does your hairstyle require lots of attention or does it often look unsatisfactory to you? If so, you can waste time and positive energy by laboring over it. Do you usually walk into your closet in the morning, having no idea what you want to wear to work? Then when you decide upon something, do you find that it needs ironing, that a button is missing, and so forth? This too can cause stress, which you could sidestep by inspecting and setting out your clothes the night before.

If you share your morning getting ready with children, you may long for the luxury of getting only yourself off to work. So let's look at some successful strategies for the complexity of family organization. First, schedule some quiet time for yourself *before* children wake up. It could be your private time to do imaging, take an unhurried, relaxing shower, sit on the patio reading the paper and having a cup of tea, stroll around the neighborhood, or do TV aerobics. Once you establish a peaceful feeling inside, you are far less likely to be negatively affected by the commotion of the children getting ready for school. Playing soothing music in the background may help you sustain that restful state of mind. Second, have a planning meeting with all family members to brainstorm positive solutions to problems which keep mornings from going smoothly and pleasantly.

Mary Beth Hoesterey, research consultant, writer, college teacher, one of our team members, and working mother of five children between the ages of six and twenty-one, has some other good suggestions:

> *"Keep in mind that each person has a different pace in the morning. Some of us are morning people and others are not. With my children who move slowly in the morning I know that helping them make decisions on which clothes to wear and whether to make their lunch or take lunch money happens best the night before—when they are alert.*
>
> *We encourage one child to help another. Jim (age fourteen) may hear Sarah's spelling words while he eats his bowl of cereal.*
>
> *I think it's important not to think of mornings as a disciplined drudgery but rather an opportunity to get off to a good start. We look for ways to make mornings fun and energizing. I stick a newspaper quiz on the refrigerator door and we enjoy seeing who can come up with the most answers. I give the kids a ten-point advantage and they often beat me. I also lay interesting articles, quotes, or inspirational pieces out on the breakfast table and in the bathroom. I say nothing about them. It's my way of surrounding the family with positive material but without being preachy.*
>
> *We feel it is important to respect the differences in our five children. One son likes to leave his room letter-perfect before he leaves for school. His brother's room is generally a disaster, but then he straightens it up somewhat when he gets home in the afternoon. Taking on the role of a heavy disciplinarian who is in charge of making everyone do right can be a big energy drain to all, especially the parent. Instead we put our energy into becoming positive role models and respecting each child's need to grow and learn in his or her own way.*

I take a walk each morning, and one morning a week I invite one of my children to walk with me. This is a wonderful time for us to talk. At evening meals we play fun games such as inviting each person to tell one good thing that happened to them that day. We find that when we proactively listen to our children as they need to be heard, and support them in learning to plan ahead and think through options, make their own choices, and live with the results of those decisions (so that they can learn from their decisions) and when we honestly share our mistakes so they learn that everyone makes mistakes—all of these are important investments toward making mornings go smoothly and helping children get off to a good start."

As we learn to express anger, disappointment, or any other negative feelings openly, as they happen in ways that communicate our needs without blaming or accusing others, the situation can be resolved and the bad feelings dispelled. If this is an issue for you or your family, you might want to read John Bradshaw's *On Family* or other books on codependency. Squelching negative feelings while forcing an appearance of a positive attitude can only delay the problem. And in the meantime, the suppressed feelings can damage our performance and relationships in ways difficult to identify.

Think in terms of compounding time. Basically this is a strategy of getting two or more benefits from one time period.

Mary Beth tells us she agrees with Tom Peters, author of *Thriving on Chaos*. The secret is to learn to thrive on chaos! She helps her children learn from this business theme. One older brother doesn't like the routine commotion of younger kids jabbering over breakfast. So he takes a long shower and listens to music in his room until school time.

This is all good preparation for the next part of the day. The secret to high energy is to respect and provide for your own inner needs while equally respecting and creatively making room for the differing needs of others.

Rewarding Commute to Work

Many professionals consider their commute to work as wasted time or, worse, as an anxiety-provoking experience that delivers them to the office feeling tense and tired. If either is the case for you, consider several ways of making your commute a calmer experience, if not a truly rewarding one.

It might be helpful to think in terms of compounding time. Basically this is a strategy of getting two or more benefits from one time period. If you drive to work, of course reading is out of the question, but listening to something stimulating is not. Rather than simply listen to the news, consider what other things might be more invigorating to hear. Here are ways in which some people we know use their commuting time positively:

- a client plays motivational sales and confidence-building tapes;

- a friend listens to language lessons on tape in preparation for a summer vacation in Italy;

- a graduate student listens to tapes of her professors' lectures as a review session;

- a writer plays library tapes of famous poets reading their own work;

- a friend listens to scripture on tape as a way of studying the Bible from start to finish;

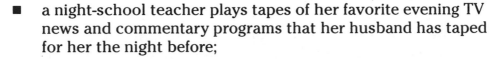

- a night-school teacher plays tapes of her favorite evening TV news and commentary programs that her husband has taped for her the night before;

- a business writer subscribes to "Books on Tape" and listens to scores of wonderful novels, both contemporary and classic;

- a client listens to life-style-changing lectures geared toward weight loss; and

- an author of children's books brainstorms plot lines and characters.

To find out the huge array of topics and books available on tape, visit your public library or bookstore. In addition, some offices are purchasing inspirational or skills-building tape series for their staff to hear at their leisure. There are so many different subjects, lectures, well-known speakers, and books available on tape these days that you could almost create a college-level correspondence degree for yourself if you desired. But regardless of what piques your interest and energy levels, the purpose is to change your daily commute from being a period of drudgery or frustration to a time of learning, fun, and inspiration.

Now if your daily commute involves heavy traffic and dangerous driving conditions, you probably won't be able to devote sufficient attention to a foreign language tape or other demanding listening. In that case, perhaps soothing classical or New Age music would be the best aid for keeping you in a peaceful mental set.

And when you arrive at work, if you have to wipe your brow and peel your hands off the steering wheel, your freeway driving at that hour probably isn't worth it. Could you leave home half an hour earlier to avoid the worst traffic? Could you pick a less busy route, one that may take you a little out of your way or may add fifteen minutes to your drive but one that will offer you a scenic, relaxing route rather than a harrowing one? Try this alternative route for several days and see whether you don't agree with the college president quoted at the beginning of this chapter. In addition, if you use your commute to listen to worthwhile tapes and appealing music, you won't begrudge the extra minutes you spend in your car; in fact, you may even come to value them as one of the few times each day when you are guaranteed private time to yourself.

Finally, if you ride on some kind of mass transit to and from work, you can still avail yourself of these tapes by using a tape recorder and earphones. In addition, some people are able to read on a train and bus. They catch up on their professional journals and other reading during this time.

Early Arrival at Work

The final suggestion for a high-energy morning is to arrive at work at least ten or fifteen minutes early. To begin with, this strategy provides you a buffer if you run into delays on your commute to work or if you need to catch up on a few unfinished details from yesterday's projects. Second, this early arrival time is a quiet period to settle in and get organized for the day. You might use this time to

- look over your schedule for the day and think of ways to enlist the help of co-workers on certain tasks;

- plan for ways to tuck fun into your morning and afternoon to keep energy high;

- review the items waiting on your desk and straighten up if you did not have time to do it the night before;

- write an encouraging note to a co-worker who is facing a demanding assignment that day;

- briefly visualize challenging parts of the day as being highly successful;

- make a prioritized list of goals for the day;

- do some troubleshooting if you anticipate any snags for that day;

- spruce up your office with fresh flowers or something else nice;

- have a conversation with a co-worker over a fresh cup of herb tea; or

- return a phone call to a friend.

Arriving early is especially important if you have business outside the office. If, for example, you are involved in an evaluation, presentation, meeting, or interview, it is very helpful to familiarize yourself with the setting. Not only will this extra time give you a chance to rectify any problems (such as a malfunctioning microphone or overhead projector), it will also allow you to get your bearings, assess the new environment, and prepare yourself for your task. Furthermore, by arriving early you can have some impromptu, candid conversations with clients that are usually not possible during the normal hustle-bustle of the day. You may also find that you can use this time to sharpen your intuition by being fully ready before anyone arrives. Then you can take the fifteen to thirty minutes of group arrival time to talk with others, listening carefully for any clues that will help you be more on target. We find this makes an enormous difference in our ability to be direct and to the point with client needs. We are amazed at the wonderful serendipity (some call it lucky coincidence) that takes place during this time.

Rather than letting your mornings be a haphazard, catch-as-catch-can experience or a stressful, 100-meter dash to the office, program them to fill you with vitality and confidence. Getting some exercise and eating a light but healthy breakfast will prime your physical energy reserves. Imaging, reviewing your schedule, and having an interesting commute to the office will instill you with mental energy. And arriving early will get your day off to a relaxing start.

Summary

1. Think of your morning routine as the launching pad to your day. It will establish your mental set, your energy levels, and your productivity.

2. Your high-energy morning menu might include a wake-up imaging session; exercise; a high-carbohydrate breakfast; a stress-free positive mental set; a rewarding commute to work; and early arrival at the office.

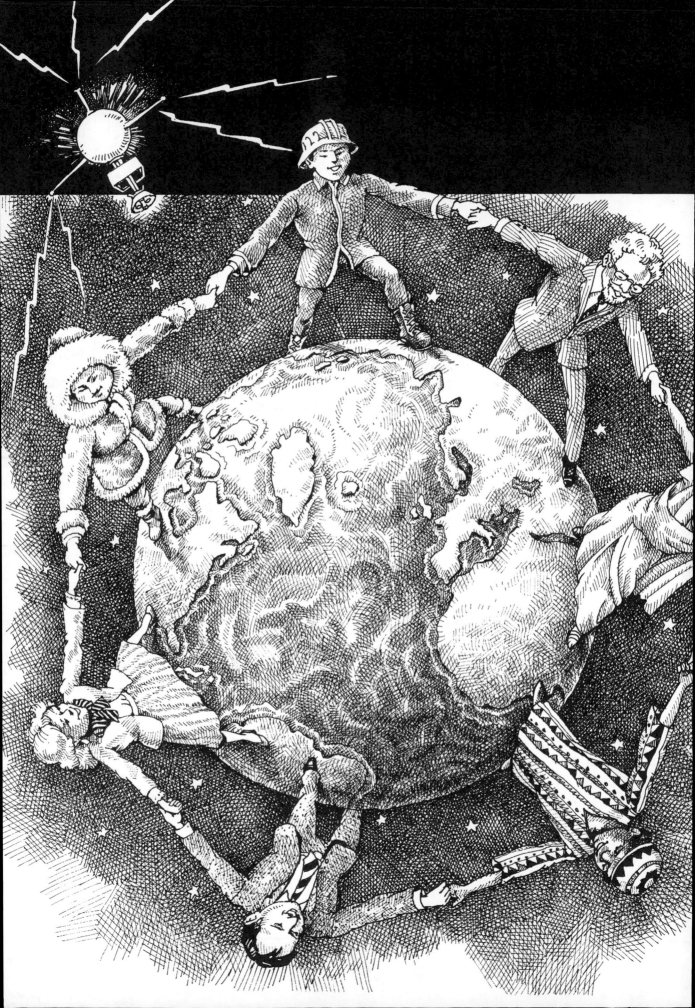

20

ENERGIZING YOUR PERSONAL POWER AND POTENTIAL:

The Unlimited Growth Of Balance

" Fatigue makes cowards of us all. "
—Vince Lombardi

" The best way to predict the future is to invent it. "
—Alan Kay, fellow, Apple Computer

" Your best this week should be your worst next week. "
—Jimmy Young, age 17

" The biggest risk is to do nothing when the world is changing rapidly. "
—Walter B. Wriston, Retired Chairman, Citicorp

W hen we are tired, our bodies and brains are filled with toxins which block the effective processing of new ideas. And even if we had a new set of winning strategies, when we are exhausted even a winning new plan can seem more like an adversary's plot to keep us on the treadmill than a path to new, innovative successes. When we are tired we are most likely to duck and avoid risk, new roles, and new ways of thinking. At a time when continuous performance improvement is essential for each of us in order to move our corporate and family teams forward to greater success and health, a refreshing and dependable source of high-energy strategies and life habits is the key.

It has been five years since we began our research on personal energy, and so many new insights have built one upon the other. We have learned clearly that there is no ceiling on our energy potential. It is not unusual for clients to estimate personal energy gains and increased productivity at four or five times their entry level (and all participants began as pace-setting leaders in their fields). In addition, there is the network effect. When your partners and peers bring increased energy, innovation, and flexibility to the team, the momentum becomes synergistic. Our clients teach us about energy as we teach them. In each of the past five years we've significantly increased our productivity, energy level, fun quotient, and balance.

The quest for unlimited energy is a never-ending journey. The more we learn, the more skillful and resourceful we become. When we ask former Perspective III participants what differences Energy Engineering has made in their life, they typically list more fun at work, more joy breaks, more quality time with family, less pressure and more enthusiasm, more creative solutions to problems, and lots more positive imaging as primarily life changes. And as we interview family and work partners, we hear similar reports of far less pressure, more effective communication, better teaming, more celebrations, better listening, and lots more creative options coming from everyone.

There is a "neural network" in the making as groups of people are learning to be so intuitive to each other's needs and meanings that they often know without being told. People are listening on behalf of one another. Spouses and other family members are contributing in some unique and creative ways to enrich the "corporate family." Family and personal needs are becoming a higher priority in some creative, win/win planning. And as a result, corporate goals receive the benefit of the enthusiastic energy of balanced employees supported by healthy families.

Abundant energy can only come by giving up victim behavior and adopting proactive, self-actualized options. Blaming and accusing others is being replaced by creative problem-solving sessions at home and at work. Becoming empowered with a new sense of unlimited personal potential is contagious and a clear benefit to all. In essence, as more and more people are bringing balance into their work and life-

The old ways of doing things are no match for the high-energy demands of leading a quality life in today's atmosphere of rapid change.

style, a creative resilience is forming a solid foundation necessary to support the rapid change taking place across the globe.

As we move toward the year 2000, the pace seems to be quickening and the changes keep coming, faster and faster, even in areas which we thought would never change. All around us we are hearing paradoxical thinking:

"You must slow down to go faster."

"If you want to change others, change yourself first."

"To become a more productive worker, make sure you take time regularly to enjoy refreshing play."

"If you want to increase your success rate, increase your failure rate!"

"To succeed in a competitive global business environment we must learn not only to survive in this chaos of rapid change, but thrive on chaos," warns Tom Peters, author of *Thriving on Chaos*. Information is doubling, maybe even tripling, every decade. Technology is changing so rapidly that all of us must keep learning monthly to even stay current.

In short, the old ways of doing things are no match for the high-energy demands of leading a quality life in today's atmosphere of rapid change. And when we are threatened, we typically shift into a defensive mode and become entrenched in familiar, time-tested, habitual ways of thinking and behaving (which may have become obsolete but nonetheless feel right). With threat and change we are most likely to withdraw into half-brained duality, blaming and accusing those not like us.

Yet those who are different from us or strong where we are weak (the left-brain masters of organization, details, and logic or the right-brain artists of innovative, flexible, and divergent thinking) become precisely the personalities who threaten us most. *We need most what we find most threatening.* To find the balance so critical to mental and physical well-being and to create the synergy of whole-brained creativity and energy, we need not only to make friends with our opposites but also to become interdependent team players, both with our own shadow side and with those around us who see what we can't, who think in ways that we find threatening to us.

But the rewards of all this upheaval are tremendous! As we learn to change our mental set, recognizing that the freedom to choose our attitude is one key to discovering new energy, we discover that our work can be fun and a sincere "get to." Problems do become opportunities. Indeed, none of us would have jobs or perhaps purpose in life without problems to solve. As we learn the secret of making paradigm shifts as ways to see the world anew and to make what seemed to be impossible possible, we learn the secret of unlocking new and significant energy.

We are talking about a holistic process. Our brains and bodies are "hard-wired" into each other. As we integrate our two brain hemispheres into a mutually supportive team, we discover not only that any problem can be an interesting and exciting challenge but that we can even have lots of fun in the process. We discover an abundant energy and enthusiasm coming as a result of all the fun and satisfaction we get as we make one breakthrough after another. And we learn the deep spiritual joy of servant leadership as we discover that by quietly listening to, supporting, and empowering others, we become more valuable and fulfilled.

One added benefit to whole-brained integration and teaming is the gift of a stronger, more active immune system which leads to more energy and therefore better physical health. We know that long periods of distress or anxiety-producing stress release floods of adrenaline into our system, which blocks our immune system. But as we learn to thrive on chaos, to think of problems as opportunities, to turn distress into positive eustress, and to have fun and feel enthusiastic about the unlimited potential of ourselves and each other, our bodies produce positive chemicals which activate our immune system and thus bring us to greater health. Nobel chemist Ilya Prigogine has described this whole system with his theory of dissipative structures. As we learn to become open systems and allow the powerful flood of change to *move through us*, adding to our energy and trusting our amazing brains to integrate the rich differences into a higher order of innovative structure, we become new each day, evolving into a higher and more effective order.

> **B**e gentle with yourself. Nurturing yourself with unconditional love, listening to your body, and rewarding yourself with frequent celebrations can put you in touch with your inner passion and power. Most Americans try to high-pressure themselves into higher performance. Instead, be gentle and trust yourself to find your own way.

The ideas and principles offered in this book are inviting you to explore givens in your life not previously questioned. Why would you want to challenge your present system? It's like shooting an arrow first and then drawing the target around it. You're in the bull's-eye every time because you have the answers to questions that haven't been asked. By tapping whole-brained energy and establishing synergy habits before the crisis hits, you are prepared for the worst and can make it the best.

"Your best (today) is not good enough (tomorrow)!" cautions Bob Gary, one of the leaders of Texas Utilities. As everything continues to change and accelerate around us, technology either bombards us, or it annoints us with multiple opportunities to accomplish everything faster. Can the human brain keep up? This is our challenge, and energy is the key to this. Bob also inspired and supported us along this journey by telling us that time for action can be thought of as a restraint or as a resource:

**"It's what you do now
when you don't have to do anything
that makes you what you want to be
when it's too late to do anything about it."**

—Bob Gary

ACKNOWLEDGMENTS

Although we three had the fun of writing the book, we have many to thank for making this vision a reality. Our business partners, Diane Bullard Cory, Mike Griffin, Jonnie Haug, Marybeth Hoesterey, Jackie Maxwell, Rayo McCollough, Karol Omlor, Kay Russell, Billie Snider, Georgia Ulrich, and Stevie Womack have all been active members of the Research and Development team as well as the production process. No one could ever imagine the dedication, energy, and imagination they brought to this task. Judy Lambert also spent days on early edits.

We found a marvelous team to produce the book headed by Ray Bard. They include:

Michael Donahue	marketing consultant
Stan Kearl	photographer
Mike Krone	illustrator
Suzanne Pustejovsky	art director, text/cover design
Alison Tartt	editor

Again, this team not only contributed their professional talent to make the book unique and communicate through fun and imagination as well as the written word; they also tested many of the concepts in their lives as the project went forward. We thank them for bringing their professional polish to the project and for agreeing to break lots of rules.

Over seventy clients, friends, and friends of friends read and critiqued the early drafts, and we are indebted to each of them for their insights.

Our families have been patient and supportive as we have involved them in all sorts of crazy, fun, and innovative experiments in our search to learn the secrets of whole-brained energy.

Perhaps our greatest debt is to our clients over the past five years who have participated in Energy Engineering seminars and given us generous feedback on what worked for them, and how and why. A special group has gone through the ten-month process called Perspective III, which invited participants to discover their own process for personal brain transformation. Much of the material in this book belongs to these pioneers, their families, and learning partners who taught us through their lives, imaginative leadership, and creative sharing.

TEXAS UTILITIES PERSPECTIVE III PARTICIPANTS

Group 1

Bob Gary (Sponsor)
John Janak
Bob Payne
Glenda Benson
John Carlson
Dick White
Frank Meyers
Larry Hearn
Bill Klotz
Tommy Thompson
Hal Collins
Leon Loveless
John Martin

Group 2

Doug Hobbs
Ed Platt
Brian Ballard
Ned Baker
Bob Clark
Tom Talley
Joe Thompson
Al Smithson
Larry Kinard
Carmen Baker
John Dorsett
Buddy Shaw
John Janak (Sponsor)
Bob Payne (Sponsor)
John Carlson (Sponsor)

Group 3

Larry Ivy
Walt Frazier
Wilfred Schaeper
Jim Hanrahan
Carroll Graves
Bill Harper
Karl Maynard
Boyce Harp
Ralph Dick
Jim Kuykendall
Rose Sharp
Jim Gregory
John Martin (Sponsor)
Leon Loveless (Sponsor)

Group 4

Gene Sellar
Paul Williams (Sponsor)
Mike Ozymy
Steve Swiger
Bailey McNutt
John Prickette
Diane Carpenter
Terry Griffin
Grant Whitt
Danny Collard
Walter Goodenough
Bill Ranton
Roy Bench
Bill Klotz (Sponsor)

Group 5

TU Electric
Al Boren
Bennie Cornutt
Steve Brewton
Larry Turpin
Bob Lewis
Mike Jarboe
Don McFadden
Tommy Thompson
  (Sponsor)

Fluor Daniel, Inc.
Joe Lanzafame (Sponsor)
Marc Walton
Roger Smith
Lloyd Hartsell
David Fincher
John Iacovini

Group 6

Tom Baker
Tom Blakey
Bob Campbell
Jerry Farrington (Sponsor)
Bob Gary (Sponsor)
John Janak (Sponsor)
Erle Nye (Sponsor)
Dale Scarth
Mike Spence
Max Tanner
Wes Taylor
Eddie Watson

Group 7

Gary Clinton
Steve Collins
Wayman Flynn
Randy Newsom
Ken Price
Gene Rand
David Reedy
Abo Schwarzer
Pat Slay
Lonnie Smith
Rob Trimble
Vic Zemanek
Paul Smith
John Janak (Sponsor)

Group 8

Will Bennett
Liz Brehm
Philip Burke
Jim Byrd
Dave Chapman
Ron Coker
Charles Fairchild
Lynn Griffin
Jeff Hardgrave
Jim Leonhart
Elizabeth Pickens
Pitt Pittman
Robert Rodgers
Butch Ross
Ronnie Skerik
Max Tanner (Sponsor)
Bill Ranton (Sponsor)

Group 9

Mike Arrington
Melvin Ball
Bob Browder
Helen Burt
Billy Clements
Larry Garner
Jarrell Gibbs (Sponsor)
Mike Greene
Bill Griffin
Jerry Larmay
Pitt Pittman
Harold Raines
Jim Trimble
Dennis Tucker
Grant Whitt (Sponsor)
Paul Williams (Sponsor)
Richard Wipf

AT&T PERSPECTIVE III PARTICIPANTS

John Agee
Bill Bennett
Diane (Bullard) Cory
Mike DeMas
Joe Giliam
James Irvine
Patricia Kellett
Dick Lombardi (Sponsor)

Tom Long
John Petrillo (Sponsor)
Gary Phipps
Ron Powers
Loren Sprouse
Jerry Vitt
John Braid
O. E. Philpot

PERSPECTIVE III+ PARTICIPANTS (AS OF 2/1/89)

Group 1

Larry Hearn (Sponsor)
Nancy Tolson
Kelly Root
Glenda Benson
Art Hodge
Jerry Johnson
Wade Stansell
Paul Zweiacker
Liz Brehm
Dick White (Sponsor)
Robert Johnson
Dick Robertson
Karen Spalding
Bill Klotz (Sponsor)
Jim Hanrahan (Sponsor)

Group 2

Jon Black
LeNae Davis
Harvey Harrison
Leah Hogue
Sylvia McCormick
Carla Meadows
Ron Nickels
Steve Ragland
Robert Turpin
Larry Williford
Diane Carpenter (Sponsor)
Boyd Andress
David Ballard
Danny Collard (Sponsor)
Steve Mankin
Larry McLain
Bill Ranton (Sponsor)
Barbara Curry
Bailey McNutt (Sponsor)
Ken Scott
Bill Klotz (Sponsor)

Group 3

Jon Black
Darlene Hardman
Steve Houle
Walt Jordan
Clyde King
Bob Laningham
Denise Miller
Dwight Royall
Judy Voss
David Westbrook
Diane Carpenter (Sponsor)
LeRoy Bryant
James McGinnis
Danny Collard (Sponsor)
Bill Ranton (Sponsor)
Ken Crook
Roy McCann
Bailey McNutt (Sponsor)
Vic Travis
Bill Klotz (Sponsor)
Hollis Hutchison

FLUOR DANIEL, INC. PERSPECTIVE III PARTICIPANTS

Group 1

Chuck Bradley
Hugh Coble
Rick Dean
Eileen Delasandro
Gerald Glenn
Larry Hart
Vince Kontny
Les McCraw (Sponsor)
Charlie Oliver
Emil Parente
Jim Stein
Peter Van Nort
Paul Varello
Joe Lanzafame

**Combined Group
with TU Electric**

David Fincher
Lloyd Hartsell
John Iacovini
Roger Smith
Marc Walton

Group 2

Phil Asherman
Dennis Bernhart
John Berra
Jim Byron
Dave Cole
Mike Epprecht
Lance Frankham
Don Gurney
Betty Hudson
Stan Kimmel
Otto Kjos
Tom Merrick
Frank Moore
Jimmy Pittman
Mark Streeter
Steve Tappan
Phil Tevis
Larry Hart (Sponsor)

Group 3

Jim Barry
Charlie Cox (Sponsor)
Roger Elton
Horst Engleitner
Richard Fenny
Harry Fidder
Dan Friedman
Al Gasper
Steve MacLeod
Sandy McArthur
David Myers
Chuck Pringle
John Schubert
Richard Shenfield
Carel Smeets
Wolfgang Subklewe
Henry Van Dyke
Frank Van Ginhoven
Paul Wiget

Group 4

Jerry Allen
Peter Bickham
Don Buck
Dick Carano
Larry Copeland
Anna Marie Cwieka
Joe Davis
Dave Eads
Jake Easton
Steve Gilbert
Ron Green
Larry Lineberger
Bill Mazilly
Phil Osterlind
Lou Pardi
Stan Spears
Dick Teater
John Thatcher
Chris Tye
Karen Vari
Tom Vaughn
Bill Zelle
Dave Cole (Sponsor)

INDEX

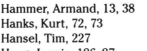

O · R · D · E · R · F · O · R · M

lease send me **You Don't Have To Go Home From Work Exhausted!**
The Energy Engineering Approach   (Hard Cover - $29.95 – Paperback - $19.95)

Quantity	Title	Unit Price	Amount
	Shipping & Handling ($2.00 First Book) 50¢ each Additional Book		
	Applicable Sales Tax (Texas residents only)		
	TOTAL		

DISCOUNT SCHEDULE
Save on Quantity Orders

Quantity	Hard Cover	Paperback
1	$29.95	$19.95
2 – 5	27.95	17.95
6 – 19	25.95	16.95
20 – 99	22.95	14.95
100 +	19.95	12.95

PLEASE MAKE CHECK PAYABLE TO

**Ann McGee-Cooper
and Associates, Incorporated**
P.O. Box 64784
Dallas, Texas 75206
OR CALL
1-800-477-8550
214/357-8550

Name_____

Organization_____

Address_____

City_____ State _____ Zip_____

Phone (_____) _____

❏ Payment Enclosed   ❏ MC   MasterCard   ❏ VISA   VISA

Card # | | | | | | | | | | | | | | | | |

Exp. Date | | | | | | |

Signature _____

Titles	Price Each	Quantity	Total
I. CREATIVITY Series - all 6 tapes	$63.00	_____	_____
"Defining Creativity and Hemisphericity"	$10.50	_____	_____
"5 Characteristics of Creative Thinking & Brainstorming"	$10.50	_____	_____
"Creative Problem-Solving Process"	$10.50	_____	_____
"Blocking Assumptions & Play & The Physiology of Creativity"	$10.50	_____	_____
"Imaginology and Practicing Creativity With Your Family"	$10.50	_____	_____
"16 Traits of Highly Creative People"	$10.50	_____	_____
II. NEW LEARNING TECHNIQUES Series - all 5 tapes	$52.50	_____	_____
"Teaching Music through the Whole Brain"	$10.50	_____	_____
"Imaging 1 & 2" (2 tapes)	$21.50	_____	_____
"Awaken Your Creativity"	$10.50	_____	_____
"Double Your Potential"	$10.50	_____	_____
"Discovering Your Brain Dominance Profile" (Tape and Self Test)	$15.00	_____	_____
III. OPENING DOORS TO GIFTEDNESS Series - all 8 tapes	$84.00	_____	_____
"Discover the Giftedness in Your Child"	$10.50	_____	_____
"The Gifted Child With Learning Differences" (2 tapes)	$21.00	_____	_____
"The Link between Learning Disabilities and Giftedness 1 & 2" (2 tapes)	$21.00	_____	_____
"Discover Your Giftedness"	$10.50	_____	_____
"Nothing Much Happens without a Dream"	$10.50	_____	_____
"Parenting the Gifted"	$10.50	_____	_____
IV. LIFE ENERGY Series - all 7 tapes	$73.50	_____	_____
"Burnout: The Superhuman Syndrome"	$10.50	_____	_____
"The Power of Play 1 & 2" (2 tapes)	$21.00	_____	_____
"Dealing Creatively with Loss"	$10.50	_____	_____
"Moving On: Tips for Times of Transition"	$10.50	_____	_____
"Woman to Woman: My Best Life Lessons"	$10.50	_____	_____
"Chaindumping vs. Positive Ventilation"	$10.50	_____	_____
V. JOURNEYS IN FAITH Series - all 5 tapes	$52.50	_____	_____
"Time Management as Christian Stewardship"	$10.50	_____	_____
"Why Teach Sunday School?"	$10.50	_____	_____
"Positive Discipline in the Sunday School 1 & 2" (2 tapes)	$21.00	_____	_____
"The Courage to Be One of a Kind"	$10.50	_____	_____
VI. SEMINARS Series			
"Awaken Your Creativity" (6 tapes, Album, Worksheets)	$80.00	_____	_____
"Time Management for Unmanageable People 1-5 (5 tapes with worksheets, album & *Joy Journal*)	$70.00	_____	_____
"Awaken Your Sleeping Genius" (5 tapes with worksheets, album & *Journal of Giftedness*)	$70.00	_____	_____
"Energy Engineering 1-6" (6 tapes with worksheets, album & *Energy Ideas Journal*)	$80.00	_____	_____
"Dyslexia & Time Management 1-5" (5 tapes with worksheets & album)	$70.00	_____	_____
"A Teambuilding Seminar" (3 tapes & worksheets & album)	$45.00	_____	_____
"Energy Ideas" (2 tapes & worksheets & album)	$35.00	_____	_____
"Chocolate Covered Hot Dogs—Unlikely Partners in the Future"	$10.50	_____	_____

Books by Dr. Ann McGee-Cooper

	Price Each	Quantity	Total
BUILDING BRAIN POWER	$11.50	_____	_____
TIME MANAGEMENT FOR UNMANAGEABLE PEOPLE (not available, in re-print)	$15.70	_____	_____
YOU DON'T HAVE TO GO HOME FROM WORK EXHAUSTED - THE ENERGY ENGINEERING APPROACH (Hard Cover – $29.95 – Paperback – $19.95)		_____	_____
Energy Ideas Journal with worksheets	$ 8.00	_____	_____
Journal of Giftedness with worksheets	$ 8.00	_____	_____

No extra charge for postage & handling on all prepaid orders mailed in the U.S.A. All others will be billed for shipping on a return invoice.

SHIP TO:

Name _____

Address _____

City _____ State _____ Zip _____

Sub-total	_____
Applicable Sales Tax (Texas Residents Only)	_____
TOTAL	_____

Please make check payable to: **Ann McGee Cooper & Associates, Inc.**
P.O. Box 64784 · Dallas, Texas 75206 · (214) 357-8550 · 1-800-477-8550